ALL THE KINGS AND QUEENS
OF THE BIBLE

ALL THE KINGS
AND QUEENS
OF THE BIBLE

Tragedies and Triumphs
of
Royalty in Past Ages

14974

by
HERBERT LOCKYER, D.D., R.S.L., F.R.G.S.

"Entire and sure the Monarch's rule must prove
Who founds her greatness on her subjects' love."
— Matthew Prior
(On Her Majesty's Birthday, 1704 —)

ZONDERVAN
PUBLISHING HOUSE OF THE ZONDERVAN CORPORATION
GRAND RAPIDS, MICHIGAN 49506

ALL THE KINGS AND QUEENS OF THE BIBLE
Copyright 1961 by
Zondervan Publishing House
Grand Rapids, Michigan

First printing	February 1961
Second printing	October 1961
Third printing	1965
Fourth printing	1967
Fifth printing	January 1969
Sixth printing	March 1969
Seventh printing	1970
Eighth printing	1971
Ninth printing	1973
Ninth printing	January 1973
Tenth printing	December 1973

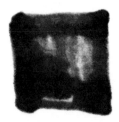

Printed in the United States of America

DEDICATED

to

A. B. R.

of queenly character,

and

whose kind heart

is more

than a coronet

Preface

Abraham Lincoln is credited with having said: "God must like common people. That's why He made so many of them." The common people "who heard Jesus gladly" certainly dominate Bible history, yet strewn across its sacred pages are the records of so-called "noblemen," kings and queens, princes and princesses, dukes and lords, many of whom were not very noble in the influence they exerted.

In Holy Writ you can read of thrones, palaces, empires and dominions; and of royal pageantry as gorgeous and glittering as any of more modern times. In this great Book of royalty you have the rise and fall of mighty dynasties and kingdoms and all the subtle intrigues of court life.

With the advent of communism and the upsurge of nationalism, crowned heads are becoming scarce in the world and kingdoms have given way to republics. It was never truer than it is today — "Uneasy is the head that wears a crown." It is, therefore, enlightening to go back to the Bible and in its gallery of royalty, look at those great rulers who exercised wide influence in their time. What stories, noble and notorious, revolve around those monarchs! Many of them were mighty as they reigned, but came down to dishonored graves, reminding us of the words of James Shirley, of the Fifteenth Century—

> The glories of our blood and state
> Are shadows, not substantial things;
> There is no armor against fate;
> Death lays its hands on kings,
> And in the dust be equal made
> With the poor crooked scythe and spade.

While the author has found the preparation of this volume a profitable exercise, no one is more conscious of its limitations than himself. Yet, although it is far from the ideal presentation of such a theme, he sends it forth with an adaptation of the wish of Robert Southey —

> Go, humble book! from this my solitude;
> I cast thee on the waters, go thy way,
> And if, as I believe, thy vein be good,
> The World will find thee after many days.
> Be it with thee according to thy worth.
> Go humble book! In faith I send thee forth.

Introduction

Requirements, Responsibilities and Rights of Kings

The notion that kings reign by divine right, quite independent of the people's will, goes back to those Old Testament days when kings were called "God's anointed," or His representatives on earth. Alexander Pope wrote of —

"The right divine of kings to govern wrong."

Mark Twain, however, in *A Connecticut Yankee in King Arthur's Court* speaks of "Those transparent swindles — transmissable nobility and kingship."

This notion of "divine right" gave rise to proverbs like — "The king cannot deceive or be deceived"; "The king can do no wrong." But both sacred and profane history give the lie to such sentiments, for many monarchs were, as Tennyson expresses it, "By blood a king, at heart a clown." We find ourselves in hearty agreement with Benjamin Disraeli who, in *Lothair*, set forth the right of kings in this manner —

The divine right of kings may have a plea for feeble tyrants, but the divine right of government is the keystone of human progress, and without it governments sink into police, and a nation is degraded into a mob.

Herbert Spencer under *Education*, Part 2, chapter 6, has the sentence — "Divine right of kings means the divine right of anyone to get uppermost."

Further, as Samuel Boyse of the Seventeenth Century expressed it—

"From Thee all human nations take their springs,
The rise of empires and the fall of kings."

All monarchs, whether godly or ungodly, owe their exaltation to God who "putteth down one, and setteth up another," who "raiseth up the poor out of the dust, that he may set him among princes" (Psalm 75:7). Kings themselves have been apt to forget that God is able "to do whatsoever his hand and his counsels determined before to be done" (Acts 4:28). It is by Him that "kings reign" (Proverbs 8:15) and it is He who is able to smite "great kings" (Psalm 136: 17-18).

The significance of the term, *king*, is of interest. Its Hebrew word, *melek*, is associated with an Assyrian root meaning, "to advise," "counsel," "rule or reign." The Latin form is "consul." The Arabic word implies "possessor as lord and ruler." The root is also found in *Molech*, tribal god of the Ammonites. Thus, at the beginning *king* signified "the wise man," then "the ruler"; and the rise of kingly power was due to intellectual superiority rather than to physical prowess. The "king" was the intellectual head of his clan or "city-state," and well able to direct its affairs. Matthew Prior of the Sixteenth Century asked the question —

> "What is a King? A man condemned to bear
> The public burden of the nation's care."

It was not long, however, before the emphasis was transferred from intellectual to physical prowess. *The International Standard Bible Encyclopaedia* has this comment on the Biblical signification of the title, *king* —

> The earliest Biblical usage of this title in consonance with the general oriental practice, denotes an absolute monarch who exercised unchecked control over his subjects. In this sense the title is applied to Jehovah, and to human rulers. No constitutional obligations were laid upon the ruler nor were any restrictions put upon his arbitrary authority. His good or bad contacts depended upon his own free will.
>
> The title "king" was applied also to dependent kings. In the New Testament it is used even for the head of a province (Revelation 17:12). To distinguish him from the smaller and independent kings, the king of Assyria bore the title "king of kings."

In olden times then, and in times not so ancient, kingship was acquired by conquest, by superior physical prowess. One etymology of one word, "king," means, "the able man," "the one who can," as admirably set forth in Carlyle's great passage. How expressive are the lines of John Milton of kingly qualities!

> For therein stands the office of a king
> His honour, virtue, merit and chief praise
> That for the public all this weight he bears.

The Responsibilities of Kingship. With the settlement of Israel in the land of Canaan, the tribes became open to hostile invasion. In order to preserve them from extermination it ¯became necessary to bind the tribes together under a leader. To all points and purposes, Joshua acted as a king of the people. Then, with the development of the nation as a monarchy, by popular acclaim Saul was appointed first king of the nation.

In those far-off days, the king had to be a fearless leader, a general in war with courage sufficient to lead his troop to battle (I Samuel 8:20; 31:2). He was not autocratic in the Oriental sense or a constitutional monarch as we understand it. Israel's kings were supposed to be responsible to God, who had chosen them to be his vice-regents and servants. God was Israel's true King, and kings were His earthly representatives as well as the representatives of the people. Control of ambition had to be exercised lest the king should lift up his heart about his brethren (Deuteronomy 17:20).

The king also acted as supreme judge (II Samuel 14:5; 25:2). He was the final court of appeal. As "The Judge," the most humble had to be able to approach him, and it was his responsibility to dignify his office. John Milton in his *Tenure of Kings* says —

INTRODUCTION

"Who knows not that the king is a name of dignity
and office, not of person?"

The king was likewise the chief person from the religious point of view who had to regard himself as a supreme, religious director, a chief priest. He could appoint priests at his pleasure (I Samuel 13: 9-11; 6:13; II Samuel 8:17) and pray for and bless the people (II Samuel 6:18). The king was assigned a place of honor in the Temple (II Kings 11:4). Latterly the priestly functions were less frequently exercised by kings.

The Range of Sovereignty. Israelitish kingdoms differed from Oriental despotisms in that the power of kings was limited (I Samuel 11:4). The Law and ancient customs exercised considerable restraint on Israel's kings — although a few of them were guilty of despotic violence. Solomon was practically a despot who ground the people down by taxation and forced labor. Yet public opinion, expressed by the prophets, resulted in restraint over the kings.

The principle had never to be lost sight of that the office of "king" was instituted for the good of the nation as a whole.

"The power of kings, if rightly understood
Is but a grant from Heaven for doing good."

The Law was above kingly authority, thus Ahab could not compel Naboth to sell his vineyard. The king was under the Law (Deuteronomy 17:14-20). Josiah swore allegiance to the Law (II Kings 23: 1-3). Cowper says —

"We love
The king who loves Law."

The king held office by divine grace, and therefore was under oath of loyalty to his Supreme Lord. Saul failed in this way and lost his throne because self usurped the place of God's will.

The Heredity of Kings. The fixed ideas of kingship passed from father to son, as judgeship passed from Gideon to his son (Judges 9:2). The king selected his successor under God's direction. According to the Law of Moses, God chose the king to be His representative, yet the people's choice was not excluded. When Samuel presented Saul as "God's anointed," the people acknowledged him as king (I Samuel 10:24; II Samuel 2:4).

Hereditary kingship began with David and succession in Judah remained all along in the House of David. Usually the first-born succeeded to the throne (II Chronicles 21:3-4). David, however, chose Solomon before his elder son, Adonijah. In the kingdom of the Ten Tribes son succeeded father, unless violence and revolution destroyed the royal house and brought a new adventurer to the throne.

INTRODUCTION

The Royal Income. The kings of old had demesnes, flocks, tenths, levies, as well as large revenue by "presents" which virtually became a regular tax. Saul and David did not subject the people to heavy taxation. Saul's prime sources of support were his ancestral estate, booty taken from enemies, gifts from friends and subjects (I Samuel 10:27; 16:20). Crown lands were held by David (I Chronicles 27:25). Caravans passing from Egypt to Dan had to pay toll (I Kings 10:15). Foreign trade by sea was another royal monopoly (I Kings 10:15). Some kind of property tax existed (I Samuel 17:25), and special taxes were imposed to meet emergencies (II Kings 23:35). The kings of Judah made free use of Temple treasures. Kings, in the days of Amos, laid claim to the first cutting of grass for the royal horses (7:1).

Symbols of Royalty. The anointing of kings was an ancient custom by no means peculiar to Israel (Judges 9:8-15). The act signified the setting apart of the elected sovereign to his high office. Shakespeare in *King Richard II*, gives us the couplet —

> "Not all the water in the rough, rude sea,
> Can wash the balm from an anointed king."

The insignia of royal dignity included beautiful robes (I Kings 22:10), the diadem or crown (II Samuel 1:10), the scepter, sign of dominion and authority (Genesis 49:10), the throne, symbol of majesty (I Kings 10:18-20), palace (I Kings 7:1-12), and a bodyguard (II Samuel 8:18).

Within the royal court there were the princes, often the king's advisers and counselors (I Kings 4:2); recorders who wrote the annals of his reign (II Samuel 8:16); scribes or secretaries who wrote dispatches and cared for correspondence (II Samuel 8:17); overseers to care for labor and larder, and minor officials as cupbearers. Confidants and friends were chosen by the king and given many favors. At times they betrayed the royal confidence reposed in them. Edmund Burke reminded us that, "A king may make a nobleman, but he cannot make a *gentleman.*" Some of the confidants of kings were far from being gentlemen.

Contents

Part One
Bible Kings

I

Mesopotamia and Ancient Monarchs

After the flood the sons of Noah parted and settled in different parts of the uninhabited earth to begin a new civilization. Thus, the oldest document extant for the *chronologist* is Genesis, with chapter 10 as the one for the *historian*. Whatever details profane history may provide, it is the Book of Genesis alone from which we have divine sources of information. The accounts, therefore, of the rise of nations, peoples and tongues; and of the dispersion of mankind as given by Moses, leave no ground for guesswork. Ethnology resolves itself into three fountain heads, namely, Japheth, Noah's eldest son, then Shem, and the youngest, Ham — all of whom originated in ancient Mesopotamia.

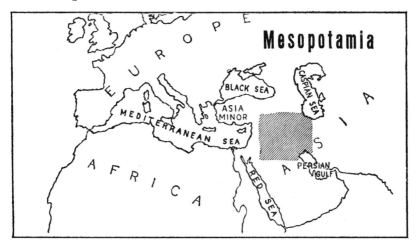

Generally speaking, the principal peoples descending from Noah's sons are —

From Japheth — *Medians, Greeks, Romans, Russians, Gauls, Britons.*

From Shem—*Hebrews, Persians, Assyrians, and many Arabian tribes.*

From Ham — *Egyptians, Africans, Babylonians, Philistines, Canaanites.*

17

Once these three progenitors of the new human race settled in their divinely-directed parts of the flood-swept earth, various clans came into being, and with the increase of population and possession of surrounding country, civilizations developed and leaders and kings appeared.

While it may be interesting to read the conjectures of both anthropologists and archaeologists as to prehistoric and primitive men who roamed the earth tens of thousands of years ago, the Bible is the only authoritative history in the world regarding the creation of man and has nothing to say about a race of beings before Adam.

The Biblical account of man's creation gives the lie to a great deal of nonsense talked and written about "evolution" which teaches that man gradually evolved from a protoplasm, or, as Darwin put it, the origin of life can be traced to "electricity and albumen." Adam was a direct, immediate creation of God — one moment a handful of dust, the next a perfectly formed body. And he was in no way "primitive" as the term is used. His was maturity at the outset and he found himself in a perfect environment.

As to the theory of a race of pre-historic men, that is, a world of beings existing before Adam, the Bible makes it perfectly clear that Adam was "the first man" (I Corinthians 15:45) and that before him there was no human being to "till the ground" (Genesis 2:51). That he was alone is further confirmed by the fact that "there was not found an help meet for him" (Genesis 2:18, 20).

All races of men, then, descended from one father, Adam (Malachi 2:10). Eve, the wife of Adam, is likewise spoken of as "the mother of all living" (Genesis 3:20). Paul speaks of all the nations of the earth as being "one blood" (Acts 17:26).

At the flood "every man," with the exception of Noah and his family, was destroyed (Genesis 6:7; 7:19, 21). After the flood, *all* generations sprang from the three sons of Noah (Genesis 9:19; 10:32). Our concern is not with the antiquity of the globe but with the creation of Adam. The Bible has no reference to kings before the flood. Not until the development of civilization, springing from the dispersion of Noah's sons, do we find mention of kings (See Nimrod).

Therefore, records of dynasties as given by so-called authorities as having exercised dominion in ancient times, even before Abraham's day, must be treated with reserve. While much can be learned from profane history, cuneiform inscriptions and archaeological discoveries of kings and kingdoms, it must be reiterated that the purpose of this volume is to deal with those monarchs specifically mentioned in Holy Writ.

Further, while it is absorbing to find out all we can of the kings of various nations and dynasties from the beginning of kingdom rule and discover how they can be woven into the texture of Scripture, it must not be forgotten that the supreme aim of Scripture is not to give us an historical account of all the kings of the past, but to focus attention on the Jewish nation and kingdom as being necessary for the coming of God's Holy King, the Lord Jesus Christ. The presence and accounts of Gentile kings in Scripture in their relationship to Israel, are only incidental.

Dr. R. K. Harrison in his most illuminating and absorbing work, *A History of Old Testament Times,* provides us with interesting material, documented from archaeological sources, of the rise and expansion of dynasties and kingdoms in ancient times. Mesopotamia, the rich tract of land between the Tigris and Euphrates rivers, northwest of Babylonia and southwest of Assyria, saw the development of human activity. Dynasties, before and after the flood, are cited by Dr. Harrison — a fascinating study outside the scope of our present study. The strip of country known as Ancient Mesopotamia, passed successively under the Babylonians, Medes and Persians. After the battle of Issus, B.C. 333, it came under the Macedonians; in A.D. 163, under the Romans; in 363, under the Persians; in 902, under the Carmathians; in 1514, under the Turks.

The first Biblical king was Nimrod (Genesis 10:8-10; see under name) the recognized founder of the Babylonian Empire. The Prophet Isaiah reminds us that it was the pride of Egyptian princes to trace their lineage back to ancient kings (Isaiah 19:11). The Canaanites and the Philistines had kings as early as the times of Abraham (Genesis 14:2; 20:2). The Edomites were related to Israel (Genesis 36:31), and the Moabites and the Midianites had kings earlier than the Israelites (Numbers 22:4; 31:8).

The kings before Israel's monarchy appear to have been autocratic and despotic, as is seen in Pharaoh's slaughter of Jewish male babies and the cruel bondage inflicted upon the Jewish people. The use of slave labor built large cities and magnificent structures like the *Pyramids* — wonder of the ages. Sir John Denham of the Sixteenth Century, in his ode on *The Earl of Stafford's Trial and Death,* has the lines —

> "Happy when both to the same centre move,
> When Kings give liberty, and subjects love.
>
> ❋   ❋   ❋   ❋
>
> Thus, Kings, by grasping more than they could hold,
> First made their subjects by oppression bold;
> And popular sway for subjects to receive,
> Ran to the same extremes: and one excess
> Made both, by striving to be greater, less."

That kings and wars go together is proven by the chapter of ancient kings and the story of the first war (Genesis 14). The first men to make war were kings (14:1, 2). Lust for power has ever been char-

acteristic of rulers (James 4:1). Too few were "worthy to receive power." Power, for selfish ends, has produced some of the darkest pages of human history. Cowper wrote —
> "But war's a game, which, were their subjects wise,
> Kings would not play it."

The chapter above (Genesis 14) provides us with two alliances of kings — four against five, with the small group victorious. God is not always on the side of majorities. Let us look, first of all, at the united forces led by the King of Elam. Assyrian tablets show that Elam had conquered and overrun Babylonia.

1. Amraphel, King of Shinar

Although a subject king, Amraphel is placed first. His name, an Accadian one, may signify "the circle of the few." Many Assyriologists identify Amraphel as *Hammurabi,* one of the greatest and most famous of early Babylonian kings — contemporary with Abraham around 2,000 B.C. Dr. R. K. Harrison affirms the identification of Amraphel, King of Shinar, with Hammurabi of Babylon.

In 1902, one of the most important archaeological discoveries was made with the unearthing in the ruins of Susa of the *Hammurabi Stone* which is now in the Louvre Museum. This finely polished block of hard, black diorite stone, eight feet in height, carries the cuneiform writing of the Semitic Babylonian language and represents the laws received from the sun-god Shamach. The laws written some 800 years before Moses received The Law were called "the judgments of the righteous." Shinar, over which Amraphel reigned, is given in a cuneiform inscription as *Sumer.*

2. Arioch, King of Ellasar

A Babylonian cylinder speaks of Arioch as *Eriaku,* "servant of the sun-god," and declares his mother was the sister of Chedorlaomer. Ellasar is the modern *Senkereh,* ancient tablets of which can be seen in the British Museum.

3. Chedorlaomer, King of Elam

This Elamite overlord is sometimes identified as *Kudur-lagamar,* found on cuneiform inscriptions — a name as servant of a Babylonian deity with a similar name.

4. Tidal, King of Nations

The Syrian Version speaks of Tidal as *"Thargil, King of Gelae."* The R.V. gives us Goiim for "Nations." Ellicott says this is a proper name, spelled *Gulium* in the inscriptions, and represents the whole tract of country which extended from the Tigris to the eastern borders of Media, including the district afterward known as Assyria.

Then we have the five kings "joined together," that is united in a confederacy to destroy the four kings just mentioned. At this time, Palestine was the possession of Egypt and the Amenophic Dynasty held sway.

BERA, KING OF SODOM,

BIRSHA, KING OF GOMORRAH,

SHINAB, KING OF ADMAH,

SHEMEBER, KING OF ZEBOIIM.

The last king is unnamed, being referred to as

KING OF BELA, OR ZOAR.

The four kings defeated the five kings in "the Vale of Siddim," which was "full of slime pits" (Genesis 14:10). These bitumen pits, characteristic of the shores of the Dead Sea, became the graves of the five kings. All camp equipment and supplies were captured. Only a remnant of the armies massed together escaped to the mountains. The victorious army entered Sodom and took Lot captive (14:12); but through the mercy of God he was delivered by Abraham whose victory was attributed by King Melchizedek to the "most high God." With a small, well-trained army of 318 veterans, Abraham staged a midnight attack and recovered all the spoil taken by the four kings. Elsewhere we have written fully about the renowned King of Salem mentioned in the chapter of kings before us.

II

Assyria and Assyrian Monarchs
B.C. 1456-615

The name Assyria is a Greek word formed from *Ashur* who built its original and primitive capital, Nineveh. The country extended from Babylonia northward to the Kurdish Mountains and at times included the country west of the Euphrates and the Khabar. The whole region was known to the early Babylonians as *Subartu*. While the histories of Babylonia and Assyria appear to be interwoven from earliest times, and Assyria was once a dependency of Babylonia,

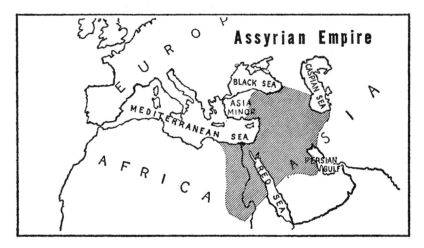

Assyria is always distinguished from Babylonia in the Old Testament and not confounded with it as by Herodotus and other classical writers. While the Egyptians were descended from Ham, the Assyrians came from Shem.

Just when Assyria became an empire is a matter of conjecture. It is assumed that it was founded around 2000 B.C. by colonists from Babylonia. From the time of Moses till the time of Solomon no mention is made in the Bible of the kings of Egypt. It was about 1300 B.C. that Shalmaneser and his son Tukulti-Mas threw off the yoke of Babylonia and ruled the whole Euphrates Valley. After a while Assyria declined, then Tiglath-Pileser I, about 1120-1100 B.C., that is around Samuel's time, restored Assyria as a great kingdom. Then followed another period of decline, during which Israel became a monarchy. Later, Assyria revived as a world empire and experienced a brilliant epoch of 300 years.

The first notice of the kingdom of Assyria since the days of Nimrod, who created a kingdom there (Genesis 10:11), is in II Kings 15:19. Assyrian history begins with the high priests (*patesis*) of Assur. The earliest known to us are Auspin and Kikia, who bear Mitannian names. According to Esar-Haddon, the kingdom was founded by Belbani, son of Adasi, who first made himself independent; Hadad-nirari, however, ascribes its foundation to Zulili.

Assyria appears to have had five dynasties stretching from about 1450-615 B.C., a period of 835 years. The Bible contacts with Assyria begin with Shalmaneser II of the third dynasty and include both kings of the fourth dynasty and four of the five kings of the fifth dynasty. Assyria was a military kingdom and the king was commander of the army, which included the majority of the male population. The prowess of Assyria's well-equipped army excited terror in Western Asia (Isaiah 10:5-14; Nahum 2:11, 13; 3:1-4).

The Assyrian Empire began to deteriorate about 625 B.C. and fell in 606-5 B.C., when it was taken by Medes, and with it Assyrian power ceased forever. About 635 B.C. Nahum predicted the fall of that city which 180 years earlier repented at the preaching of Jonah. Dean Stanley reminds us that, "The Assyrian Empire vanished from the earth so suddenly and so noiselessly that its fall is only known to us through the reduced grandeur of the palaces of its latest king, and through the cry of exultation raised over its destruction by the Israelitish Prophet, Nahum."

Religiously, the Assyrians were idolators differing from the idolatrous Babylonians in two respects —

1. The king, and not the high priest, was supreme.
2. The religious head was the national god Asur of Assur, whose high priest and representative was the king. And, originally *Asir*, leader in war, is depicted as a warrier-god armed with a bow and who, in the age when solar worship became general in Babylonia, was identified with the sun-god. Similarity of name caused him to be also identified with the city of Asur, where he was worshipped. Where religion was concerned the Assyrians were intense and intolerant.

Characteristically the Assyrians were cruel and ferocious in war, and stern disciplinarians. "They were great warriors, continually out on raiding expeditions," says H. H. Halley. "They built their State on the loot of other peoples, skinned their prisoners alive, or cut off their hands, feet, noses, ears, put out their eyes, pulled out their tongues, made mounds of human skulls, all to inspire terror."

Bas-reliefs discovered at Nineveh reveal that Assyria abounded in stone buildings and in sculpture rich in detail and delicate finish. The Assyrians also excelled in cast bronze work. Scenes hammered in relief on bronze gates were discovered at Balawat. They were also famed for work in gold, silver, ivory, glass and wood. Nineveh, the metropolis of Assyria, indicated in its vast extent and population, the magnificence and power of its monarchs.

Assyria was closely associated with Israel, as a study of Old Testament history reveals. Assyria became the place of captivity of Ephraim, or The Ten Tribes, who have never been recovered. *Who* and *where* they now are cannot be ascertained in spite of the claims of British Israelism. Assyria destroyed the Kingdom of Israel in 721 B.C. and also exacted tribute from Judah. References like II Kings 15:29; 17:6, 24; 18:13-19; 19:36; Isaiah 10:5-32; 20:1; 36; 37; 38 should be studied by the reader.

God used Assyria as a scourge in His hand to chastise His guilty and apostate people (Isaiah 10:5-34). Assyrians and Egyptians who in the past most cordially detested each other and anciently strove for world mastery at the expense of each other's ruin, are to unite in happy service and bury forever their mutual distrust and hatred. God is to unite them in blessing for His earthly people, Israel. Long-standing quarrels of Assyria and Egypt (Daniel 11) about the possession of Palestine will be healed. Situated between the two, Palestine is to be the land *par excellence*. The three leading powers in the Millennial Age will be Israel, Assyria, and Egypt — Israel being the chief, and Jerusalem the metropolitan city of the earth (see Isaiah 19:23-25).

Coming to a consideration of the Assyrian monarchs themselves, it must be said that it is well-nigh impossible to give a complete and correct list of the same. There are still wide gaps in both Assyrian and Babylonian history, but constant exploration is filling them up. The ancient *Babylonian Chronicle* gave the names and length of reign of the kings of Assyria, Babylonia and Elam from 774-668 B.C.

Commentators differ as to the number, names and order of many known Assyrian monarchs. Hastings in his *Dictionary of the Bible* sets out over 60 of them, beginning with ADASI, of 1725 B.C. Fausset in his *Bible Encyclopaedia* starts his list with BEL-SUMILI-KAPI, of about 1700 B.C., with the notation that a genealogical tablet calls him founder of the kingdom. Hastings has a most illuminating article on *Synchronous History*, in which the dynasties of Babylonia and Assyria are columnized according to their contemporary association.

In the following sketches we have, more or less, dealt with Assyrian monarchs who have a Bible contact. For information on others, the reader is referred to the above commendable study books.

ASSURUBALLID 1400 B.C.?

This most ancient Assyrian king married his daughter to a Babylonian king, thereby providing for himself a pretext for interfering in the affairs of Babylonia. When his son-in-law was murdered, Assuruballid went to Babylon and placed a grandson on the throne. Having fallen into decay, Babylon was forced to protect herself from the rising power of Assyria and formed an alliance with Mesopotamia and Egypt.

SHALMANESER I 1300 B.C.

Shalmaneser is the name of several Assyrian kings and may be derived from Shalman (Hosea 10:14). This monarch devoted his energies to crippling the Hittite power which had absorbed Babylonia. He succeeded in severing Babylonian communications with the Hittites and through several campaigns weakened the Hittite Empire.

TUKULTI-MAS

Shalmaneser's son and successor entered into the fruits of his father's labors. With the Hittites rendered powerless, the Assyrian Kingdom was left free to crush Babylonia. Babylon, the capital, was taken and for seven years Tukulti-mas was the master of all the land watered by the Tigris and Euphrates. A successful revolt, however, drove the Assyrian emperor back to Assyria and when he was murdered by his own son, the Babylonians saw in his death a punishment inflicted on the Assyrians by their god, Bel-Merodach.

BEL-KUDUR-UZUR

This Assyrian monarch lost his life in battle against the Babylonians and with his death a new dynasty mounted the Assyrian throne (for further details as to earlier Assyrian kings who do not appear in Bible history, the reader is directed to Hastings' article previously mentioned).

TIGLATH-PILESER I 1120 B.C.

Renowned for his success in extending the Assyrian Empire as far westward as Cappadocia, this first monarch to bear a familiar name, got as far as the Mediterranean and received presents from the king of Egypt. At Assur he planted a botanical garden stocked with trees from conquered provinces. With his death Assyrian power declined. Pitru (*Pethor* Numbers 22:5) fell into the hands of the Aramaeans.

Assur-nazir-pal II (III) or Ashurnasirpal 884-860 b.c.

It was under this monarch that the military power of Assyria became the terror of surrounding nations. Ashurnasirpal was a warlike and cruel man and boasted of his cruelty. J. Finegan in *Light from the Ancient East* cites this discovered cuneiform inscription of his barbarism —

> "I built a pillar over against the city gate, and I flayed all the chief men who had revolted, and I covered the pillar with skins; some I walled up with the pillar, some I impaled upon the pillar on stakes, and others I bound to stakes round about the pillar."

Ashurnasirpal welded the Assyrian nation into the best fighting machine in the ancient world. Under him, the Empire revived. He rebuilt Calah and established a seat of government at Nineveh, where he built himself a palace. The Hittites were forced to render him homage, and he laid the Phoenecians under tribute. He it was who opened the road to the West for Assyrian merchants.

Shalmaneser II (III)

Although the son and successor of Ashurnasirpal, Shalmaneser was not content, as his father had been, with mere raids for the sake of booty. He endeavored to organize and administer the countries his armies subdued. He was the first Assyrian monarch to come into conflict with Israel. Benhadad and Ahab fought against him and were defeated. Kings he conquered, like Jehu, were forced to acknowledge his supremacy (I Kings 19:15-17; 20:34; 22:1-3; II Kings 8:7-15; 9:1-5). Records of this monarch who reigned for 35 years can be seen in the British Museum.

Little is recorded in Assyrian history of the following rulers —

Shamsi-adad 825-808 b.c.
Samas-rammon IV 824-812 b.c.

The latter suppressed the two years revolt that had simmered from the time of Nineveh's capture. His chief campaign was against Media.

Hadad-nirari 811-783 b.c.

It was this son of Samas-Rammon, Jonah visited when he went to Nineveh (Jonah 3:6). Hadad-nirari claimed to have reduced to subjection the whole of Syria including Phoenicia, Edom and Philistia, and to have taken Marias, king of Damascus, prisoner in his own capital city. He also took tribute from Israel.

Two or three weak kings follow this period —

SHALMANESER (III?) 783-771 B.C.
ASSUR-DAYAH OR ASHURDAN III 771-753 B.C.
ASSUR-LUSH OR ASHURNIRARI 753-747 B.C.

TIGLATH-PILESER III (IV) 745-727 B.C.

This was the name of a military officer who became king of Assyria. His Babylonian name — he was for two years also king of Babylon — was PUL (II Kings 15:19-29; 16:10-16; I Chronicles 5:26; II Chronicles 28:19-21; Isaiah 7:1-9; Amos 7:1-3). Assyria having fallen again into a state of decay, was delivered by Pul's or Pulu's successful revolt. Bringing to an end the old time kings, he took the name of Tiglath-pileser and founded the second Assyrian Empire, making Assyria the dominant power in Asia. He re-organized his army and made it irresistible. A new administrative system was introduced. The empire was centralized at Nineveh and was governed by a bureaucracy at the head of which was the king.

"The main defect in the first Assyrian Empire," says Dr. John Adams in his book on *The Minor Prophets*, "as seen in the alternating periods of activity and decline, lay in its lack of cohesion and permanence. So long as it enjoyed the creative genius and dominating personality of some great conqueror, its armies swept out in all directions to subjugate and impoverish the nations; but the moment the conqueror died, the huge fabric he had raised crumbled to pieces, and the whole conquest had to be repeated a second time whenever a successor worthy of the nation's ideal was seated upon the throne. Even under the Second Empire, which lasted from the accession of Tiglath-pileser III to the fall of Nineveh in 606 B.C., this fatal defect in the body politic was not wholly eliminated."

While much relating to Tiglath-pileser is conjectural, owing to the deplorable state of his annals, we do know that he welded West Asia into a single empire, held together by military force and fiscal laws. His conquests were manifold and he secured the trade of the world for the merchants of Nineveh. He invaded Israel and carried the inhabitants of Galilee into captivity. Menahem paid him tribute, and Ahaz bribed him for help. Five kings of Judah and Israel are mentioned by Tiglath-pileser in Assyrian inscriptions — Azarish, Menahem, Rezin, Pekah, Ahaz and Hoshea.

SHALMANESER IV (V) 727-722 B.C.

We have scant information of the life and labors of this military adventurer whose original name was ULULA. He beseiged Samaria but did not capture it. He died or was murdered during the attempt. It was this Shalmaneser who imprisoned Hoshea for three years (II Kings 17:3), for discontinuing payment of tribute to Assyria and forming secret alliances with Egypt.

MERODACH-BALADAN 722-702 B.C.

While this king of the Chaldean State in Babylonia rightly belongs to the section dealing with Babylonian monarchs, we include him here seeing that he was tributary to Tiglath-pileser III, and because his name is conspicuous in the Assyrian Inscriptions of Sargon as having rebelled against him and set up an independent monarchy. The Inscription says that Sargon drove Merodach-baladan from Babylon after he had ruled there twelve years.

This son of Baladan made himself master of Babylon and was supported by Elam. Sargon went against the Elamites with little result. Later on, Sargon successfully overcame Merodach-baladan who was made to submit to the Assyrian monarch. Later he returned to the throne for only nine months and was then driven out by Sennacherib. Merodach-baladan managed to escape over the sea to "the islands at the north of the Euphrates." His whole family was apparently destroyed, and he himself put to death by Belib.

It was Merodach-baladan who sent princes to Jerusalem to congratulate Hezekiah on his recovery to health and made him the recipient of gifts. His real intention, however, was to secure King Hezekiah as an ally against Assyria. Isaiah rebuked Hezekiah for showing the Assyrian princes all his treasures and predicted Judah's overthrow (Isaiah 39; II Kings 20:12-21; II Chronicles 32:31).

SARGON II 722-705 B.C.

Originally a general in the Assyrian army, Sargon, who reigned for seventeen years, brought Assyria to its height of ascendency. The best part of his reign was spent fighting the alliance of Northern Nations against Assyria. Soon after coming to the throne, Sargon captured Samaria and completed its destruction and carried 27,290 inhabitants into captivity. His boast remains in the *Khorsabad* annals —

"I besieged and captured Samaria, carrying off 27,290 of the people who dwelt therein. 50 chariots I gathered from among them."

Sargon ended the Northern Kingdom, Israel, in 722-721 B.C. This warrior and builder also conquered So, king of Egypt in the battle of Raghia. Facts of his feats can be gathered from tablets, cylinders, bricks, and jars in the British Museum and also from monuments at the Louvre, France. In 705 B.C. Sargon was murdered. The fourfold mention of "The King of Assyria" (II Kings 17:3-6) is applicable to Sargon.

SENNACHERIB 705-681 B.C.

Son and successor of Sargon II, and father of Esar-haddon, Sennacherib was the first Assyrian monarch to make Nineveh the seat of government. Although he endeavored to continue the western expansion of his empire, Sennacherib was not the forceful leader his father had been. By contrast he was weak, having neither the military skill nor the administrative ability of Sargon. Babylonia was in a state of constant revolt because of his policies and rule. Out of spite he razed the sacred city of Babylon to the ground in 689 B.C.

His first attack upon King Hezekiah was unsuccessful. Attacking again, he was more successful and Hezekiah was forced to pay him tribute. He was murdered by his two sons (II Kings 18:13-17; Isaiah 37:33-37; Nahum 3:3, 14; Psalm 124:7, 8). Records of Sennacherib are to be found on bas-reliefs and cylinders in the British Museum.

ESAR-HADDON 681-668 B.C.

Referred to as "the most potent of the kings of Assyria," Esar-haddon succeeded to the throne after two of his brothers had murdered their father on the 20th Tebet (II Kings 19:37). By contrast to his weak father, Esar-haddon distinguished himself as a general and administrator. Under him the Second Empire reached the acme of its power and prosperity. He rebuilt Babylon making it the second capital of his empire.

King Manasseh was under tribute to Esar-haddon, who later took him captive but released him. He conquered Palestine and placed Assyrian governors in Egypt. Those who opposed his building of a second temple were taken to Samaria. He died on his way to put down a revolt in Egypt which he had conquered. His reign lasted 13 years (II Kings 19:37; 21:13, 14; II Chronicles 33:11; Ezra 4:2, 9).

Between Esar-haddon and Assur-bani-pal was King SHAMASH-SHUM-UKIN (668-647) of whom we have little record.

ASSUR-BANI-PAL 647-626 B.C.

Son and successor of Esar-haddon, Assur-bani-pal, whose Greek name was Sardanspalus, and probably the Asnapper of Ezra 4:10, was the most literary of Assyrian monarchs. He was the last great king of Assyria, which probably fell in 606 B.C. The virtual ruler in Babylon for more than 40 years, his reign in Assyria lasted 22 years. His brother, Samas-shum-ukin, became viceroy of Babylonia, but when dissatisfaction spread throughout the greater part of the Assyrian Empire, conscious of his guilt in the revolt, the viceroy burned himself to death in the ruins of his palace.

Assur-bani-pal was a munificent patron of learning and provided treasures for the renowned library of Nineveh where he had built a great palace. His cultural interests made him famous as the one who brought art to its climax in Assyria. This was the king who made King Manasseh along with 21 other kings pay tribute to him and kiss his feet. His conquests were many but he rested on his oars.

Extravagant luxury invaded the court, and the king conducted his campaigns through his generals, while he remained in ease at court. Constant wars, however, depleted the Assyrian treasury, and with its fighting population depleted, the nation was unable to resist the descent of the Cimerians upon it. With the death of Assur-bani-pal about 630 B.C. the Assyrian Empire crumbled, and Babylon asserted her independence, passing into the hands of Nabojolasser. Nineveh was utterly destroyed and its site forgotten. By the time of Cyrus, Asshur, the old capital of the Assyrian Empire, was still standing but only as a small provincial town (II Kings 21:2; II Chronicles 33; Ezra 4:2, 9, 10). Two petty kings followed Assur-bani-pal — his son, ASSUR-ETIL-ITANIA; and SIN-SAR-ISKUM.

As SYRIA is probably derived from the word *Assyria*, mention can be made at this point of Syrian kings. Herodotus says that "Syrians" and "Assyrians" were the Greek and barbarian designations of the same people. The Hebrew for SYRIA is *Aram* and refers to Aram-Na-hariam (Genesis 14:10), that is, Aram between the two rivers in Mesopotamia, part of which is Padan-Aram. Laban, who lived there, is called the *Aramaean* or Syrian. Originally occupied by the Hamites or Hittites, a Shemite element entered in the persons of Abraham, Chedorlaomer and Amraphel.

In ancient times, Syria was divided among many rulers known as "kings" — as Damascus, Rehob, Maacah, Zobah and Geshur (see Numbers 13:21; Judges 18:28). There are references to "The Kings of Syria" and "The Kings of the Hittites" (I Kings 10:29; II Kings 7:6). Joshua fought with the chiefs of Lebanon and Hermon (Joshua 11:2-18). David conquered HADAD-EZER of Zobah, and made Zobah, Rehob and Maacah tributary (II Samuel 10). In the reigns of Baasha and Asa, Syria was an ally of both Israel and Judah (I Kings 15:18). Damascus and Israel were frequently at war (Isaiah 7).

King David married Maacah, daughter of TALMAI, king of Geshur, and she became the mother of Absalom who afterwards fled to Geshur where he spent three years in exile (II Samuel 3:3; 13:18). King Ahaz of Judah was also associated with Syria (II Kings 16:10), which was evidently made up of small centers ruled by their own kings. Hamath had a single king, TOU by name, (II Kings 19:13; I Chronicles 18:9) and there were several other independent kings such as BEN-HADAD and 32 others allied with him (I Kings 20:1). All the kings combined their forces for joint expeditions against their foes. It was Tiglath-pileser, who, in 732 B.C., subdued Syria and divided the territory among his generals. When Alexander the Great died, his successor, Seleucus Nicator in 300 B.C., made Syria head of a vast kingdom with Antioch as the capital. Ultimately Syria came under the power of Rome.

III

Egypt and Egyptian Monarchs

Egypt had attained a high civilization and settled monarchy before Abraham went forth from Ur of the Chaldees to go into the land of Canaan. Egypt was in its glory when the Hebrews were there in bondage but it had passed its prime when David and Solomon sat upon the throne of Israel. By the time Rome had risen to power, Egypt had sunk in decay and at the dawn of modern history had ceased to exist as a nation. Yet it had played a large part in world affairs (Hosea 11:1; Matthew 11:14, 15).

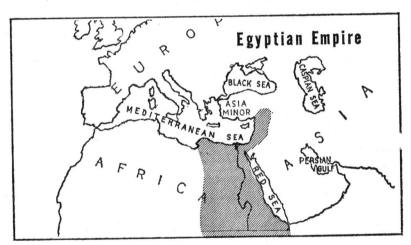

In ancient times Egypt was known as *Chemia*, the Land of Ham, Noah's son, perhaps because he lived there. Once the greatest and most fertile nation, it is now "the basest of the kingdoms" according to Ezekiel's prophecy (29:14, 15). It has been successively conquered and oppressed by the Babylonians, the Persians, the Macedonians, the Romans, the Saracens and the Mamalukes. On the Island of Elephantine, or The Island of Flowers, as the natives call it, which was an outpost for the successive lords of Egypt — Pharaohs, Ptolemies,

31

Caesars, and Saracen Caliphs — are traces of their military occupation. Today Egypt is governed by President Nasser, who aspires to be known as a modern Pharaoh.

Canon Trevors reminds us that —

"No two countries in the world offer so many claims on the attention of the Christian inquirer as *Palestine* and *Egypt*; the promised land and the house of bondage, the holy and the unclean, the type and gate of heaven, and the image of a world that lieth in wickedness. In the Old Testament they are at once connected and opposed, like the Church and the World under the Gospel. The allegory is continued into the New Testament, which opens with the announcement, 'Out of Egypt have I called My Son.' If the student of Holy Scripture gives the first place in his inquiries to the land of the Law and the Prophets, the mountains and valleys which echoed the daily psalmody of the temple, the scenes of the Saviour's life and miracles and passion — the second place is as naturally claimed by the nation from the midst of whom the chosen people were brought out 'by a mighty hand and by a stretched out arm'; a land that sheltered Israel from the famine, and Jesus from the sword."

Egypt is 600 miles long and 300 broad, and bounded on the south by Ethiopia, on the north by the Mediterranean Sea, on the east by the Red Sea, and on the west by Libya (Exodus 3:20). A few years ago it had a cultivated area of some 16,000 square miles and a population of 5,000,000. Ancient Egypt was extensively engaged in commerce and manufactures. Arts, crafts and sciences were early cultivated and maintained a degree of perfection for ages. Moses was learned in all the wisdom of the Egyptians (Acts 7:22). It was also famous for its fertility, which the overflow of the River Nile made possible. Fruits, vegetables and fish were sources of great affluence.

Religiously, Egypt was idolatrous, although in Abraham's time both the monarch and his princes recognized God and respected the right of matrimony and hospitality (Genesis 11:10-20). In Joseph's day, sovereign and nobles acknowledged the wisdom and good of Divine Providence and acted toward the Israelites with great kindness. But by the time of Moses, the government had become despotic, the people given over to the arts of magic and sorcery and to the worship of beasts and birds and natural forces. The most magnificent temples were erected to a bull, *Apis*. The Ten Plagues overtaking the Egyptians displayed God's judgment upon them for their worship of ten different heathen deities. The religion of Egypt revealed what man becomes when left to himself. *Egypt* is now a symbol of wickedness (Revelation 11:8).

Egypt — even today — stands out as the persecutor of the Jewish people. It appears either as the tempter or as the persecutor of Israel, dividing the guilt in this respect with the Babylonians and Assyrian monarchies to the east of the sacred land. Israel became contaminated by the idolatry of Egypt and was rebuked for making it her glory. Being the symbol of strength, Israel relied upon the strength of Egypt rather than upon her God. For predictions of Egypt's doom when it was at the summit of its pride and power, one must turn to Scriptures like Isaiah 19:4, 11; Ezekiel 29:3, 6; 30:4, 8, 13-19; 31; 32; Joel 3:19, 20. From the second Persian conquest, upwards of 2,000 years ago, no native prince of an Egyptian race has reigned. Although the Ptolemies, successors of the Greek, Alexander the Great, ruled for 300 years, and raised Egypt to eminence by their patronage of literature, they constituted a foreign line.

Prophetically, the ancient kingdom of Egypt is destined to play an important part in the future. It will be the theater of extensive war operations on the part of certain powers. Then because Egypt opened her friendly shores and received the Child Jesus when His own people sought His life (Matthew 2:13-15), God will be gracious unto it. During the Millennial Reign of Christ the three leading powers will be Egypt, Assyria and Israel (Isaiah 19:23-25) — "The Lord shall be known to Egypt and the Egyptians shall know the Lord in that day."

From the archaeological aspect the study of ancient Egypt is fascinating and has produced several readable books by Egyptologists. Outstanding among the relics of the past are, of course, the renowned pyramids, which Josephus, the Jewish historian asserts, were built by the Israelites while in their Egyptian bondage. These massive and ancient creations are still the wonder of the world. When Napoleon, on the eve of the battle of the pyramids, issued his famous *ordre du jour*, he exclaimed, "Soldiers, forty centuries are looking down on you!" It has been said that, "All things dread Time, but Time itself dreads the Pyramids."

Tempted as one is to linger over pyramids, temples, obelisks, tombs in which Thebian Pharaohs "lie in glory, every one in his own house," the reader is urged to consult the latest works on "Egyptology" for a full treatment of same. Mention can be made of the mummy of Rameses II, possibly the Pharaoh of the Oppression. After 36 centuries human eyes can gaze on the features of the man who had conquered Syria, Cyprus and Ethiopia, and had raised Egypt to her highest pinnacle of power, and placed its frontiers where he pleased.

As the purpose of this volume is to deal with only those kings and queens who are mentioned in the Bible, it is not within its confines to gather from outside historical sources, facts and theories of *all* Egyptian monarchs. For an illuminating insight into the dynasties, kings and cults of ancient Egypt, one is referred to the chapter dealing with same in R. K. Harrison's book, *A History of Old Testament Times*. One of the most helpful summaries we have come across of Egyptian dynasties from 2700 B.C. to 1520 B.C. and contemporary events recorded on the Monuments and Scripture Parallel Events, is that found in Fausset's *Encyclopaedia*.

THE PHARAOHS
(Genesis 12:18; 41:38-45; Exodus 14:28; II Kings 23:29; etc.)

THE KINGS WHO RULED EGYPT

Having briefly considered the land of the pharaohs let us now look at the portraits of some of the Bible-mentioned kings, who contributed to the glory and greatness which was Egypt's. About 250 B.C. an Egyptian priest wrote a Greek history of Egypt arranged under 31 dynasties from Menes, the first historical king, to the Greek conquest by Alexander the Great, 332 B.C. *Dynasties* mean the family lines of kings. Many of the aspects of this history have been corroborated by archaeological discoveries.

Of these dynasties, few records have been found and to date, only the pharaohs of three or four dynasties have been unearthed by monuments, tombs and papyri. In recent years, Egyptology has made great strides. The language of the country is better known and multitudes of stele and inscriptions have been discovered and deciphered. Dr. Samuel Manning in his most readable volume, *The Land of the Pharaohs*, vividly describes the most wonderful event in recent Egyptian history, namely the world-famous discovery at Deir-el-Bahari in 1881. Mummies of the majority of the rulers of Egypt during the eighteenth, nineteenth and twenty-first dynasties were hauled up from their long lost tombs, and one is now able to look upon the real face of the pharaoh of the oppression, as well as upon many of the now famous kings and queens of Egyptian History.

Dr. Manning enumerates the following —

King Sekerem-Ra Ta-aken, one of the Lords of early Egyptian history, and Queen Ansera, of the 17th dynasty. Queen Ahmes Nefertari, King Amenhotep I, Thothnese II and Thothnese III, of the brilliant 18th dynasty. Seti I, father of Rameses II, Rameses II and Rameses III, of the 19th dynasty.

Netem-Maut., King of Pinetem I and King Pinetem II, of the 21st dynasty.

For a consideration of the above discoveries and of more recent ones like that of King Tutankhamen's rich tomb, the reader is directed to the latest archaeological books dealing with Egyptian excavations. Fascinating as the subject of ancient dynasties and their succeeding monarchs is, we have already indicated that it is not within the scope of our study to deal with such. This we can say, that further discoveries will only go to confirm "the Scripture of Truth." Our purpose is to distinguish the *Bible* pharaohs and relate them to Egyptian and Israelitish history. In order we have seven or eight mentioned in the Old Testament.

1. The Pharaoh who reproved Abraham for lying (Genesis 12:18).
2. The Pharaoh who made Joseph ruler over Egypt (Genesis 41: 38-45).
3. The Pharaoh who, seeking to destroy the Jews, destroyed himself (Exodus 14:28).
4. The Pharaoh whose daughter married Solomon (I Kings 3:1).
5. The Pharaoh who gave protection to the king of Edom (I Kings 11:15).
6. The Pharaoh known as Shishak (II Chronicles 11:2).
7. Pharaoh-Necho associated with Josiah (II Kings 23:29).
8. Pharaoh-Hophra denounced by two prophets for his sins (Jeremiah 44:30; 46:2).

In passing, it is necessary to observe that *pharaoh* was the common designation of the kings of Egypt while the empire lasted. It was an official title like *Kaiser, Czar, Shah,* or as *Ptolemy* was a title given to kings after the time of Alexander the Great. Josephus and other writers give "king," "prince" or "supreme lord," as the meaning of the title name. *Pharaoh* enters into the composition of the names of "Potiphar" and "Potipherah." Several scholars affirm that *Pharah* was the word for "sun," to which Egyptian kings likened themselves.

PHARAOH-AMENEMHA
(Genesis 12:14-20)
The King Who Rebuked God's Friend

Abraham's contact with one of the early kings in Bible history came during a time of Egypt's prosperity. Possibly the Pharaoh mentioned here was Amenemha, the first king of the twelfth dynasty. The narrative before us makes sad reading, seeing it records Abraham's wandering from the path of obedience to God's will. The patriarch had been led to Canaan but he went, on his own initiative, to Egypt — a step resulting in the fear of man, the acting of a lie, and the placing of his wife in circumstances of great moral danger.

On leaving Haran, Abraham had Sarai agreed upon adopting the expedient of Sarai posing as his sister. Actually she was Abraham's sister, or at least half-sister, seeing that both had the same father, Terah, but not the same mother (Genesis 12:12, 13). But Abraham acted falsely because he implied that Sarai was wholly his sister and not his wife. The candor of the Bible is seen in that it does not gloss over its heroes' faults. Each saint not only falls at times, but is represented as failing in the very grace for which he was noted. Abraham was renowned for his faith yet was sadly deficient of this virtue, as grievous famine brought him into Egypt.

How we wish we might be able to throw a veil over the circumstances in Egypt which became a reproach to Abraham's character! How we should be warned by the imperfection of one of such exalted piety, namely unbelief! The friend of God gave way to a distrustful and dishonorable fear that he might be robbed and his beautiful wife and himself fall into the hands of violence.

But setting about to avoid his imaginary danger Abraham took the course which actually brought him into it. Perhaps he felt that Sarai might be clever enough to extricate herself from an embarrassing position. If Abraham was not guilty of a direct lie, he certainly was guilty of prevarication in saying of his wife, "She is my sister." Base equivocation can never be justified. Every man must speak truth with his neighbor.

The foregoing observations bring us to Abraham's contact with pharaoh, whose princes had observed attractive Sarai and spoke of her to the king. Although past 60 years of age, Sarai had retained much of the beauty commending her to the not so attractive swarthy descendant of Ham. Some years later Abraham was still haunted by the fear of the effects of his wife's attractive appearance (Genesis 20:2).

Pharaoh, impressed with the charm of Sarai, took her into his house with the intention of making her his wife. Is it not tragic that Abraham made an arrangement involving the possible sacrifice of his wife's chastity? His sin produced his punishment for he endangered the one nearest to him.

The conduct of Pharaoh was upright and dignified. He was acting upon the assurance that Sarai might lawfully become his. So he conducted himself well, bestowing upon Abraham many valuable presents, such as were given to relatives when taking a daughter or sister to wife. Yet God still watched over His erring children for good and although Abraham and Sarai were reduced to extreme distress He secured for them an undeserved deliverance.

What was the exact nature of the great plagues that came upon Pharaoh and all in his house, we are not told. Surely they could not have been very grievous, seeing pharaoh had acted in good faith. Whatever the plagues were they were God's method of preventing Pharaoh taking to himself the wife of another man. How rebuked Abraham must have been by Pharaoh's question:

"What is this that thou hast done unto me?"

"Why didst thou not tell me that she was thy wife?"

How sad it is when a sinning saint has to be rebuked by a worldling for his lapse of faith!

Pharaoh's magnanimity is seen in his willingness to let Abraham take his wife and go away, making sure that no harm would befall them because of their deception. "Go thy way" — and both of them must have left the presence of Pharaoh humiliated. They had no reply to the monarch's deserved rebuke. Alas, the repetition of this same offense (Genesis 20) reveals that Abraham did not feel much self-reproach for what he had done! We do read that Abraham returned to Canaan (13:1), where he had formerly enjoyed the divine presence and there renewed his communion with the God who pardons iniquity and heals the backsliding of His children.

PHARAOH — APEPI II
(Genesis 38:50)

THE KING WHO MADE A WISE CHOICE

What a thrilling success story Joseph's is! From earliest years his rise from a pit to Pharaoh's palace has fascinated us. What a rags-to-riches record his is!

The Bible and archaeological discoveries confirm that the dynasty of Joseph's time was one of the most prosperous in Egyptian history. It is affirmed that the Pharaoh with whom Joseph was intimately associated was Apepi II, one of the Hyksos, or Shepherd Kings of the Sixteenth Dynasty.

We are all familiar with the history of Joseph whose interpretation of his early dreams aggravated the hatred of his brethren to whom he said that their sheaves would bow down to his *sheaf* — prophetic of his future office under Pharaoh, as lord of the Egyptian granaries. The summary of his life can be found in the statement that the Lord made all that he did to prosper.

Sold as a slave to Potiphar's house, Joseph's personality soon impressed the household, particularly the wife of Potiphar who, with all the lustfulness of Egyptian women, conceived a passion for Joseph's beauty and physique and tempted him. Had he yielded to animal appetites, he would have lost a glorious future, and above all his regard for God. So the story is related in an artless manner. The pious youth flatly rejected his mistress' base proposal to sin with her.

With abhorrence, Joseph knew all that would be involved in yielding to her enticements. He could not betray his trust and act in so vile and ungrateful a way to his master. How could he do this great wickedness and sin against God? Daily the temptation was repeated but Joseph was adamant in his refusal. What a contrast is here presented of *un*faithfulness in the one, and of faithfulness in the other!

One day this over-sexed woman caught hold of Joseph's garment as he tried to avoid her, and he fled, leaving his garment in her hand. By this she accused Joseph of the very sin to which she had tried hard, but unsuccessfully, to tempt him. There is a similar Egyptian story of *The Two Brothers* to be seen in the Papyrus d'Orbiney in the British Museum. The fact that Potiphar did not put Joseph to death is evidence that he was not sure of his wife's story and that he had a suspicion that Joseph was innocent, for already Pharaoh's captain had been impressed with his slave's integrity. John Milton gave us the thought that — "He who reigns within himself, and rules passions, desires and fear is more than a king." Although Joseph became second to Pharaoh, he manifested those sterling qualities of character making him more kingly than his monarch.

God's eye was upon His faithful child in prison, and Joseph's experiences strikingly display how God, without appearing in the least to disturb the ordinary course of men's actions, causes the worst evils to bring about the greatest good. Thus the envy of Joseph's brethren, the false accusation of Potiphar's wife, the imprisonment of Joseph, all contributed to that advancement by which God enabled him to preserve Israel from famine (Genesis 50:20; Psalm 105:17).

The dreams of Pharaoh's chief cup-bearer and chief baker providentially opened the way to Joseph's elevation. For two years the cup-bearer who was restored to his position forgot his promise to Joseph, but when Pharaoh's two dreams of the seven fat kine and the seven lean kine could not be interpreted by Egypt's pretentious wise men, the cup-bearer remembered Joseph and commended him to Pharaoh as an interpreter of dreams. Thus it was these dreams that brought Joseph to the palace. Ultimately these dreams led to the salvation of Jacob and his family, one of which was to become the progenitor of Christ.

The pure and victorious Joseph was able by God to interpret the monarch's dream. He in turn acted wisely in raising the Spirit-inspired interpreter to be grand vizier over his house and his people. Pharaoh gave Joseph a signet ring bearing his name which became the seal of his authority.

As an acknowledgment of the divine wisdom Joseph manifested, Pharaoh gave Joseph the Egyptian name of *Zaphrath-Paaneah,* meaning, "Saviour of the World," or "The God of life or of the living." The Rabbini translate it, "Revealer of Secrets." Joseph's Hebrew name, means "addition," "God shall add (*yoseph*) to me another son." Then as an absolute ruler, Pharaoh commanded the marriage of Joseph to the daughter of the priest of On, thereby linking him to the noblest in the land. Doubtless the Egyptian priesthood was reluctant to admit this stranger. And of this we can be sure, that Joseph drew Asenath nearer his own faith which he openly avowed (Genesis 42:18).

Joseph became like a father to Pharaoh, and lord and ruler of Egypt (45:8), second only to Pharaoh in all of Egypt. Through years of plenty and then of famine, Joseph was eminently blessed of God as an administrator. Ultimately all his family came to Egypt, and his brethren became shepherds and dwelt in Goshen, which was afterwards known as Rameses.

Joseph died at the age of 110 years, and the Book of Genesis ends with his embalmed body in a coffin. So the book beginning with God, the Creator of the heavens above, ends with the coffin of a man in Egypt. In due course his remains were carried to Shechem and buried there (Exodus 13:19). It is sad to reflect that his two sons, Ephraim and Manasseh, followed the idolatries out of which their mother had come rather than the pure faith of their godly father.

Joseph, it must be noted, stands out as one of the most perfect types of the Lord Jesus Christ in Old Testament Scriptures. Comparisons between Jesus and Joseph form a most fascinating study. Thus the history of Joseph, one of the most lengthy in the Bible, is one of the most beautiful and attractive ever written. He displayed an exemplary pattern of goodness in different situations of life. What else can we do but admire the grace of God in giving Joseph such excellent wisdom and contentment, whether full or hungry? Joseph knew "both how to abound and to suffer need." As a son, as a slave, as a courtier, and a brother, he exhibited strictest regard to truth and true nobleness of mind. He is one of the faultless human heroes of Scripture, and one that Pharaoh had a profound regard for.

> With faith robust his dear integrity
>   He held with iron grip;
> Though pressed by passions' urgent sophistries
>   To let the treasure slip.
>
> The wrath of base desires ungratified
>   He boldly dared to face;
> And deemed the bondage of a prison cell
>   His better than disgrace.
>
> Though skilful archers aimed their shafts at him,
>   His bow abode in strength;
> And nerved by an all-conquering faith in God,
>   He overcame at length.
>
> Until some word from God was brought to him,
>   The hero's faith was tried;
> But, by the process of the purging fire,
>   His soul was purified.
>
> This stirring old-time story of a soul
>   That dared to do the right,
> Is rife with helpful inspirations still
>   That move toward the light.

PHARAOH-MENEPHTHAH
(Exodus 1-15)

THE KING WHOSE DEFIANCE MEANT DESTRUCTION

The phrase opening the Book of Exodus, "There arose up a new king which did not know Joseph" (1:8), suggests the introduction of a new dynasty. Bullinger suggests that the word "arose" meaning *stood* up, denotes a standing in the place of another whom he removed (Daniel 2:31, 39, 44; 3:24), and that "new" suggests a fresh dynasty and of a different kind from that which preceded it. This Pharaoh, then, was of a different race and dynasty, as shown by Josephus, who says, "the crown being come into another family." He was the Assyrian of Isaiah 42:4.

His desire to "deal wisely," or diplomatically, with the Israelites is worthy of note. The wisdom of Egypt ended in Pharaoh having to bring up, educate and prepare the very man who was to accomplish what he feared (Job 5:13; Proverbs 19:21; 21:30; Psalm 33:10, 11). Zom was the capital of Egypt and noted for wisdom and it was there that Moses declared the higher wisdom and power of God.

Not knowing Joseph means that the new Pharaoh felt under no obligation to him. He must have known of Joseph's wise and wonderful administration of Egypt's welfare, but he viewed the political situation apart from all personal predilections and saw danger in it. He paid no regard to the memory of Joseph and felt no gratitude toward the eminent benefactor of the nation. This pharaoh beheld with a jealous eye the rapid increase of the Israelites and as a cruel tyrant ordered the utter extermination of all male children at their birth.

Just who was the pharaoh whose daughter brought up Moses as her son? Egyptian annals are, at best, limited and fragmentary; and it is not always easy to follow the connection of sacred history with profane. This is why expectation will always be rife as to the identity of the Bible pharaohs.

As to the "new king" before us, some suppose him to be Arhmes I, the founder of the eighteenth dynasty of Manetho; others say that he was Rameses II, one of the greatest monarchs of the nineteenth dynasty. Still other scholars suggest that the weight of evidence seems to be in favor of regarding him as Seti I, the father of the above Rameses and the son of Rameses I, who reigned for the brief period of one and a half years. Seti, though not the actual founder of the nineteenth dynasty was the originator of its greatness.

The long reign of the pharaoh from whom Moses fled seems to agree with what we know of Rameses II. Not only did Manetho assign him a reign of above 60 years, according to all accounts that

have come down to us, but his 67 years are noted upon his monuments. Very few Egyptian kings reigned even as long as 40 years.

Fausset identifies Aahamas I as the king at the beginning of the
oppression and Thothmes II as probably the Pharaoh who perished
in the Red Sea. When Moses returned from Midian he found the latter at Zoan. This pharaoh was weak, capricious and obstinate. Ellicott, on the other hand, says that no other king in the Egyptian list
answers to the Exodus description except *Menephthah.* If Seti I be
the king who commenced the oppression, and Rameses II the monarch
from whom Moses fled, the pharaoh whom he found seated on the
throne upon his return must have been *Menephthah.*

The character of this king, as depicted on the Egyptian monuments,
bears a considerable resemblance to that of the adversary of Moses.
He was proud, vain-glorious, disinclined to expose his own person in
war, yet ready enough to send his soldiers into positions of danger.
Whoever the pharaoh was Moses encountered, he was one to use
slave-labor to complete his plans. Lenormant's remarks of Rameses
II are true of almost any pharaoh, "During his reign, thousands of
captives must have died under the rod of the taskmaster or have fallen victims to over-work or privations of every description. In all his
monuments there was not, so to speak, a single stone which had not
cost a human life. There is a marked contrast between the tranquil,
gentle faces or deified pharaohs in stone and the deeds of savage
ferocity ascribed to them." This we know, the nation's character, by
its experience under the pharaohs, was prepared for the high place
it assumed under Saul, David and Solomon.

The opening chapter of Exodus reveals something of the bitter life
the Israelites had under their taskmasters. But the more they were afflicted, the more they multiplied and grew. The sight of the oppression of his own people provoked the indignation of Moses and led
him to murder the Egyptian, a rash act forcing his flight from Egypt.
As long as this cruel king of that time lived, Moses the exile felt he
could not return to the land, the wisdom and ways of which had
become such a part of his life.

The weariness of a forty-year exile shows itself in the name Moses
gave his eldest son. "Gershom, for he said, I have been a stranger in
a strange land" (Exodus 2:22; 18:3). But in process of time, around
63 years, "the king of Egypt died" (2:23) and Moses, divinely informed of the fact, returned to Egypt to his brethren (3:19). Whoever the pharaoh was Moses came back to, he was the one God raised
up and by whom He manifested His power (9:16), yet the one who
refused to humble himself before God (10:3).

Divine attributes are revealed in the lives of the pharaohs in
Exodus. God's providence is seen in Pharaoh's daughter adopting the
coming deliverer of Israel from Pharaoh's oppression. The long-suf-

fering of God to Pharaoh is no less observable (8:13, 31; 9:33; 10:10). The very plagues of Egypt were calculated to expose to this pharaoh the folly of his idolatry and thus lead him to renounce it. The Egyptians were guilty of worshiping ten heathen deities and each plague was directed against a particular object of worship.

The Nile and the fish in it were the objects of idolatrous worship: God turned the waters of the Nile into blood, and the fish died.

The wind was also one of the deities of Egypt: God made the wind the messenger of His wrath in bringing the locusts, and again of His mercy in removing them.

The Egyptians worshiped the sun: God brought upon them for three days midnight darkness. In Goshen, where the Israelites dwelt, it was light.

The plague of flies was a severe blow to all idolatrous worship and worshipers. Cleanliness was imperative. For this cause, the priests, unclean in heart, wore linen and shaved daily. This plague also destroyed the worship of Beelzebub, *the god of flies*, and manifested his impotence (12:12).

Beasts, particularly the bull, were the representatives of some of their chief deities. God sent a murrain among the cattle, which destroyed them.

The successive plagues, however, proved that Pharaoh's obstinacy was irreclaimable, whether by judgments or by mercies. The plagues, and the removal of them, were insufficient to subdue the pride and haughtiness of his spirit. Any relentings were only momentary. Ultimately Pharaoh agreed to let the Israelites go to sacrifice to God *in the land* — not in the wilderness as Moses demanded. Then he said they could go into the wilderness, but not *too far*. Further the men could go, but *without the women or children;* then the women and children could leave, *but not the flocks.* Thus the world, typified by Pharaoh, would prescribe limits to the service we should pay to God.

On the hardening of Pharaoh's heart. The Bible says that God hardened his heart, but that he also hardened his own heart. "I will harden" is used by God six times, but not till Pharaoh had done it seven times. It was in each case God's clemency and forbearing goodness which produced the hardening. That goodness leads to repentance (Romans 2:4), just as the same sun which softens the wax hardens the clay.

God left Pharaoh to the bent and tendency of his own disposition, and thus left, he made his heart stubborn against God. God had not infused any evil disposition into his mind. He never can do this to any creature (James 1:13). Pharaoh had been invested with regal authority, but in the wrong use of it displayed the wickedness of his heart. When a man obstinately rebels against the light, he invariably follows his own heart's lusts (Romans 1:24-28).

It is a somewhat debatable question whether Menephthah, if he was Pharaoh with a hard heart, actually perished in the Red Sea as final judgment overtook the Egyptian host. Ellicott observes: "The chariot and cavalry force alone entered the sea, not the infantry. If all of Pharaoh's force entered, he could not well have stayed behind; if only a portion, he might have elected to remain with the others. Menephthah, the probable pharaoh of the Exodus, was apt to consult his own safety. . . . If he had been killed, would the Egyptian annals have retained no trace of it? Must we not have had some account of a great king cut off in the flower of his age, after a reign of two, or at the most three, years? . . . It is quite probable that he would remain with the reserve of footmen when the chariots and horsemen entered the bed of the sea. . . . Two years after he may have succumbed to revolutionary movements consequent upon the losses which he suffered in the Red Sea catastrophe."

The language of the Bible on the disaster at the Red Sea, however, suggests that Pharaoh perished with the Egyptians who pursued the Israelites (14:8). "Not so much as one of them remained" (14:28), clearly indicates that Pharaoh himself did not escape. His body may have been washed up on the shore (14:30 with 15:4, 9, 10). See also Psalm 106:11; 136:15. No wonder it is said that God wrought a "great work" for His people. The destruction of the Egyptian army in the sea and the preservation of all the Israelites was indeed a miracle. A pharaoh had destroyed the male children of the Israelites in the River Nile: now God visited his iniquity on another pharaoh in the Red Sea. Thomas Gray, bard of the Seventeenth Century, wrote:

> "Ruin seize thee, ruthless king!
> Confusion on thy banners wait!"

Moses' song of deliverance is one of the most remarkable in literature. Moses, it will be noted, began and ended his wilderness career with a song. The song of Deuteronomy 32 is the one referred to in Revelation 15:3.

PHARAOH-NECHO

(II Kings 23:29-35; II Chronicles 35:20-27; 36:4; Jeremiah 46:2)

The King Who Was Over-Ambitious

The brief glimpses the Bible gives us of this Egyptian king are sufficient to mark him out as an over-ambitious monarch. This pharaoh is identified as Neko or Nekoru, the Nechoh II, sixth king of the twenty-fifth dynasty, whose father, Psammetichus I, sixth king of the twenty-sixth or Saite dynasty was a tributary to Assyria but had secured independence for Egypt.

Early in his reign Necho endeavored to revive the dominion of Egypt in Syria and seized the opportunity afforded by Assyria's collapse. Thus he went up against the ruler of what had been the Assyrian empire, who had conquered Nineveh the rival capital, to share the spoils of the falling empire. Josiah, a vassal of Assyria, went out against Necho. Possibly he resented the king of Egypt's desire to possess what he regarded as his territory. Unwillingly, Necho encountered Josiah, a feature of the kindly relations which all along existed between Israel and Egypt after the exodus. Egyptian archers, however, killed good Josiah while riding in his chariot, and he was buried amid deep national mourning in Jerusalem. Juvenal, the Latin philosopher, wrote: "Few kings and tyrants descend to death without violence or bloodshed, or by a natural death."

A year or so later Necho set out on a second expedition, this time against the King of Babylon, but he was utterly defeated at Carchemish. Necho's ambition was to win dominion of Asia but his forces were routed by Nebuchadnezzar, who took from him all his Syrian possessions. Jeremiah's prophecy of the defeat of the King of Egypt has a near and a far fulfillment, namely, the historical defeat of the Babylonian invasion, and also the judgment of Gentile nations as predicted by Christ (Matthew 23:32).

The recognition of God in Necho's request to Josiah is somewhat remarkable —

> "God commanded me to make haste:
> Forbear thee from meddling with God,
> Who is with me, that He destroy thee not."

Ellicott observes that "Egyptian kings, like those of Israel, consulted their prophets before undertaking any expedition. So did the Assyrians, as it abundantly appears from their inscriptions. These facts sufficiently explain the text, without assuming that Necho had received an oracle from Jehovah or was referring to the God of Israel." It would seem as if the warning of Necho was really divine, as the events proved. For "words of Necho," II Esdr. 1:26 has, "words of the prophet Jeremiah," but there is no trace of such a warning in the extant prophecies bearing his name.

To Necho must go the credit as a forerunner of the Suez Canal, developed by the Frenchman, M. Lesseps, at enormous cost. Dr. Samuel Manning says that "the canalization of the isthmus is no modern project. It had been commenced whilst the Israelites were yet in Egypt and probably formed part of their labors at the period of the exodus. It was carried forward almost to completion by Pharaoh-Necho, who defeated King Josiah in the great battle of Megiddo. And a hundred years later it was finished by the Persian conquerors of Egypt."

Necho is the only Egyptian monarch whose name appears in connection with maritime enterprise. In his zeal for the promotion of navigation he projected the formation of a ship canal connecting the

Nile with the Red Sea, but was warned by an oracle to desist. It was left to M. Lesseps to fulfill the dream of the Pharaoh. For the undertaking of many projects heavy taxation was imposed (II Chronicles 36:3) to which the LXX adds, "They had given the silver and gold to Pharaoh: at that time the land began to be taxed to give the money at the command of Pharaoh; and every one, as he could, kept demanding the silver and the gold of the people of the land, to give it to Pharaoh-neckhao."

PHARAOH-HOPHRA
(Jeremiah 44:30; 46:25; Ezekiel 29; 30:21)
THE KING WHOSE SIN WAS PRIDE

The language the Prophet Ezekiel uses of Hophra is characteristic of his pride, "My river is mine own, and I have made it for myself." Herodotus says that Hophra was accustomed to say that "not even a god could dispossess him of power." He had not learned the proverb that "Pride goeth before a fall." Both Jeremiah and Ezekiel denounced him for his arrogance, impiety and treachery. How different the reign and death of Hophra might have been had he but exhibited the sentiment Seneca expressed —

"Where there is not modesty, nor regard for law, nor religion, reverence, good faith, the kingdom is insecure."

The dynasty he represented had improved the river and encouraged commerce with foreign nations, thereby acquiring great wealth.

Hophra or *Afries* of Herodotus, was the son of Psammis, and as successor of Necho, the fourth king of the twenty-sixth dynasty. Little is known of his reign which lasted for 25 years. Perhaps he relied on the Greek mercenaries and maintained himself in a forced co-regency in Lower Egypt until the third year of Anasis. He it was who "tempted Zedekiah to rebel against Babylon and thus lured Judah to ruin." He temporarily raised the siege of Jerusalem as Zedekiah's ally but was afterwards attacked by Nebuchadnezzar in his own country and defeated in an attempt to resist the progress of the Babylonian army.

Jeremiah announced the fate of this Egyptian king, which came before the fugitives as a "sign" that the prediction of their doom also would in due course be accomplished. The issue of Hophra's campaign was disastrous and his subjects revolted. He was deposed, kept in honorable imprisonment at Sais for a time and afterwards strangled. Jeremiah and a remnant of the Jews went to Egypt, to Tahpanhes, where Petric the archaeologist found the building in which Jeremiah placed the prophetic stones.

As we take farewell of the pharaohs of the Bible brief mention should be made of one or two of lesser fame.

First we mention the pharaoh, father of Bithiah, wife of Mered (I Chronicles 4:18). Bethiah, a Hebrew name, suggests she was a convert to the religion of Israel. "Daughter of Pharaoh," if the nomenclature be tribal, need only mean an Egyptian clan which amalgamated with that of Mered. Pharaoh is not used in the literal sense as is the next reference.

We also have the daughter of Pharaoh, whom Solomon married (II Chronicles 8:11; I Kings 9:24; 11:1). Solomon's Egyptian consort was probably a princess of the twenty-second Bubastite Dynasty, founded by Shishak, which was of Semetic origin, a confused period of which little is known. Was the foreign alliance with an Egyptian woman to whom Gezer was given as a marriage present, the beginning of Solomon's declension? This daughter of Pharaoh is distinguished from "the strange woman" who seduced Solomon to idolatry (I Kings 11:1). As a foreigner, she was not allowed to stay in David's palace, sanctified as it was by the presence of the ark. Solomon built her a palace.

We must take cognizance of the pharaoh mentioned by the Prophet Isaiah (19:11; 30:2, 3; 36:6). Probably the Pharaoh mentioned by Isaiah was Shapatoka, or Sabaco II, father of the Tir-Lakah of chapter 37:9, one of the Ethiopian dynasty that reigned in Egypt from B.C. 725-665. "The shadow of Egypt" and "strength of Pharaoh" are phrases descriptive of his kingdom. Alas, such power was a "broken reed" which only pierces the hand of him who leans on it! Sargon describes the embassy as "carrying presents, seeking his alliance, to Pharaoh, king of Egypt, a monarch who could not help them."

While the pharaohs, through pride and ambition, developed a mighty empire, and brought to Egypt great glory, little remains of their achievements. Montesquieu, the French writer, gave us the saying, "It is always the adventurers who accomplish great things, and not the monarchs of great empires."

SHISHAK
(I Kings 11:40; 14:25; II Chronicles 12:2-9)
THE KING WHO WAS A BOLD ADVENTURER

Shishak, the bold adventurer and powerful king of Egypt who, in the reign of Rehoboam, invaded Judah with a mighty host and plundered the temple of its treasures, bears the heathen name of *Susachim,* the meaning of which is hard to discover. He is to be identified with Sheshenk I, of Egyptian monuments, and the *Sesonchis* of the Greek historians. He reigned for at least 21 years.

Shishak was not of the old royal line and thus is not spoken of as having the ancient title of pharaoh. He was the founder of a new dynasty, the twenty-third, known as the Bubastite Dynasty. He united the lines of the two dynasties which previously ruled feebly in Lower and Upper Egypt and so inaugurated a new era of prosperity and conquest. He appears in the Temple at Thebes as "Lord of both Upper and Lower Egypt." In 1939 Shishak's mummy was found at Tanis in a sarcophagus of silver encased in solid gold — possibly some of the gold he took from Jerusalem.

Shishak's invasion of Judah in the fifth year of Rehoboam is referred to in the monuments as being in the twentieth year of his reign. He was thus king in Egypt for the last 15 years of Solomon's reign and was still in Egypt when Solomon died. Hostile to Solomon because of his alliance with a daughter of a previous Egyptian king of another dynasty, Shishak favorably received Jeroboam, the political exile, fleeing from Solomon. His close political alliance with Jeroboam, both as an exile and as a king, suggest a natural change of attitude toward Israelitish power.

Shishak's conquests were remarkable and receive a remarkable confirmation in the celebrated inscription on the South Wall of the court of the Great Temple of Amon at Karnak. One of the greatest warriors of antiquity, he mustered 1200 chariots and 60,000 horsemen with which he took Judah's fortified cities. *Shishak's Relief* in the Oriental Institute depicts him as presenting 156 cities of Palestine to his god Amon.

Shishak was preserved from destroying Jerusalem — this was reserved for Nebuchadnezzar. Jerusalem did, however, surrender to Shishak on the repentance of the people at the call of Shemaiah. He plundered the Temple and carried away the accumulated treasures of David's and Solomon's reigns, which must have been enormous. There is no record that he desecrated the Temple in any way. The view advanced therefore, that like the capture of Rome by the Gauls, the invasion of Shishak destroyed all ancient monuments and archives, is without foundation.

The philosophy Shishak forgot was that —

"The king exists for the sake of the kingdom, not the kingdom for the sake of the king. Power is only given for good purposes."

As we conclude our sketch of Egyptian monarchs, a paragraph regarding one of them, *Ptolemy Philadelphus*, might be in order. It was he who nearly 300 years before Christ gave order for the translation of the Old Testament into Greek, the language then most generally understood. During subsequent reigns this translation was completed and widely circulated.

As we approach the important section of study dealing with the commencement, continuation and consummation of Gentile monarchy, it is imperative to consider Nebuchadnezzar's dream and Daniel's visions as found in the book of Daniel, seeing they vividly portray —

THE RISE AND FALL OF GENTILE EMPIRES

Although some 62-65 years separate the visions from the dream, the two must be taken together, seeing they represent the long period of Gentile domination which, commencing with Nebuchadnezzar, has continued through the centuries down to our own time. Synchronizing the dream of Daniel 2 with the visions of chapters 7, 9 and 10, we have a twofold estimation — *Earth's* estimation of Gentile supremacy is that of a Colossus — all-powerful and unconquerable: *Heaven's* estimation of the same form of monarch is that of a beastly form of government.

A good deal predicted in the dream and visions has been fulfilled, but the end is not yet. *The Stone* out of the mountain is yet to come. With the emergence of the New Babylonian Empire, a new era in world government was introduced which still exists after some 2,500 years, for we are still in "the times of the Gentiles" (Luke 21:24). But Man's Day or Era is to end with the coming of God's Man, the Messiah. Returning to earth He will inaugurate a universal and an abiding Kingdom (Daniel 2:34, 44; 7:12, 14, 17). Gentile domination began with an *Image* and is to close with another (Matthew 24:15; Revelation 13; 15).

THE DREAM OF NEBUCHADNEZZAR (DANIEL 2:1)

The remarkable dream, troubling the king for awhile, faded from his mind. When he wanted to recall the dream and understand its significance, Nebuchadnezzar sent for his wise men and astrologers to re-enact the dream and describe its meaning. But to them this was an impossible task. Had they known the answer they would never have dared to announce the end of a Gentile supremacy which had just commenced so auspiciously. The revelation of the dream and its meaning were given to Daniel by God (2:19). The dream was of an image "great, bright, excellent, terrible" — adjectives used of a Gentile king (2:31).

The image Nebuchadnezzar created was man-like because what it represents covers and controls man's day (I Corinthians 4:5). It was also composed of four metals, namely, gold, silver, copper (not *brass* as same was unknown then), and iron with a mixture of baked clay and iron. Thus the image, beginning with a head of gold ends with toes of iron and miry clay. Each metal represents a kingdom and the four follow one another in order — Babylonia, Media-Persia, Greece and Rome (2:27-45; 8:20, 21; Luke 2:1-4; 3:1).

The political history of the Four Great Empires is given us in Daniel 2 and 3 — the former chapter symbolizing them as *metals* and the latter chapter as *beasts*. Thus we have a depreciation in value and weight but not in tenacity, which increases. God had values and weight in mind when He said, "Another kingdom shall arise after thee, *inferior to thee*" (5:39). Thus we have a gradual decline of governmental power the first form of which was derived from God (2:37). The Medo-Persian Empire was inferior to Babylonia in value, but not in power and tenacity. The last metal mentioned, "iron," is more perishable, more easily corroded or rusted than brass, silver or gold, but in the form of *steel* is harder and cuts through any other metal. Rome was the synonym of iron rule. So although the character and quality of government is depicted in the different parts of the image, their corresponding metals suggests no shrinkage of power and territory.

The Visions of Daniel

The prophet, divinely instructed, supplies and fixes his own chronology. The dates he gives were God-given —

The first vision was in the first year of Belshazzar (7)

The second vision was in the third year of Belshazzar when Babylon fell (8)

The third vision was in the first year of Darius (9)

The fourth vision was in the third year of Cyrus (10).

As *prophecy* is simply *history* stated beforehand, let us bring the dream and the vision together and note the significance underlying their combination. First of all, here is a bird's-eye view of the contents of the most important chapters in Daniel, whose entire book can be generally divided thus —

1. The dream of Nebuchadnezzar and their interpretation by Daniel, unfolding the history of Gentile power from its rise till its close. Chapters 1-7.

2. The visions of Daniel and the connection of the Grecian and Roman Empires with the prophet's people (8-9) — the Jews in their latter-day history (7-12).

The Great Image Represents Gentile Authority or Government

The gold represents the Babylonian Empire.

The silver represents the Persian Empire.

The brass represents the Grecian Empire.

The iron and clay represents constitutional governments.

The stone out of the mountain represents Christ in judgment.

The Four Beasts Represent the Four Universal Empires

The Lion Represents Babylon.
The Bear Represents Persia.
The Leopard Represents Greece.
The Four Wings or Four Notable Ones represent the fourfold partition of Greece on the death of Alexander.
The Goat from the West represents Alexander the Macedonian.
The Great Horn was broken representing Alexander's death and breaking up of his Empire.

The Beast represents Rome.

The Ten Horns represent the Ten Kings of the Roman Empire.
The Little Horn represents the personal head of the Empire, for example, Antiochus the Syrian King (8:9).
In passing we observe that the "days" of Daniel and also of the Book of Revelation are *literal* and apply to the time of the end. *Horns* signify "kings" — *Beasts*, "empires" — *Heads*, "governing powers." The image was prophetic, not only of the four successive world empires and of their comparative duration, but also of the form of government which should characterize them. We now come to an exposition of these details.

The Head of Gold — Babylonia 606-538 b.c. Despotic Government

Once Nebuchadnezzar received the content and interpretation of his dream, he erected in the Plain of Dura a huge image, 100 feet high and 10 feet broad — a lifeless, characterless colossus of metals. This top-heavy image he worshiped and commanded all others to do the same. Nebuchadnezzar was a despot, "Whom he slew he would" (5:18, 19). He represented absolute monarchy whose word was law. "I make a decree" (3:29).

Nebuchadnezzar was the first of the Gentile world-rulers as the Antichrist will be the last. Gentile universality began with the Babylonian monarch. "Thou, O King, art a King of Kings" (Daniel 2:37, 38) — language used of Jesus who ends Gentile rule and ushers in His own reign. "King of kings, And Lord of lords" (Revelation 19: 16). Absolute power and autocracy are seen in his edicts and decrees (3:4). *The head of gold* suggests the highest and purest character of governmental power. The king was to be responsible and subject to God *alone* from whom he directly received his kingdom and power.

The Monarchy Vision of Nebuchadnezzar (Daniel 2) covers the same historic order as the Beast Vision of Daniel, but with this difference. The king saw the imposing outward power and splendor of "the times of the Gentiles" (Luke 21:24; Revelation 16:14), while Daniel saw the true character of world-government as rapacious and warlike, established and maintained by force. Beasts are God-given types. It is somewhat remarkable that the heraldic insignia of the Gentile nations are beasts or birds of prey. The four beasts by the way, arise out of the Great Sea (Daniel 7). In the Old Testament "the great sea" is the Mediterranean Sea (Numbers 34:6), which has a great part to play territorially in the future.

Babylonian government is described as a *lion*, the king of beasts. The beasts, each a type of terribleness, are God's own choice to represent the kingdoms as He sees and judges them. The coming King is the *Lion-Lamb* (Revelation 5). The *lion* had *eagle's wings*, and the combination of the king of beasts and the king of birds indicates the royalty of Nebuchadnezzar and the swiftness of his armies in their conquests. "The plucking of the wings" refers to the cessation of the king's dominion because of his "beastly insanity" (4:20-27).

BREAST AND ARMS OF SILVER, MEDIA-PERSIA 533-333 B.C.
BUREAUCRATIC GOVERNMENT

After some 65 years of gold, silver takes its place. As silver is inferior to gold, so we have typified the inferior character of power, which was lodged in hereditary nobles of the empire. *Bureaucracy* means "a system of government with departments, each under the control of a chief." Nobles and princes made the laws, which the king confirmed. So although he reigned, he did not rule. The effect of this form of government is seen in the helplessness of King Darius to save Daniel even though he longed to save him (6:14). The laws and decrees of the realm were irrevocable, binding even the king himself — a clear departure from God's original which placed the king above the law he made, God above being his Lawgiver (6:7-15). The limited monarchy is also witnessed in Darius by hearkening to the princes, suggesting a monarchy dependent on the support of an hereditary aristocracy. The arbitrary will of one man alone had vanished.

The two arms of silver signify the *dual* nature of this second empire — Media and Persia, the beast corresponding to the *bear*, the strongest beast after the lion and renowned for its voracity. While having little of the agility and majesty of the lion, the bear, awkward in its movements, effects its purpose with comparative slowness and by brute force and sheer strength. These were the characteristics of the Media-Persia Empire, ponderous in its movements and gaining its victories not by bravery or skill but by the hurling of vast masses of troops upon its enemies. Bears are known for their death-like hug. The Persian Empire maintained its grasp upon its conquered dependencies.

The "Three Ribs" of the bear stood for the three kingdoms of Lydia,

Babylon and Egypt, which formed a triple alliance to combat the rising Media-Persia power, but all of whom were destroyed as the second empire trampled over west, north and south. The *ram* is also used to describe Median and Persian power (Daniel 7). The "two horns" of the ram represent the two nations, Media and Persia. While the two horns were high, one was higher than the other, and the higher came up last (8:3) signifying the supremacy of Persia, the younger nation, seen in the last and higher horn. "Raised up itself on *one side*" should read, "Raised up *one dominion*," and indicates the unifying of the two nations into one kingdom.

THE BELLY OF BRASS. GREECE 333-63 B.C. MILITARISTIC GOVERNMENT

After 207 years of silver, brass or copper appears. As copper is cheaper than silver, so we come to an inferior order of power, namely government by military authorities. While the age of one despot recedes, many despots take his place, each guided by his own ends and ambitions. Generals and officers of the army held sway in the Grecian Empire, especially after the death of Alexander the Great. Essentially warlike, as we shall see, this empire was only permitted to remain in power during the life of its first king and lasted for only twelve years and eight months. A descent in the grade of metals — gold, silver, now brass or copper, suggests a lower form of power.

The Grecian Empire is portrayed as a *leopard* and as an *he-goat*. Discovered Persian coins display a "ram's head" on one side, and a resting ram on the other. The leopard had "four wings" — "four heads" (Daniel 7:6). The most agile and graceful of creatures, the leopard, slight of frame, is yet strong, swift and fierce and fittingly symbolizes the rapid conquests and marvelous celerity by which Alexander and his armies subdued the civilized world. The "four wings of a fowl" is a suggestive simile. A "fowl" does not fly high — the armies of Alexander were fitted mainly for lowland fighting. "Four," being the number of the earth, may denote the four quarters of the earth to which Alexander sought to extend his kingdom. The "four heads" represent the four kingdoms into which Alexander's Empire was divided by his generals namely, Egypt, Syria, Thrace and Macedonia.

Of the leopard it is said, "dominion was given to it," and of the he-goat, "over the face of the whole earth" — both phrases implying world conquest. The "he-goat" came from the West (Daniel 8) and had one "notable horn," meaning that Alexander, the greatest warrior king who ever lived, was a king of renown and purpose. Then it had "four horns," reminding us that 15 years after Alexander's death the whole dynasty was wiped out by intrigue and murder, and true to phophetic vision, his four generals took the kingdom, as shown in our next chapter, "The great horn was broken."

LYSIMACHUS took Thrace and Bythinia.
CASSANDER took Macedonia and Greece.
SELEUCUS took Syria, Babylonia and the East.
PTOLEMY took Egypt, Palestine, Arabia and Petrea.
LEGS OF IRON. ROME 63 B.C.-400 A.D. AUTOCRATIC GOVERNMENT

After a broken and fragmentary history of many years, copper gives
way to iron, a stronger metal. "Iron breaketh in pieces and subdueth
all things" (Daniel 2:40). The Roman Empire was essentially military and aggressive. "The Emperor, however, was a mere puppet in
the hands of the lawless soldiery, and the Imperial Crown was generally bought, and its continuance secured, by currying favour with
the legions," says Walter Scott. As iron is a lower metal than brass
or copper, we have represented the lower character of governmental
power characterizing the Roman Empire. Roman emperors were independent monarchs, yet, normally at least, the power of the people
was a controlling influence as seen in the letters "S.P.Q.R." on Roman
standards. *Senatus, populusque 'Romanus* — "The Senate and the Roman people."

The two legs of iron signified the eastern and western power of
Rome over which she ruled. The *beast* describing this fourth empire is nameless — a nondescript. It was "dreadful and terrible, and
strong exceedingly, and it had great iron teeth . . . was diverse from
all the beasts that were before it and it had ten horns." This *beast*
was the accumulation of every form of terribleness represented by the
former three beasts and represents the cruel and extensive absorption
of near and distant kingdoms and states into the empire. This hideous
monster then, seen by Daniel, represents "Imperial Rome" and as
Jerome, writing in the fourth century put it, "This dreadful beast
heads up, and fills up, all the terribleness that ever has been seen or
known in former beasts" — as to its rule, blood-thirsty in the extreme.
"The beast which I saw was like a leopard (Greece) and his feet
were as the feet of a bear (Media, Persia) and his mouth as the
mouth of a lion" (Babylonia) Revelation 13.

THE TOES OF IRON AND CLAY. PRESENT AGE
SOCIALISTIC GOVERNMENT

"Democracy" describes our present civilization which is a somewhat brittle formation — "partly strong, partly brittle (2:42). The
mixture of iron and clay represents the combination of monarchy and
republics. As the toes are at the end of the image they indicate the
last and final stage of Gentile dominion. Our much approved and
vaunted "Democracy" is one sure sign of our Lord's return. As Walter Scott expresses it: "We are rapidly near the *final* form of human

government on which like a mighty avalanche the Lord of Glory shall descend and grind it to powder, and on the ruins of which He will establish His Kingdom, wide as the globe, stable as the Throne of the Eternal, and everlasting in its duration."

The Ten Toes (2:41-43) do not describe a new kingdom but a development of the fourth empire in the extremity of the image, and is the last days. Fragments of the Roman Empire still exist and are to be seen in *Demos,* the power of the people seen in "democracy." "What is more brittle than clay, and what is more fickle than the *Vox Populi?*" asks one writer. "Today it is 'Hosanna,' and tomorrow it is 'Crucify Him!'" The clay mingled with iron and forming part of the feet and toes attached to the legs suggests democracy entering into the governmental power with the iron — Rome.

The first appearance of this in its attempt to depose and dethrone monarchy, was at the French Revolution in the eighteenth century, when "the divine right of the kings" was ruthlessly brushed aside and scornfully denied. Since this appearance of clay in the feet, monarchies have tumbled until the true sovereigns in the world can be counted on the fingers of one hand. Clay principles have spread and are rapidly spreading. The upsurge of nationalism is freeing countries from imperial rule. Communism and socialism — handmaids of atheism — with their gospel of nationalization, preach that society organized as a state should own all wealth, direct all labor, and compel the equal distribution of all produce. The masses must obliterate the classes. In the industrial world the "clay" dominates and dictates its own terms. Refusal of same means the paralysis of commerce.

Scripture teaches that the culmination of this Gentile age — the ten toe period — will witness the universal confederation of all the world's great schemes — national, political, commercial, social, and religious, under one head, to be administered by one great figure, who will himself be under the guidance and support of the prince and god of this world.

THE STONE OUT OF THE MOUNTAIN. MILLENNIAL AGE. RIGHTEOUS GOVERNMENT

This stone is not a triumphing Gospel, but the personal appearance of Christ descending in power and glory to wind up the times of the Gentiles in judgment (Revelation 19:11-21). The complete destruction of Gentile power originally granted to Nebuchadnezzar by God but abused, is necessary in order that the vast Kingdom of our Lord may be established. Thus the stone cut out without hands descends with crushing force upon the extremities of the image — the toes and feet. Presently two great forces are at work. *The image* and *the stone,* and the question is, which are we in and labor for? If our eyes are on the Eternal, then "in the days of those kings when the

God of Heaven sets up His Kingdom" ours will be the privilege of assisting Him in the governmental control of all things in an empire in which peace and righteousness are to prevail.

> Thou art my Rock, when Kingdom and Nation,
>   Ruler and Crown, have crumbled to dust:
> Thou shalt be my Rock of Salvation,
>   Rock Everlasting, Thee will I trust.

IV

Babylonia and Babylonian Monarchs
B. C. 606-538

In ancient times, the histories of Babylonia and Assyria were merged and it is often difficult to separate them. Excavations in primitive Babylonia brought to light such cities as *Erida* — the traditional "Garden of Eden" — possibly the first city ever built. Another old city was *Erech*, one of Nimrod's cities. *Larsa* (the Biblical *Arioch*) was another whose king was one of those defeated by Abraham (Genesis 14:1). *Accad*, capital of Sargon's Empire also known as *Sippar*, "the book town," so called because of its famous library, was another of Nimrod's cities.

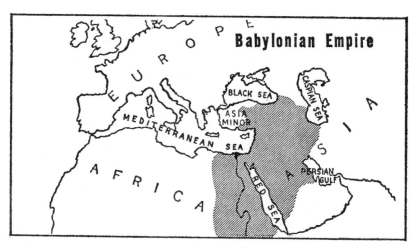

Babylon and Egypt — 1,000 miles apart — were the two principal centers of civilization in the ancient world and were populated by the descendants of Ham. Ancient Babylonia is of deep interest then to all Bible students, seeing it is the cradle of the human race, "the gate of the gods," the original home of Abraham who came out of Babylon, sojourned in Egypt, and settled in Canaan. Situated at the head of the Persian Gulf, between the rivers Tigris and Euphrates, Babylonia, some 400 miles long and 100 miles wide, was for ages the center of a dense population. Cuneiform inscriptions and dynastic tablets list the kings and dynasties from early times down to Hammurabi of Babylon, which brings us to the time of Abraham.

Babylon, capital of the Chaldean Empire, was founded by Nimrod, the son of Cush, who also founded the Assyrian monarchy (Genesis 10). This first and most ancient of all cities occupies a conspicuous place in the Bible and is undoubtedly the grandest city ever built by man and of all the seats of empire the most notable in the display of the pride and power of man. Babylon was founded by Nimrod in self-will and independence of God, and the love of power and conquest characterizes its sad origin and stamped their features on its after history.

It was under Nebuchadnezzar that Babylon reached its highest degree of splendor and magnificence of size and strength. Herodotus, the earliest historian extant, the "father of historians" who saw Babylon soon after the zenith of her glory, gives us a glowing and probably a somewhat exaggerated description of the magnificence of the city and its buildings. From Bible history we gather that Babylon must have been the grandest and largest city built or witnessed by man. But Jerusalem, the metropolitan city of the coming Millennial Kingdom, will exceed Babylon's magnificence.

Scripture information respecting Babylon is unmistakable. Among its names it is described as "the lady of kingdoms," "the golden city," "the city of merchants," "the glory of kingdoms," "abundant in treasures," "praise of the whole earth," "the beauty of the Chaldees' excellency," and "the most proud" (Isaiah 13:19; 14:4; Jeremiah 51:13, 41). Its people were numerous, rich, commercial, idolatrous, cruel and superstitious. Babylon was also God's instrument of judgment upon Egypt, Judah, Edom, Moab, Ammon, Tyre, Zidon, Assyria, Hazor and Nineveh.

From Herodotus we learn that Babylon stood on a large plain and formed a square about 56 miles across. The Euphrates flowed through the center of the city from north to south, spanned by a wonderfully built bridge, on one side of which stood the pretentious Temple of Belus, containing numerous images of pure gold, and which was plundered by the famous Xerxes. On the other side of the bridge stood the gorgeous palace of Nebuchadnezzar. "The hanging gardens," wonderful as a work of art, constructed as terraces and rising to the height of the walls, were one of the seven wonders of the world. Fruits, flowers and vegetables were grown to perfection in these gardens and must have delighted *Amytes*, Nebuchadnezzar's Median consort, in whose honor they were created.

The walls of the city were immensely high and about 87 feet broad, thus allowing abundant space for 6 chariots abreast to run around and able to turn at any point. The city's 100 gates, 25 on each side of the city, were of solid brass, as were numerous inside gates. From each gate to the other opposite there was a straight street the whole length or breadth of the city, which in turn intersected, until in all, there were formed 676 squares. No wonder it was "the praise of the whole earth."

Babylon, in the Hebrew, is "Babel," so that "the tower of Babel," which is not a Biblical one, should be designated, "the tower of Babylon." The name as given by Nimrod means "the gate of God." Fausset remarks that, "Afterwards the name was attached to it in another sense (Providence having ordered it so that a name should be given originally, susceptible of another sense, signifying the subsequent Divine judgment), Genesis 10:9; *babel* from *balal,* 'to confound'; 'because the Lord did there confound the language of all the earth,' in order to counteract their attempt by a central city and tower to defeat God's purpose of the several tribes of mankind being 'scattered abroad upon the face of the whole earth,' and to constrain them, as no longer 'understanding one another's speech,' to disperse."

The immense structure, pointing toward heaven, was erected by the Babylonians "to make themselves a name" in defiance of God who alone has the right to "make Himself a name" (Isaiah 63:12, 14; Jeremiah 32:20). The tower was a monument of self-relying pride setting up its own will against the will of God and a demonstration of man's fancied ability to defeat God's purpose. It was an impressive instance of man's perversity (Proverbs 21:30) and marked the first era in idolatry. When God came down to see the city and the tower the people had built He took *judicial cognizance* of their act and met their "go to, let us" with stern irony, "Go to, let us" (Genesis 11:3, 4). Dispersion and the confusion of tongues, which remains a barrier to international unity came as divine judgment upon man's self-will and effort.

The close association of Israel with Babylon is a conspicuous aspect of Bible history and figures largely in the Bible as the enemy of God and enslaver of His people. Daniel was written during the darkness of the most terrible captivity the Jews endured when, by the rivers of Babylon, they sat down and wept and hung their harps on the willows (Psalm 137). The 70 years' captivity in Babylon and the miraculous events recorded in Daniel proved before the world that the Babylonian monarchs were forced to acknowledge that the God of Daniel was the Great King above all gods (3:28; 4:34; 6:26). Knowledge of the circumstances of the Jews between B.C. 606 and 586 can be gathered from the prophets (see Jeremiah 24:11; 29:10). The sins, fears and hopes of the people are clearly defined in the poetic and prophetic Scriptures.

Ezra relates the return of a certain number of Jews from their captivity in Babylon under the charge of Zerubbabel, the grandson

of Jehoiakim, King of Judah (1:11). Such a return is described as a
most glorious display of the providence of God (Isaiah 43:19; 54:17).
Israel, in the day of her restored gladness, is to celebrate the doom
of Babylon (Isaiah 14). "It was *out* of Egypt that Israel was re-
deemed, but it was *into* Babylon the people were sent for their sins,"
says Walter Scott. "They were *slaves* in the one and *captives* in the
other."

The decline and destruction of mighty Babylon are likewise portrayed in the Bible. The cities of Babylon and Nineveh — respective
capitals of the Chaldean and Assyrian monarchies — are doomed in the
prophetic word to *perpetual* desolation. Various particulars of the
doom of Babylon are specified thus —

1. Particular nations plundering it (Isaiah 21:2; Jeremiah 51:11).
2. The commander in charge of its overthrow (Isaiah 44:28; 45:1).
3. The time of its overthrow (Jeremiah 25:11, 12).
4. The manner in which Babylon was to be taken (Isaiah 44:27;
   Jeremiah 50:24, 28; 51:36, 37).
5. The utter destruction of the city (Isaiah 13:19; 14:22, 23; Jeremiah 50:13, 23, 39, 40).

Daniel predicted the fall of Babylon (5:28-31). Jeremiah cried
aloud that Babylon committed a heinous sin in destroying God's people, and for that, would in turn and time be destroyed, and remain
so forever. *Literal* Babylon, situated on the Euphrates, is the subject
of Jeremiah's prophecy (chapter 51), and is not to be confused with
mystical Babylon, whose seat will be at Rome on the Tiber, which
is the great subject of Revelation 17; 18. Peter's reference to the
church at Babylon is to be understood as the *literal* Babylon, the
center from which the Jews dispersed (I Peter 5:13).

The *symbolic* significance of Babylon also deserves our attention
(Revelation 16:19; 17; 18; 19:2, 3). The language John uses is
avowedly mystical. "The Babylon of the Apocalypse occupies the
same relation to the Babylon of the Prophets, as does the New Jerusalem to the Jerusalem of the Prophets. In the Book of Revelation,
both cities are used in a *mystical* sense; in the Prophets, the cities
are to be understood in their *literal* import." John uses the *term*
Babylon as an appellation of the false church, dominated by Papal
Rome. William Nicholson, in his *Bible Students' Companion,* comments on Babylon representing the seat and center of future ecclesiastical apostasy (Revelation 17:18) thus: —

As ancient Babylon was the chief of idolatrous cities, she is taken as a
fit emblem of the monstrous guilt and extensive influence of idolatrous
and papal Rome, each in turn being the mother of harlots, and the
abomination of the earth. See Jeremiah 1:38; 51:7 and compare with
Revelation 17; 18. Thus, as Babylon of old was the first of all idolatrous cities, it is adopted as the fittest emblem to declare the enormous
guilt and the extensive and withering influences of idolatrous Rome;

each in its turn being the mother of harlots and abominations of the earth; the former corrupting the heathen world with her idolatry and fornication and Papal Babylon corrupting the Christian world.

Because Nimrod was the founder of ancient Babylon, we have placed our study of him first in the list of Babylonian monarchs. A new era for Babylon commenced with Nabopolassar, who was appointed ruler of Babylon by the last Assyrian king when the Medes made their final assault on Nineveh. For a comprehensive survey of dynasties before the new Babylonian Empire with Nebuchadnezzar described as its "head of gold," one is dependent upon historical accounts like those of Herodotus, and upon cuneiform inscriptions and tablets. For a full summary of these, with information as to dynasties not mentioned in Scripture, the reader is referred to the excellent article under *Babylonia* in *The International Standard Bible Encyclopaedia*. As the title of our work indicates, we are confining ourselves to those kings specifically mentioned *in* the Bible who reigned during the years of its history as a great empire. Dealing with ancient Babylonian dynasties R. K. Harrison says: "After 31 years on the throne Hammurabi finally removed the threat to Babylonian imperial security and established the full glory of the Old Babylonian Period which lasted to the middle of the sixteenth century B.C."

NIMROD
(Genesis 10:8-12; I Chronicles 1:10)
THE KING WHO INSTITUTED IMPERIALISM

With the sixth son of Cush we have the beginnings of the empires of brute force. The history of Babylon and Nineveh is replete with what happens from selfish, inordinate, unscrupulous desires after possessions or power. Nimrod is the first war lord of the Bible whose prowess dazzled the eyes of men even amid the calamities following in the wake of brutal ambition.

Nimrod, the first person after the Flood of whom something more than his mere name has been preserved, is described as being of the line of Ham (Genesis 10:8), the wicked irreverent son of Noah (Genesis 9:22), whose curse Nimrod inherited and who, in turn, as the ancestor of kingdoms distinguished himself by impiety toward God and inhumanity to men. The vices of Ham were in the blood of Nimrod and also characterizes the kingdoms he founded.

Although Nimrod is not specifically mentioned as a "king," he is the first one in Scripture to be associated with a "kingdom." He extended his power until he became the king of the nations he founded — the first king to be named in Bible history. Nimrod was the founder of Babylon which was long known as "the land of Nimrod." Altogether, he created eight cities — four in Babylonia and four in Assyria.

Hitherto these were small, independent tribal communities, but Nimrod forged them into kingdoms or empires. In the southern group we have Babel, the wonder city; Erech; Accad and Calnel. In the northern group there was Nineveh, renowned capital of the Assyrian Empire, Rehoboth-It, Calah and Resen.

After his death, Nimrod was deified and his name became identical with Merodach or Mardak. He was lauded as the representative hero of the great empires of Babylon and Assyria he had founded. With Nimrod we have the beginning of a godless imperialism — one of open revolt against divine and human sanctities.

Modern Arabs in the land of Nimrod's achievements ascribe to him all the great deeds of ancient times and preserve his name in *Birs-Nimrud* near Babylon, in *Tel-Nimrud* near Baghdad, and in *Sudr-el-Nimrud*, the dam across the Tigris.

Nimrod's name reveals his character. While some scholars suggest that Nimrod means *ruler*, it would seem as if it comes from a group of proper names expressive of trouble and rebellion. "Nimrod" is from the Hebrew *Marad*, meaning "to rebel." It is further said of him that "he *began* to be mighty in the earth." Such a phrase implies that he struggled for pre-eminence and by force of will and muscularity obtained it. Greedy for power, his ambition was unbounded till it sighed with Alexander the Great that there were no more worlds to conquer.

The Biblical record of this first imperialist is often misunderstood. Nimrod, it is said, was "a mighty hunter before the Lord." But the phrase "before the Lord" does not mean the same here as it does when we read that Abraham walked before the Lord and that David danced before the Lord. There was no godward bent in his pursuit as a hunter. He was not so expert that God Himself owned Nimrod's greatness in his art.

The word "before" (*liphnee*, Numbers 16:2) means "opposition." He was rebellious before the Lord — in open defiance of Him (Genesis 6:11), sinning boldly and defiantly against divine authority. Nimrod pushed his own imperialistic designs in opposition to divine laws. As a hunter, his prowess was not limited as a protector of people from wild animals when they were in continual danger. Bishop Andrews says that Nimrod "ranged over men as over beasts in a forest."

Nimrod became a hunter of men as well as of animals. By conquest, or subjugation, he became a ruler of men, and his lust for power made him more like a wild beast than a human being, as it did Adolph Hitler. Four times over Nimrod is described as "mighty," a word meaning "chief," "chieftain" or "hero." His supreme ambition was to make a name for himself, no matter who suffered. Early Babylonian tablets represent him as a king victorious in combat with a lion. Profane history, however, records that Nimrod had as much delight in hunting men as he had in tracking down wild beasts.

Josephus, the Jewish historian says: "Nimrod persuaded mankind not to ascribe their happiness to God, but to think that his own excellency was the source of it. And he soon changed things into a tyranny, thinking there was no other way to wean men from the fear of God, than by making them rely on his own power."

The Targum of Jonathan has it: "From the foundation of the world none has even been found like Nimrod, powerful in hunting, and in rebellions against the Lord."

The Jerusalem Targum expresses it: "He was powerful in hunting and in wickedness before the Lord, for he was a hunter of the sons of men, and he said to them, 'Depart from the judgment of the Lord, and adhere to the judgment of Nimrod!' Therefore it is said: 'As Nimrod (is) the strong one, strong in hunting and in wickedness before the Lord.'"

The Chaldee paraphrase of I Chronicles 1:10 says: "Cush begat Nimrod, who began to prevail in wickedness for he shed innocent blood, and rebelled against Jehovah."

Nimrod's energy was prostituted for unholy ends. Destitute of the fear of God, he had no regard for the highest welfare of men. Acquired power was used in tyranny and oppression. King Alfred the Great is credited with having said, "Power is never a good unless he be good that handles it." Dr. Moffat's translation of Micah 5:13 reads, "You must no longer worship things you manufacture." Nimrod's folly was that his powers were not harnessed to good purposes. His strength and skill were not used, as St. George used his, for the deliverance of his weaker fellows, but against their best interests. Abusing his power, Nimrod became inhuman, brutal, cruel, God-defying.

Babylon partook of its founder's character and became the chief antagonist of God's Truth and of God's People. Then we cannot fail to see in Nimrod Satan's first attempt to raise up a human, universal ruler of men. He was the forerunner of subsequent imperialists drunk with power like Alexander, Napoleon, Hitler, Mussolini and the present cruel communistic dictators.

Nimrod is also a fitting type of the world's last brutal imperialist, the Antichrist, who, when he appears, will be the lawless or rebellious one; and who will magnify himself above every other ruler, exalt himself above God and work with all power and signs and lying wonders (II Thessalonians 2:4-9). He will be the world's idea of a hero whose brute force will receive religious veneration. His worldly power and glory will quickly vanish, however, at the coming of the King of kings and Lord of lords.

The judgment of God is unalterable. "They that take the sword shall perish with the sword" (Matthew 26:52). The doom of blood-thirsty imperialists will excite no pity, but will be rejoiced over, even by the holy and the merciful (Psalm 9:19; 58:10; James 2:13; Revelation 18:20). Nimrod, and all like him, are the antithesis of Christ, who taught that self-sacrifice, not force, is the way to real and lasting greatness (Isaiah 52:14, 15; Matthew 20:25-28).

NABOPOLASSAR

While this Babylonian monarch is not mentioned in the Bible, an outside historical account of him forms a necessary introduction to this section, seeing he was the father of the famed Nebuchadnezzar.

This Chaldean prince was the last viceroy appointed by Assyria. He appointed himself king of Babylon and became the founder of the neo-Babylonian Empire and reigned for some 21 years. In 606 B.C. the Babylonians, who, with the break-up of the Assyrian Empire asserted their independence, were under Nabopolassar allied to the Medes who reduced any remaining influence of Assyria, whose fall signally vindicated the predictions of Zephaniah (2:13) and Nahum (3:1).

Nabopolassar made an alliance with Umman Marda and strengthened such an alliance by the marriage of his son and successor, Nebuchadnezzar, to the daughter of Astyages, the king.

NEBUCHADNEZZAR
(Daniel 1-4)

THE KING WHO WAS A HAUGHTY TYRANT

The Bible teaches us to acknowledge the controlling influence or the immediate agency of a righteous, wise and almighty Governor in every event of history, whether national or personal. When kingdoms pass from one possessor to another, we must bear in mind that it is God who "putteth down one and setteth up another" (Psalm 75:7). Divine providence must never be excluded from the management of the universe, for "God doeth according to His will in the army of Heaven and amongst the inhabitants of the earth." A glimpse of the remarkable character of the pagan world we are now considering is a striking illustration of a divinity, shaping our ends, rough hew them though we may (Proverbs 21:1 with Ezekiel 29:18).

Nebuchadnezzar, which should be consistently spelled Nebuchadrezzar, the familiar use of the n being an error, is a name occurring about 90 times in Scripture. The son of Nabopolassar, Nebuchadnezzar came to the throne of Babylon at an early age and reigned for 43 years, dying in 561 B.C. when he was 83 or 84 years of age. Herodotus tells us that the king's first queen was Amytis, daughter of Astyages, and his second queen Nitveris, to whom many works are assigned, was the mother of Nabunaid. This haughty tyrant of Babylon was a bold and presumptuous offender, similar to Pharaoh in maintaining a contact with heaven till at length he came to learn that God resisteth the proud and that he who exalteth himself shall be abased (Luke 14:11; James 4:6).

Without doubt, Nebuchadnezzar was a most illustrious monarch — a prudent, brave and daring war leader who by his own personal exploits added to the extensive dominion he had inherited from his father. The best part of the then known world became tributary to him until "all peoples, nations trembled and feared before him." He it was who made Babylon the mistress and wonder of the ancient world. While an intimate account of Nebuchadnezzar's achievements as he went from one conquest to another, is outside the scope of our cameo of Babylon's greatest king, one or two aspects must be dealt with.

It was he who brought the kingdom of Judah to an end and led the nation into a state of captivity in Babylon. It was this same monarch who attacked and subdued Jehoiakim, according to Jeremiah's prophecy, and robbed him of his treasures and then left him as a vassal. Afterwards, upon Jehoiakim's revolt, Nebuchadnezzar vanquished and destroyed him (II Kings 24:1). Then he deposed the young ruler, Jehoiachin, and took him to Babylon after ransacking the city and Temple of Jerusalem. He then appointed Zedekiah as Governor, and when he violated the oath of allegiance to Nebuchadnezzar, the Babylonian ruler plundered Jerusalem and blinded the eyes of the faithless prince (II Kings 25:1). Thus to gratify his ambition or caprice he made and unmade kings.

The magnificence and splendor of Nebuchadnezzar's court were equal to his power and cruelty. Babylon, his residence and seat of his empire, was made the marvel of the world. The grandeur of its buildings, temples, royal palaces and gardens became the admiration of the age (Isaiah 13:19). The monarch seemed to have reached the sum of human greatness, and if wealth, pomp and dominion contribute to supreme happiness, then Nebuchadnezzar must have been the happiest man of his time. The sequel of his story, however, disproves the theory that riches and honor mean happiness.

We might pause to ask whence came the high exaltation of this Babylonian autocrat. Historians may single out Nebuchadnezzar's wise counsel, the sagacity of his generals, the courage of his soldiers or the king's own unusual fortitude. But prophets like Isaiah, Jeremiah and Ezekiel teach us that Nebuchadnezzar, mighty tyrant though he was, was but an instrument in God's hands, a servant through whom He accomplished His purposes. God determined to punish the offenses of His people by the insolence and oppression of this Chaldean ruler, and thus allowed him to go on and prosper (II Kings 24:2; Jeremiah 25:8-12; 27:6; 44:30). How great God is when in His governmental control of all events, He is able to render even the sinful principles and passions of men subservient to His own designs!

While Nebuchadnezzar is before us as an infamous character, proud, oppressive and an obstinate persecutor of God's ancient people and a contender against God, yet with all his perversion he had a particular regard for the servants of God. When Jerusalem was desolated, the king showed favor to Jeremiah. Daniel he elected to be his prime minister at Babylon and the prophet continued to exercise his influence through the reigns of Nebuchadnezzar and his successors. Yet even these tokens of kindness are ascribed to the constraining influences of God rather than to any goodness of disposition in Nebuchadnezzar, even though through his long reign he had ample opportunity of pleasing rather than provoking Him.

The defiance of Nebuchadnezzar is seen in that he was not satisfied with plundering and destroying the Temple of God at Jerusalem. He carried its holy vessels to Babylon and placed them in the temples of his idols. Babylon had its 53 temples and 180 altars to Ishtar. Pagan deities were honored as having overcome the God of Israel. Vile indignities were heaped upon the royal offspring who were made to serve as eunuchs in the king's palace (Daniel 1:1). Yet so despicable a character as Nebuchadnezzar was made the recipient of a divine relevation concerning the establishment of Christ's Kingdom upon the ruins of the great empires of the world — a revelation Daniel had to interpret (Daniel 2).

Although Nebuchadnezzar confessed that the God Daniel worshiped was the God of gods, the monarch remained an idolater and set up an enormous image to display his superior greatness and to perpetuate his name (Daniel 3:1). At the dedication of the colossal image all were commanded to bow before it in worship on pain of a terrible death. But Daniel's three friends, Shadrach, Meshach and Abed-nego, refused to worship the image, and we all know the thrilling story of their deliverance from the fiery furnace.

The divine preservation of Daniel and his courage mortified the pride of this mighty potentate and it seemed as if in humility he would turn to God. Prostrate at the feet of Daniel, Nebuchadnezzar represented the humility of Gentile powers before Israel's God. But no real penitence was his. He remained under the power of his former vile affections. His heart was lifted up and his mind hardened in pride (Daniel 5:20), and in a dream he learned of the judgment about to afflict him (Daniel 4:1). For seven years he was excluded from human society and became a companion of the beasts of the field. How good of God it was to allow the tyrant of Babylon to continue as long as he did!

After the predicted seven years of exile and ferocity, Nebuchadnezzar recovered his sanity and the possession of his government. He returned to all his former magnificence. With his restoration, his moral character was changed. He had a different disposition of mind. Strong marks of humility and obedience were his. He bowed before the Lord and blessed and praised God most high and recognized His right to punish him as He did. Whether Nebuchadnezzar's change was permanent is open to question. With his recovery from his beast-like conditions he was a true penitent, but whether he became a true convert to God we cannot say. This we do know, that God's mercy avails for the most presumptuous offenders (Proverbs 16:18).

EVIL-MERODACH
(II Kings 25:27-30; Jeremiah 50:2; 52:31-34)
The King Who Was Kind to a Captive King

Evil-merodach, son and successor of Nebuchadnezzar, was so named after *Bel-merodach*, Babylonian god of war, of great repute in Assyria and Babylonia. This Babylonian monarch is the *Amelmardak* of the monuments of *Marduk*, being the name of one of Babylon's gods. It is thought that he governed Babylon during his father's insanity. When Nebuchadnezzar resumed his control of the empire after his calamity, he heard of his son's misconduct in that he gloried in his father's distress, and he cast him into prison where he met Jehoiachin or Jeconiah, and became his friend.

Evil-merodach's brief reign of two years was characterized by a lawless unrestrained government. About all we know of him is that soon after his accession to the throne he liberated Jehoiachin, king of Judah, out of prison after his 37 years of confinement and heaped favors upon him and granted him peculiar immunities all the remainder of his life. Evil-merodach was murdered by Neriglissar or Nergal-sharezer, his brother-in-law, a Babylonian noble married to Evil-merodach's sister, who seized the throne.

Of NERGAL-SHAREZER little is known. He was one of those who released Jeremiah from prison (39:3, 13). Probably he had been a commander in Nebuchadnezzar's army (Jeremiah 39:3. After his murder of Evil-merodach, he reigned for four years. The only palace discovered on the right bank of the Euphrates was built by Nergalsharezer or *Neriglissar.*

LABOROSOARCHOD was only a boy when he succeeded his father, Nergal-sharezer, as king of Babylon, and was murdered after a reign of only nine months.

NABONIDUS
The King Who Was His Empire's Last Monarch

While we have no Bible reference to Nabonidus, also known as *Nabunaid,* it is necessary to place him in the Scripture gallery of kings, since he was the father of Belshazzar. We speak of him as the last king of the new Babylonian Empire, seeing that among unearthed records Rawlinson discovered there was an official document from Cyrus, King of Persia, who invaded Babylon stating that Nabonidus first fled but was later taken prisoner after Belshazzar's death. It appears to be evident that Nabonidus lived for a considerable time after the fate of Babylon.

Although Belshazzar is repeatedly mentioned by Daniel as the last king of Babylon, no mention is found of him in Babylonian records or any other history giving a list of the Empire's kings. Because of this fact and the other that Nabonidus was known to be Babylon's last king, higher critics pointed to Belshazzar as another Biblical mythical figure. But time and spade came to the Bible's aid and in 1854 Sir Henry Rawlinson discovered in "Ur of the Chaldees" some terra-cotta cylinders containing an inscription by Nabonidus which mentioned his son, Belshazzar. The full inscription reads: "As for Nabonidus, King of Babylon, may I not sin against thee (his heathen god). And may reverence for thee dwell in the heart of Belshazzar, my first born, my favorite son." Thus, as Sidney Collett puts it in his *Scripture of Truth*, this fact has come to light:

> Nabonidus and Belshazzar his son were *both reigning at the same time* which explains as nothing else could, Belshazzar's offer to make Daniel the *third* ruler in the kingdom (Daniel 5:16) — Nabonidus being the first, and Belshazzar, the Regent, the second; otherwise Daniel would doubtless have been made second ruler, as Pharaoh made Joseph. This is another case in which two apparently contradictory accounts were both equally correct. The Chaldean historian was correct in saying that Nabonidus was King, while the old Bible was equally accurate in saying that Belshazzar was King.

Nabonidus, who ruled for 17 years, one of the murderers of the previous boy-king, sought to centralize Babylonian religions and to this end brought to Babylon images of deities from other cities. This act displeased the Jews and also alienated the priesthood as well as the military party, the latter feeling that Nabonidus was neglecting the safety of the empire in his antiquarian pursuits. R. K. Harrison says of Nabonidus, who shared his throne with his son, Belshazzar, that:

> He was a man of considerable culture, and was particularly interested in archaeological pursuits. He despatched his scribes throughout Mesopotamia to collect ancient inscriptions from widely divergent sources, and ordered names and dates of Mesopotamian kings to be compiled. This is some reason for thinking that his mother had been a priestess in the temple of the moon god at Haran, and this may have influenced Nabonidus to become a religious antiquary. He was the last Babylonian ruler to attempt repair to the *Ziggurat* of the moon deity at Ur, and when his restorations were completed, he installed his daughter there as high Priestess.

While Nabonidus lived in Arabia, Belshazzar was the sole ruler in Babylon and is thus represented as the last king of Babylon (Daniel 5:30).

BELSHAZZAR
(Daniel 5)

THE KING WHOSE PROFANITY WAS DISASTROUS

The history of Belshazzar, son and co-regent of Nabonidus, illustrates and confirms the observation that the great almighty Governor of the world is not acknowledged as He should be. Is it because He is invisible that men neglect and deny Him? "Where is God thy Maker?" (Job 35:10). Manifestations of divine transactions with those of past ages and judgment upon kings and rulers for their iniquities were quickly forgotten in the court of Babylon.

Belshazzar, the grandson of Nebuchadnezzar, (Scripture calls him "son," an expression implying an immediate descendant) instead of learning righteousness from Nebuchadnezzar's pride and punishment, advanced to a higher level of profaneness than that of his grandfather. The past had no salutary effect upon Belshazzar and when at last he was suddenly destroyed he exhibited in his dreadful yet deserved end the righteous justice of God. And Belshazzar remained a solemn warning to all successive rulers that presumptuous transgression is always dealt with by the God in heaven who judgeth the earth.

The only account given of Belshazzar depicts him as a bold offender, intemperate, blasphemous, and as having a shameless sense of lewdness. His conduct is more atrocious in the light of national affairs, for Belshazzar had been defeated in battle by Cyrus, prince of the Medes and Persians, who, for two years had besieged Babylon. Instead of caring for the safety of his empire, Belshazzar gave himself over to sensual pleasures. Confident of Babylon's formidable defense and of his own fancied invincible strength, Belshazzar scorned any attempt to attack his capital. Trusting to his own arm of flesh, he forgot what his grandfather, Nebuchadnezzar, had to learn that "the most High ruleth in the kingdom of men." The monarch would not be restrained in his debauchery even in a time of national peril. Thus he filled up his cup of iniquity.

While there are many dark nights in the Bible, one of the darkest was the night Belshazzar set apart for all kinds of reveling and licentious mirth, with his wives, concubines and a thousand of his lords. To this excess was added profanity of the worst order, namely, an avowed contempt of God. The holy vessels which Nebuchadnezzar had brought from Jerusalem were used at this riotous banquet, thereby insulting the captive Jews and the God they worshiped.

Among the drunkards of the Bible, Belshazzar stands out as the most profane, for he allowed his drunken guests to smear the sacred vessels with their saliva. The king deemed it a joke to drink to heathen gods out of vessels dedicated to the worship of God. We can imagine this drunken sot holding one of the vessels and blubbering, "Where is now the God of the Hebrews? Palsied be every tongue refusing to drink to the gods of Belshazzar. Ha Ha! Where is the God of Israel?" Alas, God was nearer than Belshazzar or any of the debauchees realized!

Profane laughter was quickly turned to mourning and lewd joy to heaviness, for in the midst of his godless mirth Belshazzar was divinely sentenced and condemned. Insolence and profanity were suddenly repressed — challenging earth and heaven one minute, the next the drunken king stands and shakes as a criminal at the bar of justice. Strange fingers write upon the wall, and although the king could not interpret the writing, "his knees smote one against another." His wise men failed to interpret the unintelligible marks on the wall, and Daniel the prophet, for whom the king had little sympathy, had to explain the mysterious writing.

Daniel was not long in fixing a charge of guilt upon the royal criminal. Unflinchingly he condemned Belshazzar of his pride, profanity and intemperance. Daniel read for the conscience-stricken king the terrible sentence on the wall, *Mene, Mene, Tekel Upharsin,* which interpreted meant that the Almighty Sovereign had decreed the end of the great Babylonian Empire. God in heaven had weighed the haughty, defiant monarch in the balances and had found him wanting, and with his death, his empire would be transferred to the Medes and Persians. With Belshazzar the power and pride of Babylon perished together. "This hath God done, for we perceive it was His work."

After Belshazzar had the horror of seeing the fingers of a man's hand writing out his doom, the soldiers of Darius charged up the marble staircase and burst into the banqueting hall. A Persian soldier with drawn sword smote Belshazzar under the fifth rib and he fell down among the thousand nobles and their women already dead in the slush of mingled wine and blood. What a warning Belshazzar's death is to all drunkards not to profane holy things — even the sacred vessel of the body!

> That night they slew him on his father's throne,
> He died unnoticed and the hand unknown,
> Crownless and scepterless Belshazzar lay
> A robe of purple round a form of clay.

THE KING OF BABYLON (Isaiah 14:4)

The Antichrist is prefigured in this title because he is the end and final outcome of Babel.

V

Persia and Persian Monarchs
B. C. 539-331

Persia proper was originally a small territory. It was Achaemenes who led the Persian emigrants into their final settlement in 700 B.C. and this was an ancient kingdom of Asia. The Persians, along with the Hebrews, Assyrians and many of the Arabians, were descendants of Shem. At one time Persia stretched from India to Egypt and Thrace, with the Tigris as its chief river. It was bounded on the north by Media and the Caspian Sea, Russian Tartary, and the mountains of Caucasus, on the west by Susiana, or the Euphrates and Tigris rivers; on the east by Carminia, Carbol, Beloochestan; on the south by the Persian Gulf (Esther 1:3).

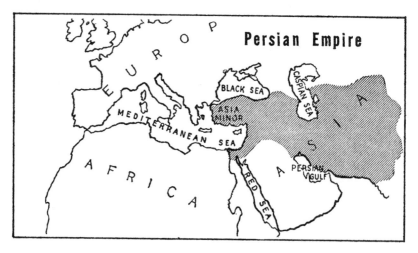

Something of the size of Persia is indicated by the boast of Cyrus to Xenophon, "My father's Empire is so large that people perish with cold at one extremity, while they are suffocated with the heat at the other," a feature still characteristic of the land, as it is of the American Continent. After 70 years subjection to the Medes, Persia revolted and became supreme in 558 B.C., hence Daniel's description of the Medo-Persian Empire.

The Hebrew word for "Persia" is *Phars*, now the modern *Parsa*, or *Parsee* (Ezekiel 27:10; 38:5), and also recognizable in *Fars*, or *Tarsistan*, one of Persia's modern provinces. To the Jews it was known by its ancient name *Elam*. Daniel calls it *Peres* (5:28). Zechariah, another prophet, began to prophesy about two months after Haggai in the second year of Darius Hystopes and continued to prophesy for two years. Like Daniel, Zechariah emblematically describes the four great empires, the chariots and horses representing the Babylonian, Persian, Grecian and Roman Empires (7:1). Daniel foretold the cessation of the Persian Empire by Alexander the Great at the moment it was rising into prominence (11:2, 4).

As a rule Persian sovereigns were kindly disposed toward the Jews, who were permitted to return from their captivity and were aided by the Persians in re-establishing themselves as a nation. The policy of the Persian monarchy was to repatriate the peoples who had been deported by their Assyrian and Babylonian conquerors. Halley points out that Israel was *nurtured* in Egypt in the days of Egypt's power and *destroyed* by Assyria and Babylonia in the day of their power, and *restored* by Persia in the day of Persia's power. The last three historical, post-captivity books of the Old Testament, namely Ezra, Nehemiah and Esther, give an account of Israel's treatment by the Persians, as well as a record of the organization of the Persian kingdom and court. Independent secular history confirms the Bible record.

When the Persians overthrew the Medes, they adopted their luxury and their gods. For an illuminating account of Persian religion the reader is directed to the exhaustive article on the subject in *The International Standard Bible Encyclopaedia*. Suffice it to say that there was the dual worship of Ormuzd, the supreme great god, the giver of life, and *Mithra*, the sun, and *Homa* the moon. The worship of the elements was common to the Persians.

Coming to the monarchy of the Persian Empire we note that its kings were despots who presided over a council. "The princes of Persia and Media who see his face and sit the first in the kingdom" (Esther 1:4; Ezra 7:14). These princes had no power in the government of the nation. The king delegated those who were to serve (Esther 3:1-10; 8:8; 10:2, 3), and service for the king was recorded and rewarded (Esther 2:23; 6:2, 3). To intrude on the king's privacy was to incur the penalty of death (Esther 2:12, 15; 4:11-16). The unalterable law of the Medes and the Persians controlled the decisions of the king (Esther 1:19), who was an arbitrary ruler with unlimited power. Let us now pass in review the Persian monarchs of which the Bible speaks.

CYRUS 558-529 B.C.
(II Chronicles 36:22, 23; Ezra; Isaiah 21:41-46; Daniel 2; 5; 7; 8; 10:1)

The King Who Illustrates Divine Sovereignty

Cyrus, whose name occurs some 24 times in the Old Testament, was a descendant of the old Persian family of the Achaemenidae, whose ancestors seem to have been chiefs or "kings" of Anshan, a district of Persia or Elam. He was the son of Cambyses the Persian, and of Mandane, daughter of Astyages, king of the Medes (see II Chronicles 36:22, 23; Ezra 1:1, 2). Bullinger advances the theory which we reject that Cyrus was the son of Astyages and Esther, and thus fulfilled Isaiah 44:28; 45:4. Thus, according to this expositor, *the book* of Esther should precede the books of Ezra and Nehemiah, and Cyrus had been carefully prepared for the part he was to play by Esther, Nehemiah and Mordecai.

Jeremiah had prophesied that the Chaldean suppression would last 70 years, which it did. Nabonidus the last Babylonian monarch to die, ascended the throne in 555 B.C., 70 years after the Battle of Carchemish in 605 B.C. Cyrus the Great captured Babylon in 538 B.C., and thus Persian history as we know it began with this brilliant conqueror, so notable for his unparalleled career of conquest and heroic behavior gaining for him the affection of Medes. Of the exploits of this energetic Persian ruler R. K. Harrison writes: "He rapidly united the people of the vassal state of Media, and in 549 B.C. he revolted against Astyages his suzerain. After a short time he conquered him in battle, and thus Cyrus fell heir to the Medo-Persian Empire. So great was his potential strength that an alliance was hurriedly formed against him. Those who participated were Croesus, King of Lydia (Asia Minor), the fabulously wealthy king who is credited with having invented coinage; Nabonidus of Babylon, and Anasis, the Pharaoh of Egypt (c.569-525 B.C.). In 546 B.C. he attacked the forces of Croesus and defeated him, thereby gaining control of the whole of Asia Minor." Then came his victory over Babylon.

When Cyrus drew near to the Chaldean capital, the known and unknown prophets of the exile were overjoyed, for the time had come for God to favor Zion (Isaiah 21:9; 24:4-25; 40-65). Isaiah expressly mentions Cyrus as the one through whom the divine purpose would be wrought out in history (44:28). After Babylon was captured without a fight Cyrus granted permission to the Jews to return to their own land (Ezra 1:1-4). Bishop Westcott remarks, "The permanent effects which Persia had wrought upon the world can be better traced through the Jewish people than by any other channel. The laws, the literature, the very ruins of the material grandeur of Persia have passed away; and still it is possible to distinguish the results which they produced in preparing the Jews for the fulfillment of their divinely given mission." The marvel is, as Dean Stanley points out,

that the document inaugurating a new era for the Jews "came not
from a Jewish lawgiver, or prophet or priest, but the decree of a
Gentile king!"

The prophets describe the virtues and vices of this Persian monarch in vivid terms. Isaiah speaks of Cyrus as being "surnamed" and
"girded" of God though he had not known Him (45:4, 5), and was
also "called" of God, as were Abraham and Isaac (46:11; Genesis
17:19). The "spirit," too, was stirred up by the Lord to do the things
he did "for Jacob My servant's sake and Israel mine elect" (II Chronicles 36:22). Cyrus is hailed as a "shepherd" of the Lord and as His
"anointed" or messiah. He is "the righteous man from the East"
(41:2), and the one ordained to restore Jerusalem and lay the foun-
dations of her ruined Temple (44:28; 45:6).

Isaiah likewise portrays the other side of the character of Cyrus.
Ambitious as a conqueror, he is "a ravenous bird from the east" and
an all-devouring "bear" as the founder of the second of the four
brutal empires Daniel describes. As "the ram with two horns," Cyrus
is symbolized as the one who would write in himself the two empires — Media and Persia — which he did (Daniel 8:3-26). God's
choice of a Gentile king to assist His people, the Jews, provides us
with three great lessons —

1. Known unto God are all His works from the beginning of the
   world (Isaiah 44:7, 8; Acts 15:18).
2. God, in what we call His ordinary providence, can make all
   things work together to them that love Him (Romans 8:28).
3. God sometimes chooses Gentiles as well as Jews, and the great
   men of this world, themselves imperfect and half-informed, as
   as well as saints and prophets, to be His instruments, and to
   further His cause. Truly His wind bloweth where it listeth
   (John 3:8)!

The character of Cyrus, who hated idols and worshiped the one
God, and therefore was profoundly affected by Israel's sense of the
power and glory of God, is not hard to trace. His generous, obliging
and heroic behavior gained him the affection of the Medes. Dr. W.
Kay in his commentary on *Isaiah* writes of this Persian monarch thus:

> The character of Cyrus has been admitted by both ancient and modern
> writers to have been singularly noble. He was energetic and patient,
> just and prudent, magnanimous, modest and religious-minded. Aeschylus
> calls him "gracious." Xenophon selected him as a model prince for all
> nations. Plutarch says that in wisdom, virtue and greatness of soul he
> appears far in advance of all kings; while a German writer, Delitsch,
> insists: "The fundamental principles of worldly politics had been grasping
> selfishness. Cyrus to his eternal honour, acted on purer principles."

If, as the oft-quoted Victorian constitutional writer, Bagehot asserts,
the three great powers of sovereigns are the right to be consulted, the
right to encourage, the right to warn, Cyrus was a sovereign who
exemplified these rights.

Before he died in July, 529 B.C., after reigning for 29 years, Cyrus had created the largest empire the world had seen up to that point in history — an empire which lasted for some 200 years. As to his death some writers say that he died peaceably in bed. Others affirm that he was killed in battle against some frontier tribe in 529 B.C. His tomb is at Murghāb, near the ruins of Pasargadae, in Persia. Plutarch recorded that the following inscription was on the tomb of Cyrus —

"O man, whoever thou art, and whencesoever thou comest (for come, I know thou wilt,) I am Cyrus, the founder of the Persian Empire. Envy me not the little earth that covers my body."

It is said that Alexander was greatly impressed with this inscription, seeing it set before him, in so striking a fashion, the uncertainty and vicissitude of worldly things. Placing his crown of gold on Cyrus' tomb, Alexander wondered why a monarch so renowned and possessed of vast treasure had not been buried more sumptuously.

CAMBYSES

This older son and successor of Cyrus is sometimes spoken of as Ahasuerus and identified as the Xerxes of Ezra 4:6 and Daniel 11:2. There is no evidence, however that he was ever called "Ahasuerus" — the name given to Astyages, King of the Medes (Daniel 9:1) and to Queen Esther's husband (Esther 1:1). The record of Cambyses, who reigned for 7 years — 529-522 B.C. — need not occupy much space. He had a brother, Bardes or Smerdes, whom he put to death secretly shortly after his accession, probably because of the fear of an attempted rebellion. Cambyses invaded Egypt and conquered it after a fierce battle at Pelusium in 525 B.C. He acted with good generalship and with clemency toward the conquered. After the subjugation of Egypt, Cyrene and Berca (modern Tripoli) surrendered to his sway. An effort to take Carthage had to be abandoned.

Later on, King Psammetichus III, of Egypt, whose life Cambyses had formerly spared, led a revolt against the Persian monarch who quelled it with great harshness. The Egyptian king was taken and executed and many of Egypt's temples destroyed. Then Gaumata, impersonator of the murdered brother of Cambyses, set himself up as king of Persia, gaining a good deal of support for his claims. With the fragments of a shattered army, Cambyses marched against Gaumata but on the way died from a self-inflicted wound. It is thought that being mentally ill, he committed suicide.

SMERDIS

A pretender, this pseudo Smerdis, spoken of as "Gomates" and thought by some to be Ahasuerus Longimanus (Persian princes had often more than one name), was the one who usurped the throne and reigned in Persia for eight months in 522 B.C. by impersonating the younger son of Cyrus, Smertis (Ezra 4:7-23; Daniel 11:2). It was the Ahasuerus Smerdis who forbade the continuance of the work commenced under Cyrus and continued by his son of establishing the Jews in Jerusalem. In his decree there is no evidence of the faith in the supreme God which characterized the decree of Cyrus. The Magian Creed of Smerdis was pantheism — the worship of the elements — earth, air, water, fire.

After his brief reign of eight months, Smerdis was overthrown and slain by Darius and his six brother-nobles whose names, as cited by Herodotus, are confirmed in Darius' Besitun Inscription.

As "Darius" was the common name of several Medo-Persian kings, it is necessary to distinguish between oriental kings thus named in the Old Testament. We have, first of all —

DARIUS THE MEDE (Daniel 5:31)

This successor of Belshazzar to the throne of Babylon dominates the sixth chapter of Daniel and is the only monarch whose age, parentage and nationality are recorded. Although this Darius is never mentioned by Greek historians, and no Persian tablet bearing his name has been found, there is a possibility that he is the *Gubaru*, Governor of Babylon, who appears on Babylonian inscriptions. Efforts have been made to identify Darius the Mede with Cambyses, or with his father, Cyrus the Persian, or with Ahasuerus, husband of Esther.

DARIUS I

Known as Darius the Great, or Darius the First, this King of Persia, son of Heptaspes, reigned for 37 years — 522-486 B.C. — and is mentioned in Ezra 5:3; 6:1-15 and in Daniel 11:2. Not recognizing the usurpation of Smertis, Darius dates his reign from 522 B.C. as the rightful heir to and successor of Cambyses. In the early years of the reign of Darius, rebellion broke out in every part of the Persian Empire headed by real or pretended descendants of ancient kings of each country.

After a three-year struggle, the authority of Darius was firmly established everywhere, and he set about dividing his empire into some 29 provinces over which he placed nobles of Persian or Median descent instead of representatives of the ancient kingdom. The empire under Darius extended from the Indus to the Black Sea, from the Jaxartes to beyond the Nile. His efforts to conquer Greece are part of Grecian history. Darius died in 485 B.C. before an Egyptian rebellion could be repressed.

The *Behistun Rock*, containing the famous inscription which supplied the key to the ancient Babylonian language, was carved by order of this Darius, who had decreed and financed the rebuilding of the Temple, 516 B.C. To him also goes the credit of being the first to dig a canal through the Suez. His inscription recounting this feat reads —

"I am a Persian, with Persia I seized Egypt. I commanded to dig this canal from the river named the Nile (Pirāva), which flows through Egypt, to the sea which comes from Persia. Then the canal was dug, according as I commanded. And I said 'Come ye from the Nile through this canal to Persia.'"

AHASUERUS
(Book of Esther; Daniel 8:7)

THE KING WHO SAVED A NATION FROM EXTINCTION

Ahasuerus, the Persian monarch who dominates the Book of Esther, is usually regarded as the celebrated Xerxes of profane history, whose invasion of Greece stirred up the rage of the mighty Macedonian monarch, Alexander (Daniel 8:7). Certainly what is recorded of Ahasuerus — his riches (1:4), the extent of his vast empire (1:1), his sensuality and feasting (1:6-10), his arbitrary and tyrannical conduct (1:13-22), agree with the character and historical account furnished by profane authors of Xerxes. Says Rawlinson —

The name Ahasuerus is undoubtedly the proper Hebrew equivalent for the Persian word which the Greeks represented by Xerxes . . . and we are at once struck with the strong resemblance which his character bears to that assigned by the classical writers to the celebrated son of Darius. Proud, self-willed, amorous, careless of contravening Persian customs; reckless of human life, yet not actually blood-thirsty; impetuous, facile, changeable, the Ahasuerus of Esther corresponds in all respects to the Greek portraiture of Xerxes, which is not the mere picture of an Oriental despot, but has various peculiarities which distinguish it even from the other Persian kings.

Ahasuerus, successor to his father, Darius I, undeterred by his late father's failure to conquer Greece, made a fresh attack but was routed and fled to Sardis. Failure to subdue Greece largely exhausted his empire, the scope of splendor of which he strove to maintain. He kept his restless subjects under rigid military control. He is represented as being capricious (Esther 3:18; 8:9). After his deposition of his queen, Vashti, because she would not violate her female decorum and expose herself to the gaze of drunken revelers, Ahasuerus, identified by some writers as the Ahasuerus of Ezra 4:6, advanced Esther to be queen. Doubtless Esther lived far into the following reign of Artaxerxes, her stepson under whom Nehemiah rebuilt Jerusalem.

The sleepless night of Ahasuerus was an important link in the chain of Israel's preservation from extinction and illustrates how the providence of God makes use of the most trifling, and what to us seem the more accidental circumstances, to accomplish His will (Esther 6:1; Romans 8:28). Wm. Broome, of the sixteenth century, in his *Epistle to Mr. Fenton* wrote —

> "None are completely wretched but the great,
> Superior woes superior stations bring;
> A pleasant sleep, while cares awake a king."

The latter course of the reign of Ahasuerus presents one broken tale of debauchery and bloodshed. After a reign of 21 years, 486-465 B.C. he was murdered by two of his officers, Mithridates and Artabanus.

Artaxerxes II; commonly called by his contemporaries
Longimanus

Artaxerxes, a name common to Persian kings, was the third son of the renowned Xerxes and reigned for 40 years from 465-425 B.C. There is general agreement that this Persian monarch was the one at whose court Ezra and Nehemiah were officials. He was raised to the throne by Artabanus, one of his father's murderers. Shortly after his accession he put his older brother, Darius, to death, and later on Artabanus suffered the same fate for trying to take the throne from Artaxerxes. Among his achievements were the re-taking of Egypt, retention of the island of Cyprus, and the granting of freedom to all the Greek cities of Asia Minor.

Doubtless influenced by his stepmother, Queen Esther, this ruler appointed Nehemiah as Governor of Jerusalem, with a commission to rebuild the walls and provide for the welfare of the Jews. For twelve years Nehemiah executed his commission with great success, amidst much opposition, consecrating both his labor and wealth to the object (Nehemiah 4:23; 5:14). Some thirteen years before, Ezra had been sent on a similar errand (Ezra 7).

Artaxerxes was noted among the Persian kings for wisdom and right feeling. Like Cyrus and Darius before him he identified Jehovah with his own supreme heathen deity, Ormuzd (Ezra 7:12, 21, 23), and supported Jewish worship by grants and offerings from the state and provincial treasures. He threatened death, banishment, imprisonment, or confiscation against opponents. Fausset further reminds us that Artaxerxes was the oriental despot "who at personal inconvenience would suffer his servant's departure for so long, to cheer him up, must have been more than ordinarily good-natured." Secular history represents Artaxerxes as "the first Persian monarch of mildness and magnanimity." The Persians admired his "equity and moderation in government." He died in 425 B.C. and was succeeded by his second son, Xerxes.

There are five letters mentioned in Ezra associated with royalty we can tabulate for our instruction in letter-writing —

1. Of Rehum to Artaxerxes charging the Jews with rebuilding the *walls* of Jerusalem (4:11-16).
2. Of Artaxerxes in reply, authorizing that the work of rebuilding be stopped (4:17-22).
3. Of Tatnai to Darius, telling him that the *Temple* in Jerusalem was being rebuilt and asking what the king's pleasure was in the matter (5:7-17).
4. Of Darius in reply, commanding that the work should proceed, and that the Jews be given every help (6:2-12).
5. Of Artaxerxes (Longimanus) to Ezra, giving permission to the Jews still in captivity to return to Jerusalem, and specially commissioning Ezra (7:2-6).

The four royal decrees can be grouped together.

1. From Cyrus, relating to the rebuilding of the Temple (Ezra 1).
2. From Darius I (Hystarpes) as to the completion of the Temple (4:24; 6:1-35).
3. From Artaxerxes, regarding the beautifying of the Temple and the restoration of its worship (7:27).
4. From Artaxerxes, about the rebuilding of the city (Daniel 9:25; Nehemiah 2:5).

As to remaining Persian monarchs who lack any Biblical reference, the following are distinguished in secular history:

XERXES II 425 B.C.
DARIUS II 423-405 B.C.

This Persian monarch with a regnal name was surnamed by the Greeks, *Aothius,* meaning "the bastard," seeing he was an illegitimate son of Artaxerxes. SOGDIANUS followed with a brief reign.

ARTAXERXES II 405-358 B.C.

Known also as Mnēmōn, Artaxerxes succeeded his father and with him we have the first signs of the decline of Persian power. Revolts in different parts of the empire threatened to bring the regime to a close. Daniel foretold the overthrow of the Persian Empire of Alexander at the moment it was rising into fame and spoke of Alexander as the first King of Grecia (8:21; 11:2, 4). Persia was to bow to Greece and the empire pass from Asia to Europe, as it did.

ARTAXERXES III 358-338 B.C.

This son of the former Artaxerxes was also known as Ochos. R. K. Harrison remarks that "for nearly 40 years (378-340 B.C.) Egypt enjoyed independence from Persian rule while Artaxerxes III was struggling to regain the ground which his predecessor had lost." He was murdered with all his sons, except the youngest, Arses, by an Egyptian eunuch, Bagōas, probably in revenge for Artaxerxes' conduct in Egypt, 338 B.C.

ARSES 338-335 B.C.

Arses was murdered by Bagōas some three years later when Darius III, Codomannus, the son of Sisygambis, daughter of Artaxerxes II, and her husband, a Persian noble, ascended the throne.

DARIUS III, the last Persian king, known also as Codomannus (see Daniel 8; Nehemiah 12:22) 335-331 B.C. After coming to the throne Darius strengthened his control over Greek cities and reconquered Egypt in 334 B.C. and to all appearances the Persian star was rising. But although the Persians looked with confidence toward the continuance of their empire, the end was near. In 334 B.C. Alexander the Greek set out to free Greek cities from Persian control and at the Battle of Arbela succeeded. This ended the history of the Achaemenian Empire, the whole of the lands composing it becoming part of the empire of Macedon. Darius himself fell by an assassin's hand.

Shakespeare speaks of "The thronèd monarch being better than his crown." Reviewing the history of many Persian kings, or of kings of other empires for that matter, we cannot say that the majority of them were better than their crowns.

VI

Greece and Grecian Monarchs

While no Greek monarch is mentioned by name in the Bible, a few are symbolically and prophetically described. Greece and Grecians are specifically indicated, hence this chapter dealing with one of the great empires of the past.

The actual beginning of Greece, as a dominating world-power through the central part of the inter-testament period, known as "The Silent Four Hundred Years," is veiled in obscurity and myth. Some historians feel that it began about 1200 B.C. and was contemporaneous with the period of the Judges and was developing during the reigns of David and Solomon. The age of Homer goes back to 1000 B.C.

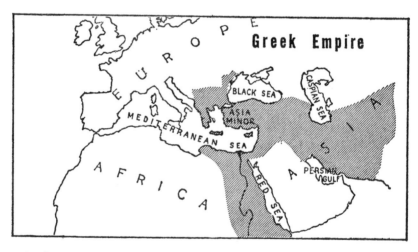

Authentic Greek history begins with the First Olympiad, 776 B.C., which was followed by the formation of the Hellenic States, 776-500 B.C. Then came the Persian Wars, 500-330 B.C. and the famous battles of Marathon, 490 B.C., Thermopylae and Salamis, 480 B.C. Greece's most brilliant eon covered 465-399 B.C. Philosophers and poets like Pericles, Socrates — contemporary of Ezra and Nehemiah — Philo,

Demosthenes, Aristotle, Diogenes and Plato exercised tremendous influence.

For 1,000 years — 500 B.C. to 500 A.D. — Athens, the most polished city of Greece, was the center of philosophy, literature, science and art, and the seat of the greatest university in the world, the "Schoolmistress of Europe." It was also the meeting place of the world's intelligentsia, yet a city wholly given over to idolatry (Acts 17:15-21). Greece had greater and lesser gods, each with its own shrine and group of worshipers. Among the greater gods were Zeus, Herta, Athena, Apollo and Artemis. Many of these gods were related to nature, e.g., Zeus had to do with the sky. Some of them were associated with human activity and emotions, as Aesculapius, who received men's prayers for relief from disease.

Athens, most distinguished for arts and learning, was the most given to idolatry. Aelian spoke of it as "The Altar of Greece." Poets, painters, sculptors and philosophers gave their sanctions to prevailing superstitions and joined the people in the impious and obscene rites of worship which they practiced. Even Socrates, greatest of the philosophers of antiquity, made no effort to reform the manners of his countrymen. He taught his disciples by precept and example to govern themselves in religious matters, according to the custom of the country.

"The god of Plato or Aristotle had little or nothing in common with the ancestral deity of the Hebrew people," says R. K. Harrison. "Hellenic society was notorious for its corruptness, coarseness and immorality, and the pursuit of pleasure for its own sake, combined with a lack of insistence on the authority of an absolute moral law, contained within itself the seeds of its own destruction." Paul's sermon on Mars' Hill was mocked by the Athenians who rejected the Resurrection. Howbeit, some believed (Acts 17:22-34).

The original Grecians were known as Ionians and in Hebrew are called after Javan, the son of Japheth, Genesis 10:2, 4. In the Apocrypha, "Grecians" and "Greeks" are used with distinction, and it speaks of Alexander the Great as "King of Greece" and his Macedonian Empire as "The Kingdom of the Greeks." When "Greeks" are comprehensively contrasted with "Jews," the reference is to Gentiles (Acts 14:1; 17:4; Romans 1:16, etc.) When the prophets write of "Grecians," it is those of Greece about whom they write (Joel 4:6; Zechariah 9:13). Grecian Jews or Hellenists were those Jews of the Dispersion who spoke Greek and used the Greek Scriptures, thereby distinguishing them from Palestinian Jews who adhered to the original sacred Hebrew tongue (John 7:33; Acts 6:1; 9:29).

Balaam, in a wonderful prophecy, spoke of the conquests of Alexander and his successors (Numbers 24:24).

Joel mentions the Grecians as being purchasers to whom the Syrian slave merchants sold the children of Judah 800 B.C. (3:6).

Ezekiel speaks of Javin (or Greece) and Tyre as trading in the persons of men (27:13).

Daniel, as we shall more fully see, foretold the rise of Alexander the Great as the swift leopard (7:6). Daniel also foretold the overthrow of the Persian Empire by Alexander at the moment it was rising to fame and spoke of him as the first King of Grecia (8:21; 11: 2, 4). The prophet speaks of Greece as *Chittim.*

Zechariah represents Judah and Ephraim as filling God's bow to pierce Greece, meaning that Jewish Maccabees would punish Greece. The kingdom of Greece, unlike the preceding kingdoms of Babylon and Media-Persia did not fall as a whole or at once but fell in parts. The last to fall was Egypt, at the Battle of Actium, 21 B.C., when Caesar Augustus defeated Cleopatra and brought the fourth world-power into being. Perhaps the prophet also depicts a coming struggle when the sons of Zion are to vanquish Greece (9:13). Greece will be destroyed at the advent of the Lord in judgment (Daniel 2:35).

Isaiah foretold that the Jews surviving divine judgment would become missionaries to Greece (66:19).

Paul's work in Greece, during his second missionary tour, 50-53 A.D., was not as successful as elsewhere, possibly because of the tremendous impact of Grecian religion and philosophy.

The Greek language through the influence of Alexander the Great and the dynasties of his generals that followed became the one universal language from Spain to the Euphrates. Thus Greece performed an important function for the Gospel in that it furnished the language for use among the nations. It was during the reign of the enlightened Ptolemy II (285-246 B.C.) that the tremendous task of translating the sacred Hebrew Scriptures into the Greek language was begun, being encouraged by Ptolemy who took interest in the history and culture of his Jewish subjects.

This translation, known as the *Septuagint* meaning "seventy," and indicated by the Roman numerals LXX, is a term derived from the seventy scholars who were chosen to undertake the translation which was completed in the middle of the second century B.C. Thus Greece was God's instrument in preparing the way for the New Testament Scriptures — sole medium of the written Word — to be spread over and understood in all the living world.

The unique language of the Greek, with its marvelous flexibility, its capability of forming new theological terms, its power of expression and most delicate shades of meaning all combined to convey to the world — with the most minute precision — the glad tidings of salvation through Christ Jesus. Orally, it was the language used by the apostles in preaching, because Greek was widely spoken, and likewise because it was the fittest lingual vehicle for imparting the Scripture to mankind.

Having briefly mentioned the fact that no Grecian king is referred to by name in the Bible, let us now examine those Scriptures presenting some of the rulers of Greece in a typical fashion. In the brass or copper *leopard* of Daniel's image we have a symbol of Greece (2:32; 7:6). Brass or copper, inferior to the two previous metals of the image, gold and silver, represents the inferior order of power characterizing the Third or Grecian Empire in which the government was ministered by the military authorities who were created at the will and pleasure of Alexander.

The beautiful beast, the leopard, portrays the art, culture and civilization of the third great power which dominated the greater part of the then known world, and was responsible for all the nobler traits of Rome. The leopard is remarkable for the impetuosity with which it seizes its prey, and symbolizes the crafty and bloodthirsty conquests of Greece. By "the four wings," we understand the incredible swiftness of Alexander's conquests. What rapid expansion was his! Like a leopard, he was swift in his movements. In twelve years his conquests extended to the Ganges.

As to the leopard's *spots*, the same can imply, as Fausset suggests, the variety of nations incorporated in Greece and also the variability of Alexander's own character, by turns mild and cruel, temperate and drunken, lawful and licentious.

In the "he-goat" with a notable horn waxing strong and breaking "the rough goat" (Daniel 8:20, 22), we have a symbol of the agility and strength of Alexander, the greatest warrior-king who ever lived, who accomplished his ambitions and wept because there were no more worlds to conquer. But we read that "the great and notable horn was broken," symbolizing the death of Alexander in the zenith of his glory and power. Fifteen years after his death the whole dynasty was wiped out by intrigue and murder and, true to the prophetic vision, his four generals came to power.

The "four heads" refer to the four divisions of the Grecian Empire after Alexander's death. The "four notable horns or ones" typify Alexander's four generals who controlled the partitioned kingdom, which partition continued till the kingdom passed under the sway of Rome in 146 B.C.

Lysimachus took Thrace and Bythinia.

Cassander took Macedonia and Greece.

Seleucus took Syria, Babylonia and the East.

The capital of the Seleucid Empire was Antioch which became a famous center of Christianity. It was here that Christ's disciples were first called *Christians* (Acts 11:26).

Ptolemy took Egypt, Palestine, Arabia and Peterea.

From the last two partitions, the king of the north and the king of the south are to appear.

ALEXANDER THE GREAT
(Daniel 2:39; 7:6; 8:7, 8; 11:13, 19)

The King Who Was Born to Victory

If ever a man was born to conquest, that man was the son of King Philip of Macedon with whom the rise of Greek power commenced. It was Philip who united part of Greece before his assault to recapture other Greek cities from Persian domination. He died in 336 b.c. before accomplishing his purpose, but Alexander, his son, who succeeded him, achieved his aim. He launched his military campaigns against Persia and conquered much of the globe before he died at the age of thirty-three. Then world-power passed from Asia to Europe.

Alexander believed himself divinely chosen for the great mission of Greece to the civilized world, to join east and west in a union of equality. Arian says: "Alexander was like no other man, and could not have been given to the world without the special interposition of God. He was the providential instrument of breaking down the barrier wall between kingdom and kingdom, of bringing the contemplative east and the energetic west into mutually beneficial contact."

Words are inadequate to describe this genius of victory who conquered half the known world in some twelve years, and who left traces of his swift conquests stamped upon the fabric of Western Asia. Although a victorious general and leader of armies, his colossal victories were followed by sympathetic and understanding administration. He won the loyalty of the defeated and conquered them again with the culture of Greece.

Without doubt, Alexander was greatly influenced by the renowned philosophers of his time. Among his tutors would be Aristotle, one of the world's greatest thinkers, whose teaching was doubtless a potent factor in molding the mind of the soldier-statesman. It was Aristotle who implanted in the young Alexander a love of Homer which lasted him all his life. He confessed it was to Aristotle that he owed "the knowledge to live worthily." Taught to "live worthily," Alexander had a well-thumbed copy of the Iliad under his pillow at night, but its companion was a dagger. At Corinth, Alexander met the eccentric philosopher, Diogenes, and asked him to name any boon he craved. The philosopher replied, "Stand out of my sun." Afterward Alexander remarked to his followers: "Were I not Alexander I should like to be Diogenes."

When Alexander succeeded his father on the Macedonian Throne in 336 B.C., he was not quite twenty and was dead before he was thirty-three. Yet in the intervening twelve years or so, he accomplished a vast and glittering panorama of conquest still dazzling men after twenty-three centuries. By 328 B.C. the Macedonian was master of all the Persian Empire and was tolerant to all the conquered provinces.

Alexander the Great died in his palace at Babylon in 323 B.C. after a brief illness following a short and merry time of godlessness and dissipation. Rumor had it that he poisoned himself. It is more probable that after having crowded into half the normal life span a score of lifetimes Alexander "burned himself out." He had reached "an eminence of human grandeur." Yet the empire he founded, like himself, passed away.

The celebrated city of Alexandria was so named after Alexander the Great who founded it in 332 B.C. It became a city of great commercial importance, as well as a center from whence emanated the intellectual and religious life of the world. When Rome became the mistress of the world, Alexandria maintained her high reputation as a seat of learning, for here lived Origen, Clement and other distinguished scholars during the first six Christian centuries. The eloquent Apollos was born here (Acts 18:24) and its shipping trade supplied Paul with a vessel to take him to Rome (Acts 27:6). Alexandria, celebrated home of the Septuagint, or Greek Translation of the Old Testament, was successively the Greek, Roman and Christian capital of Lower Egypt. The Apostle Mark is said to have been the first to preach and found a Christian church in Alexandria.

ANTIOCHUS EPIPHANES
(Daniel 8; 11:31-45)

THE KING WHO PREFIGURES THE ANTICHRIST

Because of his association with a fragment of the Grecian Empire, and the fact that "the little horn" of Daniel 8:9 *historically* represents Antiochus Epiphanes, whose rage and cruelty toward Israel knew no bounds; and *typically* "the King of the North" (Daniel 11) or Assyria (Isaiah 10), the future northeast power who will oppress Israel in the coming crisis of her history, we include a brief profile of him in this section. The language is used in Daniel 11:31-45 which applies in history and type to Antiochus but exhaustively to the Antichrist yet to come.

The changing fortunes of the Jews after Alexander the Great, as well as the political history of the Jewish nation, are given in the Book of Maccabees and by Josephus, the Jewish historian. Crises under the dynasties of Ptolemy and of Antiochus are given in detail in the Apocrypha. The only member of the dynasty of Antiochus concerning us is Antiochus IV, known as Antiochus Epiphanes, who succeeded Seleucius IV in 175 B.C., and who is typically and prophetically mentioned by the prophet Daniel. *The Feast of Dedication,* instituted by Judas Maccabeus, was a grateful memorial of the renewed dedication of the Temple to God's service, after it had been profaned by Antiochus Epiphanes (I Mac. 4:52-59). Our Lord's attendance on this feast (John 10:22) justifies the observance of correct religious seasons of human appointment.

When Alexander the Great died, 323 B.C., and the Empire he founded was divided among his generals, Egypt was placed under the control of Ptolemy, with the Ptolemaic dynasty lasting for almost three centuries. Ptolemy I invaded Syria and annexed it to his possessions. He then marched on to Jerusalem and occupied it, deporting many of its inhabitants to Egypt. Thus Judaea fell between the hammer and the anvil of Syria and Egypt.

In 168 B.C. Antiochus reclaimed Syria after a bloody battle, and two years later plundered Jerusalem and for three and a half years deprived the Jews of their civil and religious liberty. Out of the remnant of the fourfold division of the Grecian Empire, Antiochus arose to destroy the Jews, so kindly treated by Alexander and by those succeeding him. Antiochus was a proud, extravagant, crafty ruler whose character is reflected in the cynical play on his names. The royal title, Epiphanes, means *The Illustrious,* so surnamed for establishing the royal line against Heliodorus. But he was nicknamed "Epimanes," meaning "madman," because of behavior far from kingly. He would carouse with the lowest, bathe with them in public and throw stones at passers by. Because of the crafty way he supplanted Demetrius, the rightful heir, he is called "a vile person" (Daniel 11). And he it was who "came into the kingdom by flatteries."

It was in the year 170 B.C. that Antiochus plundered Jerusalem, profaned and pillaged the Temple, enslaved great numbers of Jews, and murdered thousands of others. He was determined to eradicate Judaism. Jews remaining were made to take part in pagan worship. The sacrificial Temple worship of Judaism was prohibited. A Greek altar was erected to Jupiter and a sow was offered upon it. The Jews were compelled to eat swine's flesh. Those failing to participate in the heathen rites of the Greek religion were put to death. Allusion to martyrdom under Antiochus Epiphanes can be found in Hebrews 11:35-37. Compare Daniel 12:2. Gruesome details of the horrible deaths many died can be found in II Macc. 6 and 7.

This "desolation" (Daniel 8:13) affords a type of final "abomination of desolation" of which Christ spoke (Matthew 24:15). The terrible persecution of the Jews lasted three years, until the Maccabees defeated the troop of Antiochus, and the Jews were "holpen with a little help," that is, saved from extinction until the times of the Romans.

Prophetically, "the little horn" was fulfilled in Antiochus Epiphanes and is not to be confounded with the other "little horn" of Daniel 7 who is yet to come and dominate the earth. Antiochus is certainly a remarkable type of "the little horn" of the last days. Both "horns" are alike in their hatred of God and of the Jews, and in their profanation of holy things. Scofield's Bible comment says that, "Antiochus Epiphanes was insignificant as compared with historical personages whom the Bible does not mention, but he scourged the covenant people and defiled God's altar, thus coming into prophetic light. We see in him a partial fulfillment of 'the king of a fierce countenance yet to come.'"

VII

Rome and Roman Monarchs

The Romans were descendants of Japheth, the eldest son of Noah, and the Herods represent an Edomite line of kings, who under Rome's power assured control of Judaea shortly before the close of the Inter-Testament Period, around 47 B.C. Halley, in his remarkable *Bible Handbook,* which every Bible lover should possess, dealing with "Church History," reminds us that the Church of Jesus Christ was founded in the Roman Empire. He then sets forth the following outline of Roman history —

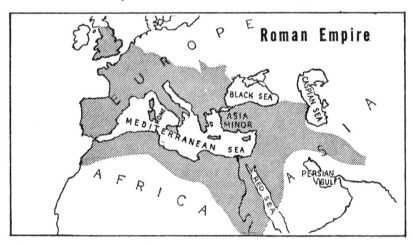

Rome was founded, 753 B.C.

Subdued Italy, 343-272 B.C.

Subdued Carthage, 264-146 B.C.

Subdued Greece and Asia Minor, 215-146 B.C.

Subdued Spain, Gaul, Briton, Teutons, 133-31 B.C.

Reached zenith of her glory, 46 B.C.-180 A.D.

Extended from the Atlantic to the Euphrates and from the North Sea to the African Desert. Population then about 120,000,000.

The Twelve Caesars

Julius Caesar, 46 B.C-44 B.C.
Chief lord of the Roman world.
Augustus, 31 B.C.-14 A.D.
During his reign Christ was born
Tiberius, 14 A.D.-37 A.D.
Christ was crucified during his governorship
Caligula, 37 A.D.-41 A.D.
Claudius, 41 A.D.-54 A.D.
Nero, 54 A.D.-68 A.D.
Cruel to Christians. Executed Paul the Apostle.
Galba, 68 A.D.-69 A.D.
Otho-Vitelius, 69 A.D.
Vespasian, 69 A.D.-79 A.D.
Titus, 79 A.D.-81 A.D.
Domitian, 81 A.D.-96 A.D.
Persecuted Christians. Banished Apostle John.

Five Good Emperors

Nerva, 96 A.D.-98 A.D.
Trajan, 98 A.D.-117 A.D. One of the best emperors
Hadrian, 117 A.D.-138 A.D.
Antonius Pius, 138 A.D.-161 A.D.
Noblest of emperors during the golden age of Rome's glory.
Marcus Aurelius, 161 A.D.-180 A.D.
A characteristic feature of all of these emperors was their hatred for and persecution of early Christians.

Decline and Fall of the Roman Empire 180 A.D.-476 A.D.

"Barrack Emperors," so-called because appointed by the army, operated during a period of civil war and widespread internal disaster, 192 A.D.-284 A.D.
Septimus Severus, 193 A.D.-211 A.D. Against Christians
Caracalla, 211 A.D.-217 A.D. Tolerated Christianity
Elagabalus, 218 A.D.-222 A.D. Tolerated Christianity
Alexander Severus, 222 A.D.-235 A.D. Favorable to Christianity
Maximin, 235 A.D.-238 A.D. Persecuted Christians
Philips, 244 A.D.-249 A.D. Very favorable to Christianity
Decius, 249 A.D.-251 A.D. Intense persecutor of Christians
Valerian, 253 A.D.-260 A.D. Persecuted Christians
Galienus, 260 A.D.-268 A.D. Favored Christians
Aurelian, 270 A.D.-275 A.D. Persecuted Christians
Diocletian, 284 A.D.-305 A.D. Intense hatred of Christians
Constantine, 306 A.D.-337 A.D. Became a Christian

Julian, 361 A.D.-363 A.D. The Apostate. Restored Paganism
Jovian, 363 A.D.-364 A.D. Re-established Christian truth
Theodosius, 378 A.D.-395 A.D. Made state religion of Christianity

THE ROMAN EMPIRE DIVIDED. 395 A.D.

West	East
Honorius, 395-423 A.D.	Arcadius, 395 A.D.-408 A.D.
Valentinian III, 423-455 A.D.	Theodosius II, 408 A.D.-450 A.D.
	Anastasius, 491 A.D.-518 A.D.
	Justinian, 527 A.D.-565 A.D.

The Western Empire fell in 476 A.D. at the hands of the barbarians, ushering in the Dark Ages. Out of the ruins of the Western Empire arose the Papal Empire.

The Eastern Empire fell in 1453 A.D.

The rise of the Roman Empire was foretold by Moses, some 800 years before its existence (Deuteronomy 28:49, 50). All the time, the Jews were surrounded by many nations whose language they understood, who were often attempting their destruction, and of whom it was foretold that they would be the instruments for their correction. But for this final dispersion and punishment, it was predicted that a nation should come from afar, whose language they did not understand. Such a prediction was literally fulfilled when the Romans overthrew the Jews.

Balaam foretold the end of Roman power. His prophecy (Numbers 24:24) of the conquests of Alexander and his successors, and of the Romans over the Assyrians and Jews, and of the destruction of the Macedonians and Roman Empires, is unintelligible to those who do not know that the family of Chittim, or Kittim (the son of Javan), settled in Macedonia and Italy; that Asshur refers to the Assyrians, and Eber to the Jews (Genesis 10:4).

Between the Old and New Testaments world power passed from the Medo-Persians to the Greeks and from the Greeks to the Romans so that the Gospel story opens under the aegis of Roman rule.

Prophetic references to Rome prove that it will be as an empire in a ten-kingdom form, with a unity and integrity as a whole secured and distributed by a coming ruler known as "the little horn" (Daniel 7; Revelation 13; 17). When the empire was broken up its unity vanished. Prophecy demands a strong, compact and united empire which will be effected by its ruler. The peoples comprising the Roman earth, if not those of a wider area, will express their hatred of Christ. A solemn future and a terrible end waits these people (Revelation 17:14; 19:1-12).

Peter described Rome by the figurative title of *Babylon.* John also speaks of it in the same way and denotes it in a manner so true of Rome (I Peter 5:13; Revelation 14:8; 16:19; 17:5, 9; 18:2, 20, 21).

Its command over all nations.

Its cruelty toward the saints.

Its situation on the seven hills.

Paul came twice to Rome, first when he appealed to Caesar; then a year before his martyrdom. There is no Scriptural evidence that Peter visited Rome or was buried there.

As to the significance of the name, *Rome*, it is suggested that it is from Romulus, who founded the empire in 753 B.C. Others indicate that it is an aboriginal word, *Rumon* — "the town by the river," from Rome's location on the Tiber. It has also been pointed out that *Rome* in Latin and Italian is "Roma," which when spelled backwards is *amor* meaning "love." All who visit the ancient city fall in love with her. Once conquering by the sword, but conquered by the Cross, she now conquers hearts by her unusual charm.

Rome was founded in the year 753 B.C. by Romulus, its first king, and rapidly increased in wealth and extent until it spread its giant arms from the Tiber to the Euphrates, becoming the mighty, colossal power of the world. The empire extended 3,000 miles east and west, 2,000 miles north and south, with a population of some 120,000,000. Built by the Etruscans, the city was originally made up of rude huts. Romulus rebuilt, enlarged and beautified the city before the Christian era.

Its direct connection with Palestine dates from 63 B.C. when Palestine was annexed to the Roman Empire. Pompey the Great conquered Palestine and there then began the domination of the Jewish people by Rome. The ancient Romans were idolaters and corrupt in their manners. It was in the Roman Empire that Christ was crucified, the legal sanction of the Roman name being attached to His cross.

Jerusalem was destroyed by the Romans in 70 A.D. when the national hopes of unbelieving Israel perished in the awful destruction of the city and temple, and the universal scattering of the people took place after a siege unparalleled in their history. The history of the Herodian family is inseparably connected with the last flickerings of the flames of Judaism as a national power before it was extinguished in the great Jewish war of rebellion in 70 A.D.

The founding of the Roman Empire by Julius Caesar and Augustus was the grandest political achievement ever accomplished. Caesar, the most remarkable man that Rome or any other empire produced, was the founder of the *Empire*, while Augustus was the founder of the *principate*. While it is profitable to trace the ups and downs of various dynasties such as The Flavian Period, 68-96 A.D., The Antonine Period, 96-192 A.D., The Changing Dynasties 192-284 A.D., etc., a fuller profile of Caesar and Augustus is necessary. Roman Emperors took the names of Caesar and Augustus (Matthew 22:21; Acts 25:10).

Julius Caesar

It was this renowned ruler who saw the opportunity of supreme power and grasped it and succeeded in exploiting democracy for his own ends. "In 49 B.C. he crossed the Rubicon and declared war upon his country, but in the same year was appointed dictator and thus made *his* enemies the enemies of his country." Because of his achievements, as one claiming kinship with the gods, he was recognized officially as "demigod," as temples were dedicated to him.

He became Emperor, Chief of the Senate, and High Priest, and was an imperialist of the highest order. Heterogeneous populations were blended into one people and into Roman citizenship. It was after Caesar's victory in Asia Minor that he sent his famous message, *Veni, Vidi, Vici* — "I came, I saw, I conquered." His word was law and coinage bore his image and title. The month *July* is in his honor.

Shakespeare made Cassius speak of Julius Caesar: "Why, man, he doth bestride this narrow world, like a Colossus," and he did bestride the world as the dictator who made possible the existence of a Roman Empire. "Imperial Caesar, dead and turned to clay," scoffed Hamlet, but despite his mortal clay the achievements of the greatest of the Caesars have lived on.

Lord Tweedsmuir has summed up the character of Caesar in his remarkable study:

> The burden of the globe on his shoulders did not impede his lightness of step. War and administration never made him a narrow specialist. His culture was as wide as that of any man of his day; he loved art and poetry and music and philosophy, and would turn gladly to them in the midst of his most critical labours . . . Combined in him in the highest degree were the realism of the man of action, the sensitiveness of the artist, and the imagination of the creative dreamer — a union not, I think, to be paralleled elsewhere.

Octavian (Augustus)

The field of Actium on September 2, 31 B.C., decided the fate of the old Roman Republic, which had sunk in exhaustion after the protracted civil and internecine strife when it was a matter of the survival of the fittest. Advancing with more caution and shrewdness than Caesar, Augustus became the founder of the Roman Empire, which began on January 16, 27 B.C.

In Rome he emulated the example of his predecessor, taking into his own hands the reins of government and proving the potent factor of the second triumvirate. Under his republican forms, Augustus ruled as emperor, controlled legislation and administration and the armies. "His policy was largely adhered to by the Julio-Claudian line, the last of which was Nero, who died in 68 A.D.

Augustus Caesar was the second Roman emperor, reigning at Christ's birth (Luke 2:1), who decreed that all the world should be taxed, which necessitated the presence of Joseph and Mary where Jesus was born as predicted by Micah (5:2). Educated by his great-uncle, Julius Caesar, Augustus reigned for over 40 years. Before his death at 76, in 14 A.D., he associated Tiberius with himself in the empire (Luke 3:1).

Other Caesars mentioned in the New Testament are *Tiberius*, who was reigning when Christ was crucified (Luke 3:1; 20:22-25; John 19:15); *Claudius* (Acts 11:28); *Nero*, known as Caesar and Augustus (Acts 25:8, 11). This was the emperor Paul appealed to in the words "I appeal unto Caesar," or "I refer the decision of my case to Nero, the present emperor" (Acts 25:8, 11, 21). Paul's execution under Nero is practically certain.

Nero began his reign as the fifth emperor on October 13th, 54 A.D. and died on June 9th, 68 A.D. His disreputable and reckless career, the burning of Rome, the terrible persecution and murder of Christians are well known to readers of church history. A coward both in life and death, Nero, who had slain many, found it wretched to die. Condemned to a cruel death by the Senate, he put a weapon to his throat and was assisted in his suicidal act by his secretary. His last words were, "Too late — this is fidelity," uttered as a centurion came with proffered help. The last of the line of Caesars, Nero perished on July eight, 68 A.D., in his thirty-first year and in the fourteenth year of his reign. His name has remained with a stigma, for men name their sons, *Paul*, but call their dogs, *Nero*.

Coming to the Herods who were of Idumaean descent, we find eleven members of the Herodian family referred to in the New Testament. Of females, we have Salome (Matthew 14:6; Mark 6:22), Herodias (Matthew 14:36; Mark 6:17, 19, 22), Bernice (Acts 25:13, 23; 26:30), and Drusilla (Acts 24:24). See the section on *Bible Queens*.

When the first of the Herods sought and received from Augustus the governorship of Judea, Samaria, Galilee, Perea and Idumaea, he was in power when Jesus was born. Henry E. Dosker in his illuminating article on "The Herods" in the *International Standard Bible Encyclopaedia* says of the name *Herod*, a familiar one in the history of the Jews and of the early Christian church, that it signifies "heroic," "a name not wholly applicable to the family, which was characterized by craft and knavery rather than by heroism."

Some of the Herodian princes were undoubtedly talented, possessing elements of greatness, but were guilty of manifest egotism. Nearly all of them abused their vested power and position and because of their sin and shame failed to leave behind them footprints on the sands of time. While the following names are not all-inclusive, mention is made of those relevant to our purpose.

Herod the Great (Matthew 2; Luke 1)

Although this Herod supported the legend that his family descended from a renowned Babylonian Jew, the Herodians sprang from Antipas, who died in 78 B.C. This second son of Antipater, who was made king of the Romans in 40 B.C. and king of Judaea in 37 B.C., was conspicuous for his cunning and unbridled ambition — traits received from his father.

A man of great physical strength, intellect, strong will, shrewdness, architectural tastes, organizing ability, and with a conspicuous talent for statecraft, Herod belied the name he bore. Profane history speaks of him as "the great" (Luke 16:15), but he lacked the element of true greatness. He was the incarnation of brute lust and exterminated those who stood in the way of his ambitious schemes. He kept his throne by crimes of unspeakable cruelty and murder. He slew members of his own immediate family and ordered the slaughter of innocent babies in order to kill the infant Jesus.

This Herod, man of impressive personality, robbed the revered grave of David of its treasures. Nothing was sacred to him. Bitter prejudice and court intrigues were conspicuous to the end of his reign. Four days before his death he ordered the death of his eldest son, Antipater, and commanded his nobles to be slain after his decease. A victim of an incurable and loathsome disease in his stomach and bowels, he developed an irritable temper, making life for himself and his court most miserable. He became more cruel as he came to the end of his wicked course. Josephus, the Jewish historian, to whom we are obliged for details on the Herods, tells us that Herod the Great made a fruitless attempt at suicide. In the year 4 B.C. he "died unmourned and unbeloved of his people to pass into history as a name soiled by violence and blood."

Herod Antipas (Matthew 14; Mark 6; Luke 3; 8; 9; 23; Acts 4; 13)

Aristobulus, the older brother of "King Herod" as he is called by courtesy, not correctly (Mark 6:14), was in direct line but was put to death by his father in 6 B.C. He it was who married Bernice, the daughter of Salome, and sister of Herod the Great. Antipas, contraction of Antipater, was the son of Herod the Great and Malthace, a Samaritan woman, and married the daughter of Arctus, the King of Arabia, whom he forsook for Herodias, the wife of Herod Philip I.

This tetrarch of Galilee was a Sadducee and as such denied a moral government and a future state. Sadducees were also distinguished for their ferocity and inhumanity in their judicial capacity. This fact makes the remarks of Antipas concerning John the Baptist, whom he beheaded, a striking instance of the power of conscience overcoming, against a man's will, the sophistries of infidelity.

Antipas has a historical profile far from commendable. He was superstitious, inquisitive about truth without loving it, crafty, incestuous and wholly immoral, foxlike in his cunning. John the Baptist, who openly rebuked Antipas for his gross immorality and defiance of the Mosaic law, paid for his courage with his life (Matthew 14:1, 10; Luke 13:31; Leviticus 18:16).

The last glimpse we have of this Herod is during Passion Week in the final tragedy of the life of Christ — Pilate and he, previously estranged, became good friends over Christ. Antipas mocked and ridiculed the Saviour by dressing Him in a gorgeous robe. Through the machinations of Agrippa I, accusations of high treason were preferred against Herod Antipas and he was banished to Lyons in Gaul, where according to Josephus, he died in great misery. Fausset says of Antipas, who, like his father was cruel yet cunning, that —

> He was the very type of an oriental despot, sensual, capricious, yet with a sense of honour and having respect for piety in others; but like Ahab too weak to resist a bad woman's influence, under which false scrupulosity outweighed right conscientiousness, to be succeeded by superstitious terrors. Tiberius, which he founded and named after the Emperor, was one of his greatest works.

Herod Philip I (Matthew 14:3; Mark 6:17; Luke 3:19)

This Philip was the son of Herod the Great and the second Mariamne, daughter of Simon, the high priest, who married Herodias, sister of Agrippa I. Salome, their daughter, danced before Herod Antipas, paramour of her own mother and dishonorer of her father. Through his own mother's treachery Philip was excluded from any share in his father's dominions and lived privately. Being without the pomp and glory of a kingdom was, perhaps, the reason why his ambitious wife, Herodias, deserted him for his brother, Antipas. Nothing is known of Philip's later history. Our study of the wicked Herodias (see *Queens*) proves how futile craft ambition can become. Antipas and Herodias ended their days in shame and exile.

"Vaulting ambition o'erleaps itself and falls on the other side."

Herod Philip II (Luke 3:1)

This builder of Caesarea Philippi, near the Jordan (Matthew 16:13), was the son of Herod the Great and Cleopatra of Jerusalem. He married Salome, daughter of Philip I and Herodias. He was Tetrarch of Ituraea and Trachonitis, which he inherited from his father. He died at Julias, the city into which he raised Bethsaida, 34 A.D. As he died childless, his territory was given three years later to Agrippa I, his nephew.

Josephus describes him as being unlike the rest of the Herodian family. He ruled justly, was retiring, dignified and moderate, and wholly free from the intriguing spirit of his brothers. "It is but fair to suppose that he inherited this totally un-Herodian character and disposition from his mother."

Herod Archelaus (Matthew 2:22; Luke 19:12-27)

Because this Herod was refused the title, "king," he was known as the Ethnarch of Judaea, Idumaea and Samaria, around 4 B.C. He was the oldest son of Herod the Great and of Malthace, a Samaritan. He was first married to Mariamne and after his divorce from her to marry Glaphyra, who had been the wife of his half-brother, Alexander. By the will of his father, he was heir to the greater part of the Herodian kingdom, the rest being divided between Antipas and Philip.

Like his father, Archelaus was a man of violent temper and like his father displayed a taste for architecture. He built a royal palace at Jericho and also founded a village, which he called after himself, Archelaus. Matthew's reference to Archelaus indicates something of the injustice and cruelty of his reign. Josephus supplies details of his murderous instinct and of the way he ruled with a hard hand.

Disasters overtook him. His possessions were confiscated by the Roman power, and he was banished to Vienna in Gaul where he died. Jerome, however, says that his sepulchre was near Bethlehem. He was another Herod who reaped what he had sown.

Herod Agrippa I (Acts 12)

The son of Aristobulus and Bernice, this first Agrippa was the grandson of Herod the Great by the first Mariamne. He succeeded to the tetrarchy of Philip II in 37 A.D., and of Herod Antipas in 40 A.D. Judaea and Samaria were added in 41 A.D. For his unguarded speech he was imprisoned by Tiberius but freed when Caius Caligula came to the throne in 37 AD. Caligula gave him kingdom and kingship (Acts 12:1).

Possessing great shrewdness and tact, Agrippa restored the kingdom of Herod to great glory. He avenged his father's fate and restored the old Herodian power to its original extent. "He ruled with great munificence and was very tactful in his contact with the Jews."

Fausset says that unlike his predecessors, Agrippa strictly kept the Law, and that a legend describes him bursting into tears as he read in a public service Deuteronomy 17:15, on which the Jews exclaimed, "Be not distressed, thou art our brother," namely, by half descent from the Hasmonaeans. Yet, inconsistently, he harried the church whenever possible, and to please the Jews slew James, the brother of John. He also imprisoned Peter and intended to execute him after Easter. But Peter was divinely delivered.

"Love of popularity was his ruling principle, to which Agrippa's ordinary humanity was made to give way. Self-seeking led him to design Peter's death, but the issue was his own death." For his impious pride he was tragically punished. Josephus says that when Agrippa appeared in a robe all of silver stuff which shone in the morning light, his flatterers saluted him as a god. But the true God smote him with a dreadful disease in the bowels from which he died five days later in his fifty-fourth year. With his death Herodian power had virtually run its course. He whom men called "Agrippa the Great" is a lasting monument of warning to proud, conceited men. "Woe to him that striveth with his maker! Let the potsherd strive with the potsherds of the earth" (Isaiah 45:9).

Of the four children Agrippa left, three are known to history — Herod Agrippa II, Bernice of immoral celebrity, and Drusilla, the wife of the Roman Governor, Felix (Acts 24:24).

Herod Agrippa II (Acts 25:13; 26:1)

This last Herodian prince was the son of the former Agrippa and succeeded to the tetrarchy of Philip II, 53-70 A.D. As he was only a youth of 17 when his father died, he was considered too young to assume the governorship and the country was placed-under a procurator. When he came into his kingdom, Claudias gave him authority over the temple and sacred treasury and power of appointing and deposing the high priest — which power he held until the destruction of Jerusalem in 70 A.D. when he retired to Rome, dying there 100 A.D.

Josephus tells us that Agrippa espoused the cause of the Jews whenever he could. Paul called him "king" and appealed to him as one who knew the Scriptures. It was before this Herod and his sister Bernice that Paul reasoned so powerfully and eloquently as to make Agrippa confess that the apostle's appeal almost made him a Christian.

It would require a volume itself to gather together all the legends and traditions associated with all of Rome's rulers. There is one to the effect that the Roman Emperor Julian, known to history as "The Apostate," addressed to Christ whom he derided, the famous words *Vivisti, Galilee,* which Swinburne, also an unbeliever, translated in his "Hymn to Proserpine":

Thou has conquered, O pale Galilean.

And Christ continues to conquer, not by the sword as Rome did, but by His scars.

VIII

Palestine and Jewish Monarchs

It is impossible to follow the records of Jewish kings without considering the blood-soaked yet sacred land in which they lived, moved and had their being. Palestine, the most memorable of all lands, is where the sovereigns of Judah and Israel are interred, some of whom await the trump of God to rise and enter a glory prepared for them by the King of kings, while others, alas!, await the summons to come forth to "the resurrection of damnation."

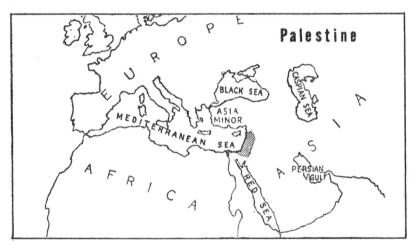

The Bible, as a whole, breathes the air of Palestine. The past, present and prospective future of "the holy land" (Zechariah 2:12) dominate the Holy Book. The ancient name of Palestine is *Philistia* (Psalm 60:8; 87:4), seeing that the long strip of sea-coast plain was originally held by the Philistines. Palestine was anciently regarded as the center of the known world and certainly its geographical situation is somewhat remarkable — "The center of the earth." God decreed that Jerusalem should occupy a central position in the midst of the inhabited world. "This is Jerusalem: I have set it in the midst of the nations and countries that are around about her" (Ezekiel 5:5).

Jerusalem, the capital of Palestine, is the most famous of all cities. Around it the pilgrim fathers of Israel lived and died. It was here, in the Temple, that God localized His presence. "Our fathers worshiped in Jerusalem" (John 4:20). Here, too, reigned David and Solomon whose power and glory were world-famous. Alas! It was also here that the King of Glory was crucified. Prophecy declares that it will yet become "Jerusalem the Golden."

Jerusalem, named in Scripture more than 800 times, has been besieged in the past no less than 34 times. It has been attacked by the Grecians, Syrians, Egyptians, Parthians, Romans and Europeans. The Bible records plunder of the historic city by Shishak, King of Egypt (II Chronicles 12:1-4); Jehoash, King of Israel (II Kings 14:13, 14); Rezin and Pekah (II Kings 16:5); Sennacherib (II Kings 18:17); Pharaoh-Necho (II Kings 23:33-35); Nebuchadnezzar, 3 times (II Kings 24:1, 10, 11; 15), Emperor Titus (Luke 21).

The protection of Palestine as a whole is unique. On the *north* there is the Lebanon range of mountains, the summits of which are almost perpetually capped by snow; on the *west* the land is washed by the Mediterranean Sea; on the *south* lies Egypt and adjoining desert; on the *east* from Jordan, stretches out the great Arabian desert to the Euphrates, a distance of some 300 miles. How precious is the promise that the Lord is round about His people even as the mountains are round about Jerusalem (Psalm 125:2)!

As geographers differ in defining the limits of the land, it is difficult to give the exact length of the country. It is about 150 miles in length from north to south, with an average width of about 40 miles, and covers an area of about 12,000 square miles. Prophetically, Palestine is to be considerably enlarged according to the limits assigned to Abram (Genesis 15:18; Ezekiel 48:1-28), from the Nile on the west to the Persian Gulf, where the Euphrates empties itself on the east. This area of about 300,000 square miles, or nearly two and a half times the size of Great Britain and Ireland combined will necessarily embrace those parts of Africa and Asia lying between the above points.

Walter Scott, to whom the writer is greatly indebted for his most descriptive portrayal of ancient empires, says:

During the time of our Lord, the whole country was divided into three parts, the northern one being Galilee — *the intellectual*—middle provinces being Samaria — *the defiled* — the southern portion was Judea — *the religious*. In the glorious reign of Solomon the country rivaled all the kingdoms of the earth for grandeur. Its population was immense (I Kings 3:8), its social prosperity great (I Kings 4:20), its commerce successful and extensive (I Kings 9:26-28). The treasures and rarities of India were imported into Palestine by a regularly established merchant navy (I Kings 10:22), and gold and silver were so abundant that the latter was "nothing accounted of" in these balmy days (I Kings 10:21).

The Bible speaks of Palestine, so named by the ancients, in suggestive ways. Each name carries its own significance —

Canaan (Leviticus 14:31).
The Holy Land (Zechariah 2:12).
The Lord's Land (Hosea 9:3).
Thy Land, O Immanuel (Isaiah 8:3).
The Land of Israel (I Samuel 13:19).
Land of the Hebrews (Genesis 40:15).
Land of Judah (Isaiah 26:1).
Land of Promise (Hebrews 11:9).
The Pleasant Land (Daniel 8:9).

For most enlightening and profitable material on Palestine's antiquities and archaeology, geology, botany, zoology, climate, the reader is referred to illuminating articles to be found in Encyclopedias like *Fausset's* or *The International Standard Bible Encyclopaedia.*

Having considered the land, let us now deal with the kings and queens intimately associated with it.

THE REJECTION OF THE DIVINE KING

The craving of the Jews for a visible, titular head was a revolt against divine sovereignty. Enamored of the pomp and glory of surrounding kings and nations, Israel wanted royalty of its own. God, however, never intended His people to be the subjects of an earthly ruler, but "a kingdom of priests" and "a holy nation" with Himself as their King (Exodus 19:6; I Peter 2:9). Thus the nation's rejection of Jehovah as their King evidenced a total absence of confidence in God. Was not His presence in their midst a sufficient guarantee that their safety and provision would be amply secured?

But the demand of the people, "Make us a king to judge us like all the nations" (I Samuel 8), was a distinct and positive rejection of God and His reign, and a step fraught with serious consequences for them. In His grace and mercy, God turned their sin into an occasion to further His purpose in royalty to be realized in Christ — God's ultimate resource in blessing for all men and creation. "Thus the reign of Saul was no part of Jehovah's *purpose,* although an integral part of His plan."

We are indebted to Josephus for the term *theocracy* to describe Israel before it became a monarchy. The *theocracy* commenced with the call of Abram and the selection of the Jews from among surrounding nations and is a term declaring the direct government of God, without the medium or intervention of an earthly ruler. This form of direct government did not fail but the people failed to appreciate its benefits and were not equal to its lofty conceptions (I Samuel 8:7). Declination from the ideal of the theocracy took place when the people demanded a king before God's time. *Theocracy* was embodied in the words, "Jehovah is our Judge; Jehovah is our Lawgiver; Jehovah is our King" (Isaiah 32:22). He was the Ruler of His people, and no one was to be appointed in His stead.

It was God's purpose to give His people a visible kingdom as predicted by Moses (Deuteronomy 17:14, 15). When Israel requested a king, Samuel alluded to Moses' direction (I Samuel 10:24). God's explicit promise was ever before the people, "Kings . . . shall be of Sarah" (Genesis 17:16). Other allusions to kings can be found in Genesis 36:31; Numbers 24:17; Deuteronomy 28:36.

A theocratic leadership characterized the days of Moses and Joshua. During the period of the Judges there was no centralized political government. "There was no king in Israel." Samuel became God's viceroy with executive power under God and the prophet saw that in the times of the Judges a theocratic commonwealth was found to be impracticable, for then every man was a king unto himself (21:25). Thus, when the elders of Israel approached Samuel with the request, "Make us a king to judge us like the nations," (I Samuel 8:5), the prophet felt the issue could not be evaded. He warned them, however, of the direct results of their request. Dominations and sore burdens would be theirs.

It was not the nation's *desire* for a king but the *spirit* of their request that was wrong. Samuel, God's appointed leader, was set aside under the pretext, "thou art old," after having directed the affairs of the people for 35 years. Such rejection coupled with impatience added to the sin of their request. They lost sight of the fact that God was their King, so in anger He gave them one after their own heart (Hosea 13:10, 11). Voltaire once said, "Heaven often gives kings in its vengeance." Milton expressed a similar thought in the lines,

"God gave quails in His wrath, and kings in His wrath, yet neither of these are evil in themselves."

With the desire for a king two ideals collided, the political and the religious. Samuel was all out for the spiritual ideal and would have used his influence against a monarchical system, but God declared it otherwise. As a necessary part of their divine training He would allow the people to become a monarchy. "He gave them their request, but sent leanness into their souls." The dream of political supremacy was corrected by the discipline of history. Through bitter experiences God taught them lessons they would not otherwise learn. In that way it came to pass that the monarchy thus constituted preserved the existence of the nation, foreshadowed the Kingdom of the Messiah (Genesis 49:16) and witnessed the reality of divine government.

The Records of Jewish Kings

The full list of monarchical government in Israel is given in the two books of Samuel, the two books of Kings, and the two books of Chronicles, which six books in ancient times constituted two books, Samuel and Kings being treated as one book. It is from these books, then, that we gather a comprehensive sketch of Jewish kingdom history. We have —

1. The founding and establishing of the kingdom in the books of Samuel.
2. The general history of the kingdom in the books of Kings.
3. The inner history of the kingdom in connection with God's sovereign grace in the books of Chronicles.

The books of Samuel and Kings tell the one story, namely, the story of the monarchy from its rise to its fall. Here we have the facts of history seen from the human standpoint. The book of Chronicles gives us the divine words and thoughts about these facts — history seen from the divine standpoint.

The books of Samuel are taken up with the king; the books of Kings with the kingdom, the political and royal aspect; the books of Chronicles with the house, the priestly and ecclesiastical aspect. Kings and Chronicles present no confusion when the full facts are borne in mind. Kings gives us the *record* of history — wars, idolatries and offenses. Chronicles gives us the *philosophy* of history — deliverances, repentances and reformations. Further:

1. The histories of the two kingdoms are given parallel with one another from I Kings 12-II Kings 17, when Israel is taken captive.
2. The history of Judah is continued along from II Kings 18-25.
3. The history of Israel (Ten Tribes) is not given in Chronicles.
4. The great period from the death of Solomon to the captivity of Judah is recorded from different and distinct standpoints.

Taking the six books in their present pairs, we can summarize them thus —

I Samuel presents the kingdom founded by Saul, but according to the *responsibility of man.* The book contains the account of the change of government from Judges to Kings, and includes the ministries of Samuel and Eli, as well as the reign and death of Saul. The book covers a period of about 100 years.

II Samuel shows how the kingdom was established in David according to the *purpose of God* and provides us with the history of the reign of David which occupied nearly 40 years. He was the only king to be born in Bethlehem as the Saviour was and reigned over the tribes of Israel as many years as the Lord lived on earth — about 33 years.

The books of Kings were originally one book and were divided by the LXX translators in their Greek version of the Hebrew Old Testament. The explanation given for the separation is that the Greek requires at least one third more space than Hebrew. Therefore, the translators were compelled to divide the book, either because the scrolls were of limited length or to make them easier to handle.

I Kings gives us the *public* history of the kingdom — from Solomon to the death of Jehoshaphat. The book embraces a period of some 126 years and can be divided in this twofold way —

1. The history of the undivided kingdom under Solomon, chapters 1-11.
2. The history of the divided kingdom, chapters 12-22.

II Kings continues the first book and describes the government and actions of successive kings of Judah and Israel from the death of Jehoshaphat to the destruction of Jerusalem and its Temple. Here we have *general* history set out thus —

1. Contemporary history of the kingdom of Judah and Israel to the end of Israel with its captivity by Shalmaneser, king of Assyria.
2. History of the decline and fall of the kingdom of Judah, 1-17, and its captivity by Nebuchadnezzar, king of Babylon, 18-25.

The books of Chronicles, originally one book and appearing at the end of the Hebrew Bible in the third division known as *The Psalms,* were probably written by Ezra after the return of the Jews from the Babylonian captivity. The LXX title for the books is "Omissions," because of supplements it supplies. Our present title, *Chronicles,* goes back to Jerome of the fourth century.

The writer of these books obviously used the books of Samuel and of Kings, as well as other records. We are indebted to Chronicles for our knowledge of the reign of David, the building of the Temple, and the history of Judah, which were written with a definite purpose, namely, to emphasize "two divine institutions — The Temple and the Davidic line of kings."

I Chronicles portrays David as the prominent personage. After tracing the genealogies of Israel back to Abraham, the whole of the rest of the book is taken up with God's chosen king. We have:

1) History of the Race, 1-9;
2) History of Saul, 10;
3) History of David, 11-29.

II Chronicles is occupied with David's house in the foreground. It begins with the reign of Solomon and contains a history of about 480 years till the return from Babylon. Its material coincides with much of Kings, with this difference: In the Kings the history of Judah and Israel is mixed, but in Chronicles we have scarcely any thing but the history of David's descendants, much of which we had not before. It is therefore necessary to compare Kings and Chronicles to have a just view of the characters described. For example, Chronicles gives no account of Solomon's apostasy, and Kings, no account to Manasseh's repentance.

The significant silence regarding many events hitherto recorded is impressive. Such silence is often more eloquent than speech. The spiritual progress of Judaism must be measured by the records and omissions of each book. It would seem as if an official recorder was attached to royal households whose responsibility it was to keep a chronicle of events preparing, thereby, the sources of future history. The names of some of these chroniclers are indicated (I Chronicles 9:29-31. See also II Chronicles 12:15; 13:22 R.V.).

A study of Jewish kings reveals a stereotyped plan of recording the facts regarding each monarch, for example —

At the beginning of a reign we are usually told how old the king was at his accession.

Then we are informed how many years he reigned and in the case of some of Judah's kings, his mother's name.

A general description of the character of the king's rule, whether good or evil, follows.

Causes of death and place of burial are sometimes stated, as well as the name of the succeeding ruler. Occasionally a reference to another authority for fuller details is cited (I Kings 11:41).

A Jewish king was not like an eastern monarch of a distinct royal caste chosen from among equals, and like predecessors, bound by the fundamental laws of the nation (Matthew 23:9). The people chose a king from among their brethren, and the king never usurped the right to legislate (I Samuel 9:15; Psalm 89:19).

For Israel, all prosperity depended upon the faithfulness or unfaithfulness of the reigning king. Individual piety ever shone through the darkest periods of Israel's history. All governmental blessing for land and people was lodged in the then reigning monarch — a principle amply illustrated and verified in the history of the kingdoms of Judah and Israel. Jeroboam I, as we shall see, cast the shadow of his evil life over the kingdom he founded. Matthew Arnold's lines are true of Jeroboam —

> "For this is the true strength of guilty kings,
> When they corrupt the souls of those they rule."

THE UNITED KINGDOM 1095-975 B.C.

While it is generally assumed that three kings, Saul, David, and Solomon, are related to the United Kingdom and that each reigned for 40 years, we must not forget Ish-bosheth, Saul's son and successor. Saul and his son were of the tribe of Benjamin — David and Solomon, of the tribe of Judah, so that the predicted Messianic line began with David (Genesis 49:10). Walter Scott says that

Saul is a type of the future anti-Christian king in Palestine.

David prefigures Christ, first nominated for the kingdom, then rejected, afterwards setting up His Millennial Kingdom on the ruin of all opposing authority of the enemy.

Solomon set forth the royal splendor and magnificence of the peaceful reign of Christ.

The United Kingdom reached the zenith of its power, prosperity, glory and influence during the forty year reign of King Solomon.

SAUL
(I Samuel 9; 11:13-21; II Samuel 1; 21:1-9)

THE KING WHOM GOD ALLOWED, THEN REJECTED

The history of Saul exhibits the tragedy of a soul, a great and gifted soul, for he was a brave and accomplished monarch and was noble in many ways — yet a soul disturbed by evil spirits who died a despairing suicide in a lost battle. Amongst all the noble creations of Greek poetry there is no single figure more vividly portrayed than that of Saul as he comes before us in the inspired records of Israel.

Saul, the son of Kish, represented the insignificant tribe of Benjamin, as did his namesake of the New Testament (Acts 7:58; Philippians 3:5). Thus *Saul* is the most distinguished name in the genealogies of the tribe of Benjamin. The Old Testament Saul became a king after man's heart, as David became king after God's heart (I Samuel 13:14; Acts 13:22), and his history is typical of the sin and rejection of the Jews, and of God raising up sons unto Abraham from among the Gentiles (Matthew 3:8-10).

The promise and disaster of Saul's reign reminds us of Macbeth in Shakespeare's profound and tremendous tragedy, for like Macbeth, Saul's career opened with a splendid victory and like him falls under hellish influences, and like him progresses through jealous fears, despair and murder.

The beginning of Saul's reign was auspicious enough. The afflicted Israelites were not content to have God as their King and Samuel as their prophet-judge. They wished to be ruled by a visible sovereign as surrounding heathen nations were, and using Samuel's evil sons as an excuse, demanded that Samuel should provide them with a king. The prophet, discerning the sin behind the people's request, rebuked them, but God overruled their sin and permitted the establishment of the Hebrew monarchy, preparing the way, thereby, for the coming and kingdom of His Son.

Saul, because of his commanding personality, appealed to the carnal Israelites and was given to them by God in His anger (Hosea 13:11). But the people were to learn by experience the difference between the kind of king they chose (I Samuel 8:18; 12:13), and the One whom He, in due time, would send (Isaiah 52:2, 3). From the time since royalty was instituted, God has punished nations by giving them rulers of the type they foolishly desire. "Heaven often gives kings in its vengeance."

Saul's befitting qualifications for kingship are impressive. Had he remained true to God he would have carved a niche for himself in the royal gallery as a mighty king.

He was tall and the kind of man people would turn round and look at with admiration. The Bible describes his hero-like beauty (I Samuel 9:2).

He was modest (10:22) and knew how to keep a secret until it was time to speak (10:16). He did not deem his kingship inconsistent with common work (11:5).

He was a brave leader except on one memorable occasion (17:24). His exploits secured for him a deep place in the hearts of his people and confirmed him in the kingdom (9:21).

He possessed the great quality of patriotism and had zeal for his people although it was not always zeal according to knowledge (II Samuel 21:2, 9; Romans 10:2).

He fought hard for the nation and in spite of long wars left the kingdom consolidated. In his early days, Saul exhibited Caesar's virtue of clemency to political opponents (10:27; 11:12, 13; Psalm 72:10). He refused to be severe because of God's goodness (11:13).

He was blessed in Jonathan with a gallant son, who tried to keep him from persecuting David (20:33). Father and son were lovely and pleasant in their lives, and in death were not divided (II Samuel 1:23).

Spiritually, Saul was also fitted for responsibility as Israel's first king: The records state —

He received the Holy Spirit on two occasions (10:10; 11:6). God endowed or anointed Saul, not in favor but in the sense of acquiescence of Psalm 106:15. David would not slay Saul seeing he was the Lord's anointed.

He was given "another heart" (10:9) — the only man in the Old Testament of whom it is said, "God gave him another heart."

He had to be followed as king. From his coronation onwards he had to be treated as the Lord's anointed (10:1-5; II Samuel 1:4). In the people's acceptance of Saul as king there arose the strain embodied in the anthem, "God save the King — or Queen," which is a prayer to God, appointed in His Word, and therefore to be sung with holy reverence (10:24; I Timothy 2:2).

He had the advice and prayers of Samuel, and the offices of the High Priest and the Ark (12:23; 14:18), and also the inspiring Psalms of Israel's psalmist (I Samuel 16:23).

In spite of all the gifts and encouragements showered upon Saul, he failed in a state of probation. "Difficulties bring out a man's abilities and reveal where his real trust is placed." Saul was proved and found wanting. His threefold failure can be summarized thus —

Self-Pride. "Saul died for his transgression which he committed against the Lord" (I Chronicles 10:13). He was a man of considerable pride, which led to his fall.

Self-Will. "Against the word of the Lord which he kept not" (I Chronicles 10:13). Solomon discourses on the fruit of presumption (Proverbs 10:8; 23:1).

Self-Aid. "Asking counsel of one that had a familiar spirit" (I Chronicles 10:13). Heaven was closed to Saul's cry. The progress of the king's sin is before us in bold relief. Contrast his humility, command of temper, spirit of forgiveness with his wounded pride, violence of temper, spirit of murder (I Samuel 9:21; 10:16; 11:5, 13; 16:27; 18:8; 19:1-15; 20:30).

At one time Saul's convictions were deep, yet he perished at last in his iniquity (I Samuel 24:16, 17; 26:21; 31:4).

How tragic was the end of Saul! The presence and influence of Samuel were withdrawn. The Spirit's anointing was removed. He became the victim of mental disturbances which the harp of David occasionally calmed. He patronized the witchcraft he once condemned and died by his own hand. The youth of giant stature who commenced his reign with great promise died 40 years later as a sinner and a suicide. The brave hero's heart failed him, and leaning upon his spear, he died of self-murder. Although David was the victim of Saul's malice, hearing of his death, he was silent on his sins. David's beautiful lament over Saul was a generous gesture (II Samuel 1:17-27).

ISH-BOSHETH
(I Chronicles 8:33; 9:39; II Samuel 2:8-12; 3:7-15; 4)

The King Who Was Slain During His Siesta

Although a usurper, nevertheless Ish-bosheth reigned over Israel for two years, and therefore deserves a place in our study of Bible royalty. His name, occurring some 13 times in II Samuel was originally Esh-baal (I Chronicles 8:23; 11:39), in contempt of Baal, from some connection of the family with whom he had been named. He was the youngest (and almost imbecile) of Saul's four sons, and his succession to the throne was according to eastern usage, though Mephibosheth, son of Saul's eldest son, Jonathan, was alive.

It was at Mahanaim that Ish-bosheth was given the throne by Abner, his valiant kinsman, after an interregnum of five years during which the Philistines and David had the country divided between them. He was forty years of age when, by Abner's influence, and after five years of effort, he became king over all Israel, except the tribe of Judah over which David ruled. But Abner was too strong a man for Ish-bosheth to have as a captain.

In eastern custom it was tantamount to a charge of treasonously aspiring to the throne when Ish-bosheth charged Abner with cohabitation with his father Saul's concubine Rizpah (I Kings 2:13-22; II Samuel 3:7). Incensed, Abner vowed to transfer his allegiance to David, which he did. But Abner's proffered help was accepted on condition that David's former wife, Michal, was returned to him.

When Abner was murdered by Joab, Ish-bosheth lost the last prop of his throne and gave up hope of retaining power. "His hands were feeble, and all the Israelites were troubled" (4-1). Baanah and Rechab, captains of marauding bands, were determined to avenge the slaughter of their kinsmen, the Gibeonites (II Samuel 21). Pretending to fetch wheat from the inner court for their men, they found Ish-bosheth taking his midday sleep on his bed and smote him.

They took the head of Ish-bosheth to David as though it was a welcome gift, seeing Saul had been the enemy who had sought David's life. But the murderers little understood the mind of David when, taking God's name in vain, they said, "Behold . . . the Lord hath avenged my lord the king this day of Saul and his seed." Doubtless they expected David to reward them for their bloody trophy. Instead they were reproached and slain for the wicked murder of "a righteous person in his own house upon his bed."

In Bible interpretation it is important to refer to the immediate context, that is, what goes before or follows a particular sentence, verse or chapter. Thus, Ish-bosheth, though in his opposition to David acted contrary to the declared will of God (I Samuel 16:12, 13; 28:17; II Samuel 3:9; 4:11) and therefore unrighteously, is termed by David a *righteous* person. The context explains the matter. Ish-bosheth was righteous as to his murderers, having done them no injury and having given them no provocation.

David commanded his young men to hang Baanah and Rechab and sever their hands and feet. The head of Ish-bosheth, brought to David by the two captains, was duly buried in the sepulcher of Abner in Hebron — a generous gesture on David's part toward one who had usurped him for so long.

DAVID
(I Samuel 16-31; II Samuel 1-25; I Kings 1-11; I Chronicles 2, 3, 10-29)

THE KING WHO WAS FAMOUS FOR BRAVERY AND BALLADS

David's establishment on the throne of Israel was brought about chiefly by the crimes of his enemies and the destruction of each other as, for instance, in the murder of Ish-bosheth and the subsequent killing of Abner and of Baanah and Rechab (II Samuel 3:8; 4:8). As we commence a brief study of David, king, soldier, poet, musician and genius, we cannot do better than set out for display the cameo J. G. Greenbough sketched of him —

> Few of the historical figures of the world have been formed in a bigger mould. In spite of his sins, awful blunders, and moral falls, he stands out in huge bulk as one of the world's master minds; a far-seeing statesman, a gifted thinker and poet, a brilliant soldier, a man of charming personality and winsome attractiveness, a man of infinite patience and unwearying energy, and every inch a king. If he had been a vain man, what a loud story he would have told of his own mighty doings and conquests of difficulties; how loftily he would have carried himself among his throngs of courtiers and flatterers. David the king, poet, soldier, genius, in one line just kneels down, strips himself of all those special gifts and distinction which makes a man bulk large in the eyes of his fellowmen, and takes his place with the rest of us, saying, "If we have any greatness at all, it is the gentleness of God that gives it to us." . . . The Bible has the greatest contempt for self-important people.

The Book of Ruth contains the origin of David's family and his descent from Judah (4:18; with Genesis 38:29; Matthew 1:8; Luke 1:32). His name occurs some 1120 times in Scripture, and because he is the greatest personal type of Christ, his name is given to Him (Isaiah 55:3; Jeremiah 30:9; Ezekiel 34:23; Hosea 3:5). Under the title of *David,* the Messiah is spoken of as the Person in whom all the promises made to David are fulfilled (Ezekiel 34:23; 37:24; I Kings 11:36). David is the only king to be born in Bethlehem, the Saviour's birthplace.

David is called "the Lord's anointed" (II Samuel 19:21; 23:1) and a threefold anointing to kingship was his:

By Samuel privately (I Samuel 16:11).

By his own tribe, Judah (II Samuel 4:2).

By all of Israel (II Samuel 5:2).

He was thirty years old when he began to reign and he reigned 40 years, over Judah for 7 years, over all Israel for 33 years. He had to wait for the fulfillment of God's promise to be king over all Israel for seven and one-half years. When ultimately all the tribes recognized David as their king they made a "league" with him and at Hebron he received his official coronation. God is not so slow in fulfilling His promises as men are apt to think.

It has been said that "a biography should be read with an endeavor to find out what were the vital forces of the man, and what were the leading principles that ruled and toned his conduct and relations. Find the one thing that most impresses you in every life, and that will suggest the message God meant to send by making, endowing and guiding that man." In David's case we have a man after God's own heart, who believed that in spite of changing fortunes, God was a living and righteous Being. David not only asked God to help him in his plans, he looked upon himself as a helper in God's plans.

David made political and moral mistakes but his humility at all times made him strong enough to subject himself to the hand of God, and this humility was based on the quality of his spiritual attitude toward God which shows itself in his Psalms. Beyond any other king, David was a connecting link between God and His people. "The distinguishing peculiarity of David as a king was that he recognized in the most loyal manner the higher loyalty to God," says Taylor, "and regarded himself as a mere human vice-regent."

Of no man in the Old Testament is there more recorded of his inmost thoughts, as well as his outward life, as of David. His life is reflected in the wonderful 77 Psalms ascribed to him. Emerson said, "The finest poetry was first experience." God made David "the inspired poet of the religious affections." He ever had the highest conception of his royal office and even in his most brilliant success did not forget that he was called to rule only as "the servant of Jehovah."

There are many ways by which we can view the record of the greatest king that Israel ever had. As a gifted ruler and organizer, David developed the strength of his kingdom from within and extended it without by overpowering jealous neighbors. Then he revealed his political wisdom by the conquest of Jerusalem and its selection as his capital city. Poetical and musical gifts were also his. As a minstrel, he was able to soothe King Saul when overcome by morbid melancholy (II Samuel 23:1-18). The words of Macaulay spring to mind as we review David's long reign, "The hearts of men are their books; events are their tutors; great actions are their eloquence."

Thinking of David as a mighty, valiant man, prudent in matters of business and speech, unique as a psalmist, and with a decided Godward bent, the reader is left to group fitting Scriptures around the following outline of his life and labors —

1. The Record of David until Saul's Death
   His Life As a Shepherd Lad
   His Life As a Palace Courtier
   His Life As an Exile from Saul
2. The Reign of David over Judah at Hebron
   His Patience with Usurpers
   His Confidence in God's Promise
3. The Reign of David over all Israel at Jerusalem
   His Period of Prosperity
   His Period of Adversity
   His Period of Tranquillity

SOLOMON
(II Samuel 12:24, 25; I Kings 1-11; I Chronicles 22-23:1; 28-29;
II Chronicles 1-9)

THE KING WHO LOVED WISDOM, WEALTH AND WOMEN

Solomon, "the king and the king's son" (Psalm 72:1), was David's second child by Bathsheba, and one upon whom God bestowed such royal majesty as had not been on any king before, or after him, in Israel (I Chronicles 29:20-25). When he succeeded his father he was "young and tender," perhaps about 20 years of age, and reigned for 40 years. Dr. Wm. Graham Scroggie speaks of Solomon as "a strange character that may be regarded in a threefold way, personally, officially and typically —

> Viewed personally, he was characterized by wisdom and wickedness: greatly gifted intellectually, he was very weak ethically. His mind and his morals were not on the same level. Viewed officially, his great work was twofold, the material development of the kingdom, and the erection of the Temple. . . . Viewed typically, it is not difficult to see an anticipation of Christ's Millennial Kingdom, when, after the extirpation of all His foes, there will be peace.

The leading events in the life of Solomon, whose name appears over 300 times in Scripture, can be gathered around the following aspects —

1. A Great Builder

In contrast to David's record of piety, Solomon's life is composed mainly of details about buildings, organizations and commerce. Through the consolidation of the throne by his father, prospects were never brighter for the nation than when Solomon succeeded David, and he took full advantage of David's preparations, especially for the Temple. Building operations are detailed for us in I Kings 6-10. Solomon practically remade Jerusalem with new streets, walls and public service buildings. It was amid the dazzling beauty of his unique architectural creations that Solomon held court in hitherto unknown grandeur.

Chiefest among his creations were the "House of God" or "Solomon's Temple," which took seven years to build, and his own gorgeous palace, taking some thirteen years to complete. As to the Temple, God Himself designed it (I Chronicles 28:12, 19) and at its dedication took solemn possession of it. One of the wonders of that time, it was a building where scarcely anything appeared which was less valuable than silver and gold. Materials used on the magnificent structure cost millions of dollars.

Having an unbounded command of wealth and labor, Solomon, the autocrat, was able to carry out his grandiose schemes. "Solomon's servants" or slaves were compelled to labor in the king's quarries as hewers of stone. Thousands of artificers were used, as well as foreign labor. Hiram, for example, was Solomon's chief artificer in brass. The people's patience was tried with hard labor, heavy taxes, levies of provisions, and conscriptions required (I Samuel 8:15; I Kings 4:13, 21-23). Rehoboam, Solomon's son, foolishly demanded more excessive and rigorous labor and taxes.

2. A Mighty Ruler

If Psalm 72 was from Solomon's pen then it reflects the wisdom, work and wickedness uniting to make him a renowned king, whose reign coupled with his father's constitutes the golden period of the Jewish state. Solomon's might and greatness of dominion permanently impressed the oriental mind. He not only strengthened his kingdom at home but made alliances with surrounding nations and engaged in extensive commerce in all kinds of goods. R. K. Harrison reminds us:

> Solomon took advantage of the decline in Egyptian and Assyrian power to expand the economic interests of his vast realm. . . . From his commercial activity he derived a great deal of revenue, partly by exacting tolls and partly by engaging in trade with other nations. . . . Failing to increase the agricultural productivity of the country to any great extent, the balance of trade was heavily offset by his ambitious building and economic projects.

While Saul and David were simple Arab warriors riding over the desert with their armies, Solomon was the mighty eastern despotic ruler with his settled capital and thousands of slaves building his palaces, thousands of women in his harem, merchants sweeping the seas and scouring the deserts to bring back gold to swell his revenue.

Solomon's glorious and wide kingdom affords a type of the Messiah's coming Kingdom, the magnificence of which will far outstrip Solomon's.

3. A Renowned Author

In answer to prayer Solomon was endowed with unusual wisdom and because wisdom was his first desire, riches, honor and life were added (I Kings 3:9). The king became known as "The Wisest Man of the East." His fame traveled far, bringing the Queen of Sheba to his palace. Solomon recognized the divine source of his wisdom (I Kings 3; James 1:5), making him "wiser than all men." Literature, botany and zoology were realms in which he reveled (I Kings 4: 32-34). Three books are commonly ascribed to Solomon:

Proverbs. Having knowledge of 3,000 of these, he was guided to set in order a selection of their number in the Book of Proverbs, which is a unique collection of moral, religious and providential precepts crystallizing the manifold aspects of life.

The Song of Solomon. This idyll tells in dramatic form of how pure love in humble life triumphed over the splendid seductions of a royal wooer. Fausset suggests that this "book represents Solomon's first love to Jehovah in youth, *Proverbs* his matured experience in middle age, *Ecclesiastes* the sad retrospect of old age."

Ecclesiastes. The key phrase of this book, occurring 30 times, is "Under the sun," and gives us a clue to its message, namely, the use and abuse of the world.

The Prayer for (or of) Solomon forming Psalm 72 is ascribed to Solomon and describes the period when the national development reached its height. This great psalm sets forth the kingly office more fully and more ideally than any other Old Testament passage. Alas, Solomon did not fulfill the aspirations of such a prayer!

4. An Apostate Autocrat

No Bible king so belied the promise of his early days as Solomon, on whom prosperity produced so fatal an apostasy. Farrar speaks of Solomon as "the brilliant soldier and trafficker who grew into an uxorious, a ruined and an apostate autocrat. The story of Solomon is the story of one whose heart was perverted and his will enervated by luxury and pride."

In a chapter on Solomon in his book on *Bible Characters*, H. V. Morton says that if he were "writing a book about Solomon, I would paint him not as we commonly imagine him, a kind, wise and pious ruler, but as a greedy and relentless autocrat who by his insatiable love for splendor sucked his people dry, overtaxed them, carried them at one bound from the simple, tribal civilization of his father, David, to the misery of a highly organized commercial state, with its ghastly extremes of wealth and poverty."

Dean Stanley once wrote that Solomon remains the supreme instance in sacred history of that which meets us so often in common history — the union of genius and crime. It was his exactions and despotism that brought to a head a sense of social injustice and a violent clan warfare that had been seething throughout his reign. Solomon was the first man to see the commercial possibility of Arabia and to realize the fabulous riches that lay waiting for any man who would organize the trade of the early world. Thus he built the first great trading fleet which ventured to the mysterious confines of Ophir — some say India.

Solomon, the ardent capitalist, had fine qualities of the mind and a certain amount of spirituality, but these broke down under or were undermined by greed, success, luxury and idolatry.

> 'Tis but the moral of all human tales,
> 'Tis but the same rehearsal of the past:
> Wealth, vice, corruption — barbarism at last.

Religious apostasy and indulgence in polygamy brought upon Solomon's ruin. His idolatrous mistresses and consorts brought into the royal household the worship of their native deities, for whom shrines were built in Jerusalem (I Kings 11:1, 7). Divine chastisement fell upon Solomon for his adultery and idolatry. Although he commenced to walk in David's godly ways, he sacrificed in high temples. He tried to mix the worship of God with heathen rites. The high places Solomon built for Ashtaroth and other heathen deities appear to have remained for more than 350 years.

Solomon's disregard of God's honor was the cause of his calamities and the raising up of adversaries against him, the division of the kingdom, and the ultimate captivity of the Ten Tribes and of Judah (I Kings 11:9-14; II Kings 17:14-20; Luke 19:42). The king had been warned that if the nation should apostatize, the Temple should be destroyed and become a by-word among the people, which it did. The Chaldeans spared "Solomon's Porch," perhaps for its strength and beauty. Our Lord walked in its shelter in winter (John 10:3).

Solomon's grievous fall provides a striking instance of the insufficiency of the highest endowments to preserve man from the grossest folly and sin (John 15:5). The apostasy of Israel's illustrious king was the more glaring, contrasted with God's goodness in appearing to him twice, blessing him so greatly, and warning him so plainly. He came to learn, as all transgressors do, that their way is hard (I Kings 11:14, 21, 26). Those who introduce corruptions into pure worship know not how far they will reach, nor how long they will last. Solomon's pride is reproved in our Lord's word about his glory being unworthy of comparison with the "lilies of the field" (Matthew 6:29). Solomon probably repented in the end; for *Chronicles* makes no mention of his apostasy.

Comparing the three great kings of the United Kingdom, Dr. F. Tuck gives us this interesting note —

Saul was self-willed; David was self-subdued; Solomon was self-contained. The religion of Saul was associational; the religion of David was personal; the religion of Solomon was official.

The story may be read in yet another light. Man is a composite being, and each man has to decide which part of himself shall rule the whole. Saul made the body rule; David made the heart rule; and Solomon made the mind rule. So these first three kings illustrate primary religious truths for all the ages.

THE DIVIDED KINGDOM 975-586 B.C.

With the death of King Solomon the kingdom of Israel was torn in parts, and the division was principally due to the idolatrous disloyalty of the nation, for which sin both sections of the kingdom were plagued and ultimately swept into captivity, Israel to Assyria 721 B.C., and Judah to Babylon in 586 B.C. So long as the strong, autocratic and wise Solomon and his advisers were at the helm, various rebellious tendencies dared not assert themselves, but after the king's decease, catastrophe came.

Heavy and prolonged taxation, to which the people were compelled to submit, was deeply felt. Expenditure on a lavish scale had sown seeds of dissension among the populace for a number of years. Domineering, illiterate Rehoboam, Solomon's son and successor, brought things to a head. Solomon had failed like his father David to respect the inherited liberty-loving tendencies. His colorful personality had succeeded in transforming the early concept of the monarchy into a typical oriental despotism.

The division of the kingdom into two unequal parts also had its rise in Solomon's adultery and idolatry. Because of his departure from the worship of the true God, the judgment went forth: "I will rend the kingdom from thee, and will give it to thy servant . . . Howbeit I will not rend away all the kingdom but will give one tribe to thy son for David my servant's sake and for Jerusalem which I have chosen." Thus the division was appointed by God as chastisement upon the house of David for the idolatries imported by Solomon's wives and for the way such a contagion had spread to the whole mass of people.

Outside factors likewise paved the way for the division of the kingdom. Rezon, the vigorous founder of the Damascus dynasty, proved to be an increasing source of trouble in the latter days of Solomon. Thus when the kingdom was rent in twain the tribes of Judah and Benjamin formed the Kingdom of Judah under Rehoboam and his successors, and the Ten Tribes became the Kingdom of Israel under Jeroboam, the son of Nebat, and his successors as predicted by the Prophet Ahijah (I Kings 11:2. See I Kings 12; II Kings 18; II Chronicles 10-28). The history of the thirty-nine kings is so given as to show mankind the certainty of the fulfillment of God's promises and threatenings; and especially that righteousness exalts a nation, and sin ruins it (Leviticus 26:31 with II Kings 25:9).

A glance at the separated kingdom shows how the two kingdoms differed materially. The Northern Kingdom, with its Ten Tribes, was more powerful than the Southern Kingdom. The latter, however, was more firm spiritually than the former. Then the dynasties of the north were only of short duration, being plagued by revolutionary forces. On the other hand, the small and often over-powered kingdom of Judah faithfully adhered to the royal line of David, and, although characterized by dangerous crises and several unworthy rulers, had a spiritual bond which kept the people united. Isaiah's forceful ministry can be studied in this light.

THE KINGDOM OF JUDAH 975-586 B.C.

The Kingdom of Judah continued for almost 400 years under 20 kings from Rehoboam to Zedekiah, many of whom were pious. For comparison and contrasts between the two kingdoms and their kings, the reader is referred to our introductory and concluding remarks under *The Kingdom of Israel.* Jerusalem was the center of the Southern Kingdom and was destroyed by the Chaldees under Nebuchadnezzar when the bulk of the people were taken into captivity.

Prophets associated with the long period of this kingdom were Isaiah, Jeremiah, Joel, Zephaniah, Micah, Nahum and Habakkuk. The prophecies of these men of God, which were literally fulfilled, form a pledge to us that those further prophecies speaking of the dead, small and great, standing before God, and being judged, every man according to his works, will be realized (II Peter 3:11-14; Revelation 20:12).

REHOBOAM
(I Kings 12:20-24; 14:21-31; II Chronicles 11-12)
THE KING WHO WAS HEADSTRONG AND INSOLENT

Rehoboam, son of Solomon and of Naamah, the Ammonitess, was 41 years of age when he succeeded his father and reigned for 17 years. He followed his father's luxurious habit in the possession of a considerable harem, for he is said to have had "18 wives and 60 concubines." During the first 3 years of the monarch's reign, king and people walked in the ways of David and Solomon, but during the remaining 14 years, the land became foul with Sodomite wickedness and idolatry. Josephus, the Jewish historian, says that in disposition King Rehoboam was a proud and foolish man and that he "depised the worship of God till the people themselves imitated his wicked actions."

The northern part of the kingdom, chafing under the heavy taxation and slave-like conditions imposed upon them by Solomon, sought relief at the hands of his son. Alas, headstrong and insolent Rehoboam rejected a just plea and thereby forfeited the unity of the throne of old Israel, and was left with only two tribes to reign over. Had Rehoboam succeeded to his father's wisdom, as well as to his throne, he would have followed the riper judgment of the elder statesmen and thus saved the kingdom from a disastrous division. Tennyson in *To the Queen* expressed the sentiment, "The king who fights his people fights himself." In his fatal decision, Rehoboam fought against his best interests as well as those of his people. He should have profited by some of his father's proverbs, like —

"The fear of the Lord is the beginning of wisdom; but fools despise wisdom and instruction" (1:7).

"Grievous words stir up anger" (15:1).

When the disruption of the kingdom was decided upon, Rehoboam, believing in his ability to deal with ten tribes seeking to dethrone him, dispatched Adoram, his taskmaster, to subdue those insulted by Rehoboam's insolence. Adoram was stoned to death, and Rehoboam, realizing for the first time the seriousness of the revolt, fled to Jerusalem to assume control of a diminished kingdom. How apt, at this point, are the lines of Daniel Defoe in *The True-Born Englishman:*

> When kings the sword of justice first lay down
> They are no kings though they possess the crown;
> Titles are shadows, crowns are empty things,
> The good of subjects is the end of kings.

Rehoboam massed an army of 120,000 men to make war against the revolting ten tribes, but the planned battle was forbidden by Shemaiah the prophet on the ground that they should not fight against their brethren, and that the revolt was of God. Yet we read that there was war between Rehoboam and Jeroboam continually (I Kings 14:30).

Then Rehoboam occupied himself in strengthening the territory he was left with by fortifying a number of cities, but when God is forsaken, fenced cities avail nothing. In the fifth year of his reign Rehoboam was punished for his sympathy with heathen abominations and immoralities. Shishak, King of Egypt, plundered Rehoboam's palace and the Temple, robbing them of treasures, including the shields of gold for which Rehoboam substituted shields of brass. Rehoboam died at the age of 58, and was buried in Jerusalem.

"The mistake of Rehoboam was the common mistake of despots. He presumed too much on privilege not earned by service, and on power for which he was not willing to render adequate compensation."

ABIJAM
(I Kings 15; II Chronicles 13)

The King Who Faced Both Ways

Abijam, or Abijah, as he is also called, was what John Bunyan described as "Mr. Facing-Both-Ways." This second king of Judah tried to do what Jesus, the greatest King of all, said was impossible, namely, serve two masters. When Abijam assembled his army of valiant men of war upon Mount Zemaraim, he expressed confidence in God and in the divine covenant to preserve the House of David. The language he used, "A light always before me," implied the continued existence of the divine purpose (I Kings 11:36).

Representing himself as the guardian of the Temple and of the priesthood against the rival, idolatrous worship of Jeroboam, Abijam's own heart was not perfect toward God. How could he protest with any measure of sincerity against the degradation of the worship of God in Israel when he himself walked in the sins of his father and

connived at the worse sin of the worship of rival gods in Judah?
It was mockery for him to chide Jeroboam's golden calves while he
himself continued to countenance the coarse luxury, idolatry and
polygamy of his father.

Abijam declared war against Jeroboam during the 18 years of the
latter's reign. In the amount of men Abijam was able to rally to his
banner we note the steady increase of Judah, and the decrease of
Israel. Abijam could assemble 400,000 men against his predecessor's
180,000. Judah's increase through successive reigns was due to the
gradual emigration of Israel from the ten tribes. Abijam totally defeated his rival. Jeroboam lost more than one half of his entire
army. How tragic civil war always proves to be! Says Cicero, "All
things are wretched in civil war." And so they are, for fellow-country-
men and relatives are found fighting against each other.

Abijam, son of Rehoboam and of Maachah, also named Michaiah,
daughter of Abishalom or Absalom, reigned for 3 years in Jerusalem,
waxed mighty and had 14 wives and 22 sons and 16 daughters. Willis
J. Beecher suggests that "the name Abijam means 'father of the west'
and that exploration has revealed the fact that the whole region near
the eastern end of the Mediterranean was known as 'the west.'
'Father of the west' is not an inapt name for Rehoboam to give to
the boy, who, he expects, will inherit the kingdom of Solomon and
David. The effect of the secession of the ten tribes was to make that
name a burlesque, and one does not wonder that it was superseded
by *Abijah*, meaning 'My father is God.'"

ASA
(I Kings 15:9-15; II Chronicles 14-16)
THE KING TURNED REVIVALIST

The third king of Judah was a pure stream from a putrid source.
Asa proves that an evil heredity need be no handicap to holiness.
He was the godly son of a godless father, Abijah, just as Manasseh
was a godless son of a godly father. Asa's heart was perfect with the
Lord all his days. The first ten years of his life were occupied in
abolishing idolatry and in religious reforms. Acknowledging God in
all his ways, Asa was divinely directed (Proverbs 3:5, 6). It was thus
that he was able to overcome the mighty host of Zerah (II Chronicles
14:9-15).

Asa was no respecter of persons, as is seen in the deposing of his
own grandmother for her idol-worship. Relying upon God, he served
Him with much zeal, breaking down all altars and images and removing the sodomites. His covenant with God is worthy of emula-
tion (II Chronicles 15). This son and successor of Abijah reigned

for forty years and would have had an unblemished record had it not been for two errors.

The first was the king's league with Benhadad, a breach of faith. Asa requested his assistance against Baasha, King of Israel. For this act of distrust of God's power, he was rebuked by the prophet Hanani. "Correction is grievous to him that forsaketh his way" (Proverbs 15:10), and so Asa, exasperated over the just reproof of Hanani, put the prophet in chains and ordered the death of many of the prophet's friends.

Then, diseased in his feet, a disorder that made Asa extremely peevish and passionate, he sought the aid of physicians rather than divine help (II Chronicles 16). The king's trust was less in God than in human remedies (Jeremiah 17:5). He died in the forty-first year of his reign and his funeral was attended by a "very great burning" — a sign of high esteem. The weakness and blemishes of his old age are a warning to all believers to take heed how they stand lest they fall (I Corinthians 10:12).

How apt are the lines of Sir Walter Scott:

> 'Twere good
> That kings would think in that
> When peace and wealth their land has blessed
> 'Tis better to sit still and rest,
> Than rise, perchance to fall.

Because the revival of true religion under King Asa reads like a romance, we deem it necessary briefly to review this oasis in the generally bad history of the kings. What world-wide interest would be aroused if a reigning king today became a flaming revivalist! "King Asa . . . renewed the altar of the Lord." Both sovereign and subjects need to get back to God.

Chapters 14 and 15 of II Chronicles must be read together, seeing they present the double aspect of Asa's reforms. In chapter 14 we have the outward prosperity of the king's reforms. In chapter 15 we are given a detailed account of the inward and religious purification and rectification. Aspects standing out clearly are —

1. *The Power of a Spirit-Endued Messenger*

"The Spirit of God came upon Azariah," and his message smote the consciences of king and people. The effects were immediate. The greatest need of national life today is a company of Spirit-filled and directed prophets.

2. *A Sad Condition of Barrenness*

We read that there was "no true God." Idols had taken His place. How true this is of our nation, in which there is a blatant godlessness to be deplored!

Then there was no "teaching priest." Those who should have had a deep, spiritual understanding of the true character and purpose of God, were satisfied with the mere performance of altar duties. Theirs was a cold professionalism.

The people also were "without law." Divine commands were forgotten, disobeyed. When nations and men trample underfoot divine laws, the lawlessness becomes rampant and ends in national disaster.

Further, there was "no peace to him that went out." Religious apostasy ever results in social disturbances, political anarchy and national conflict.

3. A Desperate Endeavor to Rectify Errors

God was gracious in that He promised restoration and blessing. It took courage to rectify all wrongs, but the thorough expulsion of all idolatry and idolaters was rewarded. Some idols must be destroyed, others must be displaced. Asa removed his own near relative from her exalted position because of her idolatrous practices. Revival was drastic; the altar was renewed; solemn vows were taken; old vessels were rededicated; old paths were re-trod.

4. Divine Blessing and Reward

Having sworn with their whole heart and sought God with their whole desire, the people declared their determination to abide by their covenant. And what streams of blessing flowed from the rectified life of king and nation! Both Jews and Gentiles felt the impact of the revived and quickened life of Asa and his people. The nation enjoyed a season of rest from war. Our restless age needs peace, but it can only come when conflict with God ends. Troubled nations will experience peace when their rulers arise and follow King Asa in his drastic extermination of all idols and evils. "Great peace have they that love Thy law."

Ours is a lawless, godless, wicked age, and nothing can stem the rising tide of iniquity like a heaven-sent revival. The enemy is in like a flood. May the Lord lift up His standard against the foe and give us rulers who will reign in righteousness!

JEHOSHAPHAT
(I Kings 22:2-33; 41-50; II Chronicles 17-21:3)

THE KING WHO WAS HOLY YET HUMAN

If the old adage, "To err is human," is true, then Judah's fourth king was not only most holy but also most human in that he erred grievously against God, the people over whom he ruled, and himself. During the twenty-five-year reign of this pious monarch, who walked in the godly ways of his father Asa, he was greatly blessed. The commands of the Lord and not the ways of Judah were the guide of his conduct and ways (II Chronicles 20). One of the godliest kings ever to sit on the throne of Judah, Jehoshaphat was yet linked to one of the worst kings in Israel's history. His association with Ahab by the marriage of his son with Athaliah led to the desecration of the Temple, the complete apostasy of the state for six years, and the almost entire destruction of his whole family (II Kings 8:18-26; 11:1).

Jehoshaphat, fourth in lineal descent from Solomon, owed much to the example and instruction of good King Asa. After the death of good Queen Victoria, her son King Edward VII, in his first speech on the opening of Parliament said:

"My beloved mother, during her long and glorious reign, has set an example before the world of what a monarch should be. It is my earnest desire to walk in her footsteps."

Jehoshaphat was duly sensible of his peculiar advantages and sought to improve them. His heart was lifted up in the ways of the Lord. A king of unusual spiritual singularity, Jehoshaphat inaugurated a system of religious instruction and judicial administration for his people. Although he evinced a prudent regard for the safety of his dominions, and put them in a proper posture of defense (II Chronicles 17:1), he was chiefly solicitous to promote the honor of God.

Jehoshaphat's zeal for God brought him and the nation much prosperity. The king became a prosperous and potent prince, and his subjects were secure and peaceable. "The Lord was with him" and the king was eager to ascribe his affluence and tranquillity to the hand of God. "The Lord established the kingdom in his hand . . . and the fear of the Lord fell upon all the kingdoms round about."

Godly and prosperous, Jehoshaphat was still human and prone to err, so we come to those sad defects in his character, which are all the more conspicuous because of his eminence as a good king. Although his lapse was only occasional and he himself was not guilty of any gross iniquity, the alliances he made had disastrous results. Conspicuous in his opposition to idolatry, Jehoshaphat was induced from worldly motives to join hands with one of the worst idolaters in Israel. Jehoshaphat joined affinity with Ahab (II Chronicles 18:1).

During his state visit to Israel, Jehoshaphat received a great reception and prolonged entertainment from Ahab and committed the greatest error of his reign by arranging for the marriage of his eldest son, Jehoram, to Athaliah, Ahab's daughter by Jezebel. Perhaps Jehoshaphat thought this union good policy in that it might result in the union of the two kingdoms under his own posterity. But this wrong step displeased God, was extremely hurtful to Jehoshaphat, and offered a mischievous example to his subjects.

One downward step leads to another, thus there came the expedition to Ramoth-Gilead which nearly cost Jehoshaphat his life. His alliance with Ahab in battle was in direct opposition to the warning of God's prophet. In mercy, the Lord spared the king and he returned to his people with a desire to repair the mischief his familiarity with Ahab had brought about. With holy ardor, "he brought back the people to the Lord God of their fathers."

A further test came when Jehoshaphat found himself facing his confederate enemies, the Moabites and Ammonites who invaded his land, causing much consternation (II Chronicles 20:1). But having learned his lesson from his wrong alliance, Jehoshaphat "set himself to seek the Lord," and persuaded his people to do the same. Through the prophet, the king received an answer of peace, and in answer to prayer, without a blow being struck, all the enemies were vanquished (II Chronicles 20:20-30).

Alas, because the best of men are only men at the best, Jehoshaphat, although forgiven for his intimacy with Ahab, lapsed again in his commercial treaty with Ahazial, who like his father was a profane character. These two kings prepared a fleet of ships to bring gold from Ophir, but God blasted the scheme and frustrated all hopes of gain. The ships were destroyed in part, and God's prophet declared a chastisement upon Jehoshaphat for his attachment to another wicked house. With his severe corrections, the king should have renounced all further alliance with God-forbidden partners. But strong is the tendency of human nature to evil.

Once more we find Jehoshaphat in confederacy with the profane court of Israel, joining in a war-like expedition with Jehoram and the King of Edom, which, but for the miracle wrought by Elisha, would have led to the destruction of their three armies for want of water. Jehoshaphat found it hard to resist the sin easily besetting him, namely, that of wrong alliances. How the question must have rankled in his soul for the rest of his days, "Shouldest thou help the ungodly?" (II Chronicles 19:2).

There is no record of Jehoshaphat again making an alliance with one of the wicked kings of Israel, and in any way helping the ungodly. What a practical illustration of the admonition, "If sinners entice thee consent thou not" (Proverbs 1:10), the experience of Jehoshaphat affords. If we are partakers of other men's sins, we shall also receive their plagues. At 60 years of age, Jehoshaphat died and was honorably buried with his fathers in the city of David. Ahab, his one-time ally, was killed in battle.

JEHORAM
(II Kings 8:16-24; II Chronicles 21)
THE KING WHO DIED IN DISHONOR

Some men, because of the pernicious influence they exert, are better dead than alive. It was thus with King Jehoram, godless son of a

godly father, who died unregretted and was buried without honor.
One day Robert Murray M'Cheyne, the Scottish saint, wrote in his
diary —

"O God, for grace to live, so that when dead,
I shall be missed."

The world never missed the wicked king of Judah, murderer and
idolator, when he died of an agonizing, lingering illness.

Jehoram reigned in consort with his father, Jehoshaphat. He was
designated as king in the seventeenth year of his father's reign, but
was crowned in his father's twenty-third year of reign. He reigned
eight years in Jerusalem, two with his father and six after his father's
death (II Kings 1:7; 8:16).

The tragedy of Jehoram lay in his decision to follow the influence
of his heathen wife, Athaliah, rather than the godly ways of his father,
Jehoshaphat. If only he had been familiar with Solomon's *Proverbs*
he would have remembered that "Whosoever findeth a wife, findeth
a good thing, and obtaineth favor of the Lord" (18-22). Jehoram
failed to find the right kind of wife.

S. K. Mosiman in *The International Standard Bible Encyclopaedia*
has the comment —

In the beginning of the reigns of Ahab and Jehoshaphat, an attempt was
made to end the old feud between Israel and Judah. At the suggestion
of Ahab, the two kingdoms for the first time joined forces against the
common foe of the North, the Syrians. To seal the alliance, Athaliah,
daughter of Jezebel and Ahab, was married to Jehoram, son of Jehoshaphat. Thus Jehoram was brother-in-law to the Jehoram of Israel. No
doubt this was considered as a master stroke of conciliatory policy by
the parties interested. However, it proved disastrous for Judah. Beyond
a doubt, the unholy zeal of Jezebel included the Baalizing of Judah as
well as of Israel. This marriage was a step in that direction.

Jehoram clave unto his idolatrous wife and "walked in the ways of
the kings of Israel, as did the house of Ahab." Alas, he not only accepted the godless religion of his wife, but became a persecutor, com-
pelling the people of the land to become apostates. As belief affects
behavior, Jehoram's idolatry came out in his character. The worship
of Baal had in it the elements of tyranny and civic unrighteousness.
Thus most heartlessly, Jehoram became guilty of fratricide. Jehoram
began his reign by murdering his six brothers and other princes of the
land, to whom his father, Jehoshaphat, had given positions and
presents.

Because of his gross idolatry and wickedness Jehoram received a
divine condemnation of his conduct, which, however, had no effect
upon his godless heart. He was punished by the revolt of the Edomites
in fulfillment of Isaac's prophecy (Genesis 27:40). The invasion of
the Philistines and Arabians was a heaven-sent stroke or divine visi-
tation in that Jehoram lost all his family save his youngest son, Jehoahaz. Jerusalem and the royal palace were ransacked. Thus Je-

horam himself was smitten *in* his people; and *in* his sons, and *in* his wives and *in* all his goods.

Having sown to the flesh, Jehoram reaped corruption. His painful disease of the bowels, some violent form, resulted in his death. He died without being desired, which means he died unregretted, unlamented. No eyes in Judah were wet with tears over his passing. Then to add to his deserved punishment and dishonor, he was buried without honor. His foul body was denied a grave in the sepulcher of kings.

AHAZIAH
(II Kings 8:25-29; II Chronicles 22:1-9)

THE KING WHO HAD CORRUPT COUNSELORS

Shakespeare in *Othello* has the question, "Is he not a most profane and liberal counselor?" The tragedy of King Ahaziah was that he had the wrong kind of counselors. "His mother (corrupt Athaliah) was his counselor to do wickedly . . . Those of the house of Ahab were his counselors." With such profane and liberal, in respect to morals, counselors, Ahaziah followed their advice to his destruction (Psalm 1:1). Plantus, Latin philosopher, said, "Counsel from divine sources comes with greater strength." What a different king Ahaziah would have been had he counseled with the Lord!

Ahaziah was 22 years old when he began to reign, and he was king for only one year. His reign coincided with the twelfth year of the reign of King Jehoram of Israel. This sixth king of Judah was coached in wickedness by his mother who was of the house of Ahab. Her influence would be used in support of the Baal worship, which was the symbol of alliance with the Northern Kingdom. Notice the threefold repetition of the words, "The House of Ahab" — a house rotten to the core. By the persuasion of his mother and her family (II Chronicles 22:4), Ahaziah engaged, with his Uncle Jehoram or Joram, in war against Hazael. Relations between the two kingdoms, established by Ahab, were cultivated by Jehoram and Ahaziah. Ramoth-Gilead was captured and held for Israel against the King of Syria (II Kings 9:14).

Jehoram was wounded and returned to Jezreel, his army being left in the charge of Jehu. Ahaziah, one in the politics of his ally, visited him in Jezreel, and while there Jehu formed a conspiracy against Jehoram. Healed of his wounds, Jehoram again joined forces with Ahaziah to meet Jehu, but Jehoram, suspecting treachery, turned to flee. An arrow from Jehu's bow, however, found its mark and pierced Jehoram's heart and he died in his chariot.

Ahaziah, persecutor of Elijah, tried to escape, but was overtaken at Ibleam and was mortally wounded by one of Jehu's own men. He reached the fortress of Megiddo where he died. His destruction was

of God because of his alliance with Jehoram. Jehu sought out Ahaziah's hiding place and slew him. He was buried but we are not told
by whom or where. Josephus has a different version of the end of
Ahaziah. He says that Ahaziah was wounded while in his chariot,
fled on horseback to Megiddo, where he was well cared for by servants until he died. The chronicler adds, "The house of Ahaziah had
no power to keep still the kingdom," meaning, there were none capable
of assuming the sovereignty.

The violent deaths of Jehoram and Hazael recall an item in Dr.
E. Cobham Brewer's *Dictionary of Phrase and Fable*. In 1894, though
a few more royal heads have rolled since then, Dr. Brewer wrote of
2,500 sovereigns who had hitherto reigned:

300 had been overthrown
134 had been assassinated
123 had been taken captive in war
108 had been executed
100 had been slain in battle
 64 had been forced to abdicate
 28 had committed suicide
 25 had been tortured to death
 23 had turned mad or imbecile.

The next in line of Judah's reigning monarchs was a woman, a
usurper, Athaliah, the mother of Ahaziah. Under *Section 2*, dealing
with "Bible Queens," a full study of Athaliah, described as "that
wicked woman" (II Chronicles 24:7), will be found.

JEHOASH
(II Kings 11, 12; II Chronicles 22:10-24:27)

THE KING WHO LACKED STRENGTH OF CHARACTER

We all know of those who appear to be good and confident when
leaning on stronger characters than themselves. But once their props
are taken from them, they quickly fall. They are clinging vines who,
when they have no one to cling to, droop and die. Judah's ninth
king was this type of person, for we read that "Jehoash did that which
was right in the sight of the Lord all his days wherein Jehoiada the
priest instructed him."

Under the moral and spiritual influence of Jehoiada, a man of
lofty character and devout spirit, Jehoash felt secure. But when the
godly priest died and his nephew was left alone, it was a different
story. Snatched from the unnatural fury and murderous orgy of
Athaliah when she massacred the royal princes, Jehoash was sheltered
for six years by his uncle, and grew up fully dependent upon the
wise counsel of Jehoiada. Through the years he clung tenaciously to
his uncle. On his death, however, Jehoash seemed to go to pieces.

The way Jehoash acted after the passing of Jehoiada reveals that circumstances show a man how little he is acquainted with himself. True character stands out. When the long and useful life of Jehoiada came to a close, the strongest pillar of the state was removed and a sad declension took place. The princes of Judah, who aided in the affairs of the state, expressed their wish to Jehoash for greater freedom of worship than had been allowed them by the aged priest. With weak compliance Jehoash hearkened unto them and idol shrines began to appear, thus both the king and the kingdom suffered.

Jehoash, also called *Joash*, the son of Ahaziah and Zibiah, a woman of Beersheba, began to reign when he was only six years of age, and reigned for forty years. Some scholars include the six years of Athaliah's usurpation in his reign. When only six, he was suddenly and dramatically presented as king, much to Athaliah's consternation, who cried, "Treason! Treason!" but who was driven out of the Temple and slain. When grown to manhood Jehoash married two wives and had several sons and daughters. He is mentioned as the father of Amaziah (II Kings 14:1) and his contemporaries in Israel were Jehoahaz (II Kings 13:1) and Jehoash (II Kings 13:10).

Joash's reign began quite auspiciously with a new covenant being made between Jehovah, the king, and the people. Later on, Joash evinced deep concern over the dilapidated condition of the Temple for which the godless reign of Athaliah was responsible. To meet the cost of restoration the king gave orders for all monies coming into the Temple to be appropriated for such a purpose. This plan failed so a new one was adopted. A chest with a hole bored in the lid was set up on the right side of the altar in the charge of two Temple officials and people were invited to put their offerings into the box. This method was overwhelmingly successful and more than enough was subscribed for the complete renovation of the Temple.

The tragedy was that idol shrines were set up throughout the king's domain and that in spite of the protest of unnamed prophets, Joash revealed his true character in his treatment of the high priest, Zechariah, a worthy son of Jehoiada. This prophet courageously testified that the nation had forsaken God and that disaster would follow. Joash was angry at the priest's rebuke and gave orders that Zechariah should be stoned to death in the temple-court. Our Lord referred to this act of sacrilege, ingratitude and murder (Matthew 25:35).

As Zechariah died he said, "Jehovah look upon it, and require it." Within a year of his death the prophecy was fulfilled. The armies of Hazael, King of Syria, laid waste Judah — God using the Syrians as His rod of punishment. To save Jerusalem from the indignity of foreign occupation, Joash collected all the hallowed things of the Temple and all the gold of the palace and sent them to Hazael.

The weak king had a sad end. His punishment is recorded in

Kings and the cause of it in *Chronicles*. Failure of his policy, both in religious and national matters, excited such adverse feeling that a conspiracy was conceived to assassinate him. His diseased body won him no sympathy. While asleep in the fortress of Millo in which he was visiting, two of his own officers murdered him and buried him in the city of David. He was deemed unworthy of being buried along with Jehoiada in the royal sepulchers (II Chronicles 24:25).

AMAZIAH
(II Kings 14; II Chronicles 25)

THE KING WHO BEGAN WELL BUT ENDED BADLY

Amaziah was like the man our Lord described who began to build but was not able to finish. Judah's king was unsteady in character and conduct. At the outset of his reign he was semi-religious, although he failed to serve God as perfectly as his forebear, David, had done. He soon forsook the Lord and because of his apostasy brought war and distress upon the kingdom and a tragic end upon himself.

The son of Jehoash and Jehoaddan of Jerusalem, Amaziah had a peaceable accession to the throne at the age of 24 and reigned for 29 years. Owing to his father's war with Hazael, King of Syria, Amaziah came to a kingdom with a depleted treasury, a despoiled palace and temple, and a discouraged people. As soon as he was firmly established and felt his power was secure, he set about slaying the murderers of his father, but observing the Mosaic Law, spared their children.

Then came the conquest of Edom, which for fifty years had practically been an independent state. The Edomites severed themselves from Jehoshaphat and elected their own king. Amaziah was determined to bring them back into the Judah-fold, and mustering an army of 300,000, slew in one conflict 10,000 men. He changed its capital, *Selah*, to *Joktheel*, meaning, "subjugated by God."

But Amaziah carried off the gods of Edom and set them up as his own and offered them incense possibly to curry favor with the idolatrous Edomites. These idols proved a snare to the victorious king, and for this act of apostasy he was warned of approaching destruction. Pride of conquest, however, proved too much for Amaziah. So we come to his challenge to the King of Israel.

Jehoahaz was called, not to a summit conference where diplomacy could have settled differences, but to battle. "Come, let us look one another in the face." Amaziah, headstrong, spurned the prophetic warning about the tragic end of such a war, because of his previous adoption of the Edomite gods. Intoxicated by his Edomite success he felt the time was ripe for the recovery of the Ten Tribes of Israel.

Under the parable of the Bramble and the Thistle, Amaziah demanded the surrender of Israel to Judah.

The challenge was accepted by Jehoahaz and Amaziah suffered an ignominious defeat. He was brought to his own capital as a prisoner and his palace was plundered of its treasures. God humbled the pride of Amaziah who was left with his throne but little else. Many of those near to him were taken as hostages for his future good behavior. His latter years were spent in seclusion and dread. A Latin proverb has it, "Truly not armies nor treasures are the safeguard of a kingdom — but friends." Amaziah was left with few friends.

There was general dissatisfaction over the king's foolish and ill-fated enterprise against Israel and in a military revolt, Amaziah, at 54 years of age, was slain. Insultingly, his body was carried on horses, not in a coffin, and buried in the royal sepulchers. The French have a saying, "Today a king — tomorrow nothing." Thus it was with Amaziah. An interregnum followed his death until his son was old enough to succeed him.

The example of Amaziah teaches us that no former acts of religion or sacrifice of self-interest will avail us as excuse for indulgence afterwards (II Chronicles 25:2, 9, 10, 14-27). Of him the proverb is true: "A prating fool shall fall" (Proverbs 10:8).

UZZIAH
(II Kings 15; II Chronicles 26; Isaiah 6)

THE KING WHOSE HAUGHTINESS BROUGHT HUMILIATION

Strewn across the sacred pages of the Bible are striking and solemn evidences of heaven's hatred of human pride. No wonder *pride* heads the list of the "Seven Deadly Sins." Arrogance, conceit, inordinate self-esteem and ostentation characterizes many Scripture personalities. William Knox, Scottish poet of 1787 in his *Mortality* asks the pertinent question —
> "Oh, why should the spirit of mortal be proud?
> Like a fast-falling meteor and a fast-flying cloud.
> A flash of lightning and break of the wave,
> He passes from life to rest in the grave."

King Uzziah suffered for his highmindedness. He came to experience that, as John Ruskin puts it in his *Seven Lamps of Literature*, "Pride is at the bottom of all mistakes." Because of his professed faith in God, Uzziah's pride was all the more offensive. Earl of Stirling wrote in *Doomsday*, in 1600 —
> "Vile avarice and pride, from Heaven accurst
> In all are ill, but in a church-man worst."

What a pity it was that Judah's eleventh king did not remember the proverb of King Solomon, "When pride cometh, then cometh shame" (11:2).

Uzziah, also called Azariah, son of Amaziah, came to the throne in his sixteenth year and reigned for 52 years, the second longest reign in Judah. His father, unpopular because of a great military disaster, met his death by mob violence (II Kings 14:19). Uzziah became king with the popular acclaim of the nation (II Chronicles 26:1). At the outset of his long reign, Uzziah determined to blot out the failure of his father in the subjugation of his enemies. Success crowned his expedition and the Edomites, Philistines, Arabians and Ammorites were subdued and Uzziah's "name spread abroad even to the entrances to Egypt; for he waxed exceeding strong."

The king strengthened the defenses of his capital and country and formed several military stations which were supplied with necessary cisterns for water storage. Uzziah gave to his small realm extension and prosperity it had not enjoyed since the days of Solomon. Amid all the success crowning the first 20 years of his reign, Uzziah earnestly sought the Lord and endeavored to walk according to divine counsels. "As long as he sought the Lord, He made him to prosper."

During the lifetime of his godly monitor, Zechariah, "who had understanding in the vision of God," Uzziah profited by the prophet's character and counsel and "set himself to seek God." But with the death of Zechariah, he found himself in a dangerous vacuum. Like his grandfather, Jehoash, who was so dependent upon the advice of Jehoiada the high priest, but who went to pieces at his death, so Uzziah, after the passing of Zechariah, acted adversely to divine instruction.

Uzziah's heart was lifted up with pride and he sinned against God. Elated over his prosperity, he sought to emulate the kings of the east who exercised priestly as well as royal functions. Why could he not exercise his royal prerogative and offer incense on the golden altar of the Temple? Thus he impiously usurped priestly functions. Deserved punishment for pride is a principle from which God never departs, as Uzziah came to learn. Scorning the remonstrances of Azariah the high priest and his associates, Uzziah, angry over such a rebuke, pressed forward, censer in hand, to offer the incense. But as he prepared to undertake this priestly office, white spots appeared on his forehead — he was a leper.

Conscience-stricken because of his pride and disobedience, Uzziah hurriedly left the Temple to begin a life of loneliness. From then on he had to live in a separate house assigned to lepers, isolated from society. Thus his kingly responsibilities and public life were ended. Lepers were freed from all social relations and duties. Loving husbandry (II Chronicles 26:10), Uzziah may have spent the rest of his life caring for his cattle and lands.

Jotham his son became his father's representative, his viceroy until Uzziah's death. "Jotham, the king's son was over the household, judging the people of the land" (II Kings 15:5). The place of Uzziah's burial is not given. Dying a leper, he was not buried in the sepulchers of kings. Isaiah, Hosea and Joel prophesied during Uzziah's reign. The year of his death brought to Isaiah a remarkable vision of the sovereignty and glory of Christ (Isaiah 6:1; John 12).

Josephus has the story that the great earthquake Amos mentions (1:1) happened just as Uzziah threatened the opposing priests; and that a ray of sunlight falling upon the king's face through the Temple room which was cloven by the shock, produced the leprosy. But the Bible says, "The Lord had smitten him."

JOTHAM
(II Kings 15:32-38; II Chronicles 27)

The King Whose Record Is Clean

Judah's twelfth king seems to have profited by the sin and sorrow of his father, for Jotham copied all the good qualities of Uzziah, but not his evil. Jotham is about the only Jewish monarch who has no sin laid to his charge. The Bible gives him a clean record. He was mighty in the administration of his kingdom because he prepared or established his heart before God.

Jotham's beautiful testimony is summed up in the words, "Howbeit he entered not into the Temple of the Lord," meaning he was never guilty of his father's sin of sacrilege. The memory of Uzziah's leprous condition acted as a deterrent of the invasion of the Holy Place. Yet Jotham's influence was not strong enough to turn his people Godward. "The people do yet corruptly." The prophets tell us of the deep-seated corruption that sapped the strength of the nation (Micah 3:10-12; Hosea 4:1, 2). Isaiah also ministered during Jotham's reign.

Good King Jotham began to reign at the age of 26 and reigned for 16 years. Some 4 years before his father's death, Jotham, owing to Uzziah's separation from society, took over control of national and palace affairs and was king in all but name. Jotham does not seem to have shared his father's interests in farming and cattle-raising but gives himself to the sterner duties of the state.

The wisdom and vigor of his administration and policy are fully recognized. Jotham, son of Uzziah and Jerusha, daughter of Zadok, the high priest, effected many public improvements. He repaired the gate of the Temple, built and re-built many towns, castles and towers of refuge. He fought vigorously against Ammon and exacted from that nation a heavy tribute imposed by his father but which the Ammonites refused to pay.

It would seem as if Jotham sought to cultivate humility, and thereby avoid the fate that overtook his father because of his presumption. He died greatly lamented and his name appears in the royal genealogies and also in the human genealogy of Jesus (Matthew 1:9). A Scottish proverb says, "He that is hated of his subjects cannot be counted a king." With Jotham it was otherwise.

AHAZ
(II Kings 6; II Chronicles 28; Isaiah 7-12)

THE KING WHO BURNED HIS CHILDREN ALIVE

We often hear the remark, "Oh, it doesn't matter what a man believes, so long as he believes something." But what false reasoning this is. Because belief influences behavior it is all-important to have the right kind of belief, for creed shapes character. Ahaz, a king by divine grace, worshiped, not the God of heaven, as he should have as a Jew, but Moloch, the god of Ammon, for whom Solomon had built a shrine.

The Valley of Hinnom was the scene of the cruel rites in honor of this imaginary deity John Milton called, "Moloch, horrid king, besmeared with blood." It was at Hinnom that the appalling custom of burning children alive was carried out. Ahaz appears to have been the first Jewish king to offer such a gruesome sacrifice. "He burnt his children in the fire." Ellicott has this comment on such an inhuman offering, "He, no doubt, regarded it as a last desperate resource against the oppression of his northern enemies. . . . Such dreadful sacrifices were only made in cases of dire extremity." The king of Moab offered up his son for a burnt offering (II Kings 3:27). In dark times of national calamity the Hebrews were prone, like their neighbors, to seek help in the same dreadful rites (see Manasseh, II Chronicles 33:6; also Psalm 106:37-39).

Doubtless Ahaz felt that such a human sacrifice would appease the wrath of the god evidently bent on his destruction. Had his whole trust been in the God of grace and mercy how differently he would have acted, and what a wholesome, instead of a wicked, influence he would have exerted as a monarch.

Ahaz, the son of Jotham, succeeded to the throne at the age of 20 or so, and reigned for 16 years. He had the reputation of being the most wicked and idolatrous of all the kings of Judah. He is also spoken of as *Jehoahaz*. Young and determined, he meant to show how unshackled he was by parental influence. Thus, at the outset of his reign, he wanted it to be known that he was wholly opposed to the religious traditions of his nation and so began by making and circulating molten images of the Canaanite god and reviving the abominable worship of Moloch.

With the shutting up of the Temple and the cessation of its divinely ordained services and the setting up of the idolatrous shrines, Ahaz entered a reign that was to prove calamitous. The invasion of Rezin,

King of Damascus, and Pekah, King of Samaria, meant serious peril to the Kingdom of Judah. A conspiracy to dethrone Ahaz was thwarted, and although the advance of the two kings was without success, the Jews were expelled from Elath on the Red Sea (II Kings 16:6).

The record says that 120,000 men of Judah were slain in one day and 200,000 were taken captive by Pekah. No wonder the heart of Ahaz and the heart of his people trembled as trees of the forest tremble with the wind (Isaiah 7:2)! In his extremity Ahaz appealed, not to God as his son Hezekiah did when threatened by Sennacherib, but to the king of Israel for help.

Twice over, the prophet Isaiah faced the godless and frivolous monarch with messages of confidence, but they were spurned. Ahaz thought more of aid from Assyria than from heaven. The Assyrian king is said to have "hearkened unto Ahaz" but we also read that he "distressed him, and strengthened him not" (II Kings 16:9; II Chronicles 28:20). Both of these opposing statements are true.

The king of Assyria did help Ahaz. He took Damascus and delivered Ahaz from the power of the Syrians. But the service was of little value, for the Assyrian monarch did not assist Ahaz against the Edomites or Philistines; and he distressed him by taking the royal treasures and the treasures of the Temple, and rendered him but little service for so great a sacrifice.

The seeming contradiction is illustrated by what happened in Britain, says Bishop Horne. The Britons invited the Saxons to help them against the Scots and Picts. The Saxons accordingly came and assisted them for a time, but at length they made themselves masters of the country.

Alliance with Tiglath-pileser increased the distress of Ahaz and brought his kingdom nigh to ruin. If only Isaiah's counsel had been followed, enemies would have crashed and Judah would have retained her freedom. The tragedy was that the more Ahaz was afflicted, the more he sinned. "He trespassed yet more in his affliction."

The congenial, yet withal, impious pursuits of Ahaz included the setting up of a sun-dial, the erection of the Damascus altar, a heathen altar of fanciful pattern, upon which sacrifices were offered. Further impieties and acts of apostasy were indulged in, bringing deserved judgment in further hostilities from surrounding enemies. Thus after 16 years of misused power, Ahaz died unlamented. While his body was buried in Jerusalem it was not deemed fit to have a resting place in the royal sepulchers of kings. But that grace prevails over wickedness is seen in the fact that Ahaz appears in the genealogy of Jesus (Matthew 1:9).

We can fittingly conclude our glimpse of Ahaz with the summary Bishop Rawlinson gives us —

Ahaz has left behind him the reputation of being among the worst, if not actually the very worst, of all the princes of the house of David. He had neither courage, nor patriotism, nor energy, nor prudence, nor piety, nor even a decent regard for the traditions of his house and nation. . . . In vain did Isaiah warn him, rebuke him, offer him signs, threaten him, urge him to rely on Jehovah; he doggedly pursued his own course, sought help in every quarter but the right one, put his trust in the arms of flesh or in the gods of the nations, cared not how he degraded his country nor disgraced his noble lineage, persisted in evil, ever trespassed more and more until God cut him off in the prime of life.

It was to a godless king like Ahaz that Isaiah gave the prophecy of the coming Immanuel (Isaiah 7:12), the One whose blood is able to make the vilest clean.

HEZEKIAH
(II Kings 18-20; II Chronicles 29-31; Isaiah 26-39)

The King Renowned for His Religion and Reform

As we look at the line of Jewish kings it would seem as if heredity, which is the transmission of character to descendants, does not always operate. Sometimes children depart from the ways in which they were trained (Proverbs 22:6). Wicked Ahab, one of the most dreadful characters recorded in Scripture, was the son of a godly father and the father of a godly son. Pious Hezekiah in turn, was the son of a wicked father and the father of a wicked son. His grandson, Amon, was also bad.

King Hezekiah, who reigned for 29 years, is more unreservedly commended than any other king of Judah. The history and literature of his beneficial reign occupy 17 chapters of the Bible. At the time of his accession to the throne, Judah was reduced to a low state. Through the wickedness of Ahaz, true religion had vanished and the people were guilty of the grossest idolatry. Then the strength of the kingdom had been exhausted by the defects and captivities which it suffered during the reign of Ahaz.

God, however, did not give His people up to utter desolation. He was not unmindful of His promise "to make the horn of David to bud" (Psalm 132:17). Under Hezekiah God made the people the recipients of His distinguishing mercy. Whenever His counsels are ripe for execution His chosen instrument is at hand. According to the law of heredity no good could have been expected of the son and immediate successor of godless Ahaz, but Hezekiah appeared eminent for wisdom, piety and zeal.

Hezekiah came to the throne in the vigor of youth when he was only 25 years of age — an age when young men are eager to gratify their passions. Hezekiah, however, early learned how to "flee youthful lusts" and although his upbringing had been extremely unfavorable, he began his reign by abolishing idolatry and calling his sub-

jects back to the worship of the Lord God of their fathers. At once
the king entered upon the arduous work of reformation and pursued
it with unwearied diligence. Hezekiah's confidence in God inspired
a like confidence in his people.

Service of the neglected and profaned Temple was restored and
Hezekiah led the rulers of the nation to the courts of the Lord for
the celebration of a holy festival of thanks. In addition to the people
of Judah, the Israelites of the ten tribes were invited to assemble
at Jerusalem so that unitedly they might renew their covenant with
God. It was the desire of Hezekiah to re-unite all the Jews into a
single community.

But only a few of the Northern Kingdom responded. As a whole,
the Israelites scorned Hezekiah's ambassadors of good-will. The
whole of Judah followed the king and for fourteen days fervor of
devotion to God prevailed. Idolatrous altars and images were destroyed and steps taken to prevent the nation from returning to their
former abominations. One wonders whether idolatry is destroyed
when idols are removed by force. Would that all present-day rulers
could realize that righteousness alone can exalt a nation!

While the Northern Kingdom was a vassal of Assyria and nearing
its end as a nation, Hezekiah was not only prosperous in the restoration and establishment of the stated administration of the divine
ordinances of the Temple, but also in the civil administration of his
kingdom and in his political enterprises. Under God, Hezekiah subdued the Philistines and cast off the oppressive yoke of the Assyrians.

Later on, it pleased God to try Hezekiah in a sharp manner by
allowing his enemies to gain an advantage over him. Reduced to the
lowest state of distress, the king revealed the peculiar excellence of
his character, namely, unreserved reliance upon God, for he was
distinguished for his faith above all others who sat on the throne of
Judah.

In the 14 years of Hezekiah's reign, Sennacherib, the proud prince
of Assyria, provoked by Hezekiah's unwillingness to submit, invaded
the kingdom of Judah and penetrated nearly to its capital (II Chronicles 32:1). Sennacherib had already led captive the ten tribes of
Israel and now threatened the entire dissolution of the sister kingdom. Hezekiah prepared for a vigorous resistance and used the
wisest precautions to annoy the enemy and fortify the town. Hezekiah believed in trusting God and keeping his powder dry.

While Hezekiah was confident of divine interposition in his favor,
several of his leaders, contrary to the directions of the prophet Isaiah,
solicited the assistance of the Egyptians. Hopes of relief from this
quarter failed and trust in the shadow of Egypt brought confusion.
Hezekiah gave way to a sinful distrust by robbing the Temple of its

treasures and ornaments that he might bribe Sennacherib to withdraw his forces. This plan likewise failed.

Sennacherib, intent upon the destruction of Jerusalem, sent his great army to envelop the city and force Hezekiah to surrender. Ridicule was heaped upon Hezekiah, not only for his expectation from Egypt but also for his trust in God. In such a time of national crisis what could the pious king of Judah do? With conspicuous tokens of humility and godly sorrow, Hezekiah went up to the Temple and soliciting the fervent intercessions of Isaiah for relief, rested his cause with God.

Another summons in a letter from Sennacherib, which expressed the most blatant irreverence and defiance of God, reached Hezekiah and seeking the throne of grace, he spread the insolent letter before the Lord and was assured by Isaiah of a speedy deliverance. That night, as Hezekiah slept, He who never slumbers nor sleeps sent forth His angel, who instantly destroyed 185,000 of the Assyrian army. Sennacherib fled, leaving immense spoil behind him, and ultimately perished miserably at the hands of his own sons. Truly, "the triumph of the wicked is short," when they defy God. Psalm 76 is generally regarded as a celebration on the overthrow of the Assyrian king.

The signal deliverance by God's manifest interposition excited the wonder and attention of surrounding nations. Hezekiah's prestige was enhanced and valuable presents and honors were bestowed upon him. A fly in the precious ointment, however, was a sharp affliction over the king's sudden and dangerous disease which brought him to the edge of the grave. The divine call came to prepare to leave this world (Isaiah 38:1). Turning to God, his only refuge, Hezekiah poured out his soul in prayer for a continuance of life.

No saint should be afraid to die or to postpone his entrance into heaven. "Blessed are the dead that die in the Lord." Doubtless, Hezekiah felt that he had to live on in order to consolidate his kingdom. How astonishing are the effects of prayer! Immediately, Hezekiah's cry was heard and Isaiah assured him that in three days he would be perfectly healed of his disease and that 15 years were to be added to his pilgrimage. Alas, it was during these added years that a son was born to Hezekiah who became a curse on the earth and an abomination in the sight of the Lord.

Hezekiah expressed warmest gratitude for answered prayer. He went up to the Temple to bless God for His goodness and his psalm of thanksgiving has been preserved for us (Isaiah 38:9-20). There was an eclipse in 713 B.C. with which the going back of the shadow may have been connected.

Soon after his recovery, Hezekiah was guilty of a defect in his obedience for which he was reproved and threatened by God Himself. Fortunately, his departure from faith was not of long continuance nor of a gross or notorious kind as to expose himself to the reproaches of the world. Jesus Sirach, the Jewish chronicler, eulogized Hezekiah as one of the three kings who alone did not "commit trespass" (Sirach 49:4), the other two kings being David and Josiah. Sirach represents Hezekiah as lapsing from the wisdom of piety only by his vainglory in revealing the resources of his realm to the envoys of Merodach-baladan.

Hezekiah yielded to a conceit of his own importance on account of the divine and human favors received. "His heart was lifted up." The king of Babylon, eager to curry favor, sent many presents and a letter of congratulation on his extraordinary restoration from fatal sickness. Carried away with pride, Hezekiah reciprocated by displaying the grandeur of his palace and treasures before the pagan monarch. "God left him to try him, that he might know all that was in his heart" — and Hezekiah quickly learned the depravity of his heart!

Hezekiah's vanity did not go unpunished. Isaiah came to him with a solemn reproof and threat of captivity and of confiscation of his boasted treasures by the very man to whom he had paid court. The king humbled himself before God and obtained a respite and was assured that the threatened desolation would not come in his time. From then on, he was stedfast in his devotion to God and increased in power, riches and honor.

Singular prosperity crowned the 29 years of Hezekiah's reign and when he died his exalted worth was seen in that "they buried him in the chiefest of the sepulchers of the sons of David and did him honor at his death." His special distinction, beyond all other Judaean kings before or after, was that he "trusted in Jehovah, the God of Israel." It is as the king who "clave to Jehovah" (II Kings 18:6) that the Hebrew mind sums up Hezekiah's royal and personal character.

Horace Greeley wrote, "Fame is vapor, popularity an accident, riches take wings, those who cheer today will curse tomorrow, only one thing endures — character." Hezekiah was a man of character, who owed much to the spiritual influence of Isaiah, whose prophetic ideals inspired the king. After all, the greatest asset of any nation is not so much its princes as its prophets — men of God, who stand out as the conscience of the nation, as John Knox did in Scotland.

MANASSEH
(II Kings 21:1-9; II Chronicles 33:1-9)

THE KING WHO PROVOKED GOD TO ANGER

A study of the history of reformation seems to indicate that each reform is followed by a more determined effort on the part of evil to undermine the good. Thus, Manasseh, in his long apostate career, destroyed the faith his godly father had established in the land.

Manasseh was the son of Hezekiah and of Hephzibah, being born to them in the third year of Hezekiah's added 15 years of trembling faith and tender hope (Isaiah 38:15). Manasseh reigned for 55 years, the longest reign of any Jewish monarch. His name is somewhat suggestive, meaning, *forgetting*. He was so named because God caused his father to forget his troubles (see Genesis 41:51). What a sad name for the one who was to become the worst of Jewish kings! His name appears second in the list of kings who brought gifts to Esar-haddon.

During Manasseh's reign, Assyria, under Esar-haddon and Assur-banipal, was at the height of its power and pride. "Manasseh's long reign was the more or less peaceful and uneventful life of a willing vassal, contented to be counted as a tributary king in an illustrious world-empire, hospitable to all its religions and cultural ideas and ready to take his part in its military and other enterprises."

Manasseh's record presents him as being conspicuous as a reactionary idolator. He filled the Temple with the vilest forms of idolatry and thereby hastened the ruin of Judah. He seduced his people to do more evil than other iniquitous nations God had destroyed. "Seduced" is a term not used of any previous king.

Through Manasseh's influence Judah had been drawn into the utmost sweep of a tremendous wave of ritual and mechanical heathen culture, proceeding from the world centers of culture and civilization. Of what a horrible catalogue of sins Manasseh was guilty! Astrology, spiritism, wizardry, wickedness, human sacrifices, seduction, erection of idol groves.

Manasseh revived all the abdominations which his father, Hezekiah, had destroyed — and added to them! He filled Jerusalem with innocent blood. He restored the debasing culture of nature-worship his father had suppressed and made Judah revert to the sterile Baal-worship Ahab instituted. "His sin that he sinned," his conspicuous sin, was the setting up of idols he had made in the House of God in which He said He would put His name forever.

Black arts flourished and all forms of wickedness were indulged in. The prophetic voice of true religion decrying all vile worship went unheeded (Isaiah 1:13). The king turned a deaf ear to God calling him to consider his ways. The long-lived monarch in spite of divine and human warnings persisted in his evil ways.

But amid all national wickedness the godly remnant, preserved and purified, as inspired by the influence of Isaiah. Manasseh persecuted the prophets and their followers, and he shed much innocent blood. Tradition has it that he killed Isaiah by placing him inside a hollow tree and sawing him asunder (Hebrews 11:37).

Punishment overtook Manasseh. The King of Assyria took him among the thorns, bound him with fetters, and carried him to Babylon. "Among the thorns," means with hooks or rings. There is an ancient monument showing King Esar-haddon leading two captives with hooks or rings through their lips, and it bears the inscription, "I transported (from Syria) into Assyria men and women innumerable . . . I counted among the vassals of my realm twelve kings of Syria, beyond the mountains, Balon, King of Tyre, Manasseh, King of Judah."

During his humiliation and repentance in Babylon, Manasseh's eyes were opened to the truer meaning of godliness. In captivity he came to see the terrible evils of a despotic idolatry. While his record in the Book of Kings gives no account of his repentance, Chronicles declares that Manasseh confessed his sins and forsaking them, found mercy (Proverbs 28:13). He came to know that Jehovah was God (II Chronicles 33:10-13) and is before us as a monument of God's grace sanctifying affliction. The prayer he prayed is not given (II Chronicles 33:19).

Returning to Jerusalem, Manasseh removed the heathen altars and restored the services of the Temple and resumed the worship of God against whom he had sinned. He permitted, however, many high places or idol shrines to remain. One commentator asks, "Was Jehovah's right to a specific culture of His own the only motive prompting Manasseh to recognize God?" That Manasseh did not succeed in committing his nation, in his evil days, to the wholesale sway of heathenism is seen in the fact that years after his death, good Josiah established yet once again the worship of the true God in the land.

As to Manasseh's end we are informed that he slept with his fathers and was buried, not in the usual sepulchers of the kings, but in the garden of his own house. "Slept with his fathers," is a beautiful description for death, "shalt lie down to sleep," and is used alike of good and evil kings, even of Jehoiakin, who had no burial.

AMON
(II Kings 21:18-26; II Chronicles 33:21-25)

THE KING WHOSE REIGN WAS SHORT AND SINFUL

The period from 20 to 25, "the fifth lustrum of life," is the time when men feel a buoyant sense of mental vigor and delight in the exercise of intellectual weapons, says Mr. Robertson Nicoll in *The Round of the Clock*. But it was otherwise with Amon, who came to the throne of Judah at the age of 22, reigned for only 2 years, and was murdered at the early age of 24 — quite long enough because of the pernicious influence of his short life!

It would seem as if the sacred historian was unwilling to give much notice to the godless monarch before us. About twenty lines only are allotted to Amon whose brief reign was a weaker continuation of the regime of his wicked father.

Amon's name was associated with the Egyptian local sun-god, *Amen*, and was given him when his fanatical father, Manasseh, was immersed in his idolatrous practices. It indicates that God had no more claim to worship than heathen deities. Amon's mother was Meshullemeth.

The youthful king abandoned the worship of God and thoroughly identified himself with his father's foreign superstitions (II Kings 21:21). Moral and religious license went hand in hand. Amon "trespassed more and more," or as the margin puts it, "multiplied trespass." A Latin proverb says, "The whole community is ordered by the king's example" — whether for good or bad.

Amon copied all his father's sins but not his sorrow over his sins. He spurned the grace shown in Manasseh. Being a youth, he doubtless thought that life was before him and that he could have his fling in all that was licentious and then in later life repent like his father. But such a day of repentance never came.

Amon was murdered by some of his courtiers or palace officials, who could have been some of the remnant eager to rid the throne of apostasy. A section of the populace arose and slew those who had conspired against the king and slain him. Such judgment against idolatry proved that a sterling fiber of loyalty still existed, seasoned and confirmed by trial, below the corrupting cults and fashions of the ruling classes.

Amon was buried in his sepulcher, not in the royal supulchers, but in one he had prepared for himself near his father's grave (II Kings 21:1). Thinking of Amon we recall the Scottish proverb, "He that is hated of his subjects cannot be counted a king."

JOSIAH
(II Kings 22-23:30; II Chronicles 34, 35)
THE KING WHO TURNED NOT ASIDE

Of no other king is it said that "he turned not aside to the right hand or to the left." Josiah kept his eye on the goal and reached it with satisfaction in a reign of 13 years. He made an early and right start and progressed and was persistent to the end. We can apply the words of Shakespeare in *King Lear* to Josiah:

"Ay, every inch a king."

The name of Judah's king was given 6 years before the death of his grandfather Manasseh, and is a royal name associated with Jehovah. *Manasseh* and *Amon*, preceding Josiah, were heathen names.

Thus of fulfilled prophecies, the most remarkable is that respecting Josiah. Some 300 years before Josiah was born, no one gave his son such a name or assumed it for himself, or attempted to fulfill the prophecy, until the appointed time arrived. It was Amon, a wicked king, who named his son *Josiah*, and evidently was not aware of the prophecy until he had fulfilled it (compare I Kings 21:23 with II Kings 9:21, 26, 36).

Josiah is a conspicuous example of early piety and its beneficial effects. With such an evil heritage it would have been no surprise had he continued the evil influences of Manasseh and Amon. But light arose for Judah, on her dark night of blatant infidelity. Josiah's grandfather had not been able to abolish all the profane practices he had introduced, and which Amon, Josiah's father, renewed and extended. Josiah was only 6 years of age when placed upon the throne, and what could one expect from a child! Manasseh began at 12 and was nurtured under godly Hezekiah. Josiah began at 6 and was nurtured under ungodly Amon. What a contrast in character! Yet through the tuition of persons of virtuous principles, while he was yet young, Josiah sought after the God of David. Zephaniah began his ministry in the first year of Josiah and Jeremiah is prominent in the king's thirteenth year. Nahum also wrote toward the end of Josiah's reign. "Those that seek me early, shall find me" (Proverbs 8:17).

As life opened to him, Josiah dedicated himself to the service of God. He remembered his Creator in the days of his youth. In the eighth year of his reign he sought and found the Lord, and four years later began to extirpate idolatry out of the land. Thereafter, his reign was characterized by close attention to the written Word of God. The Apocrypha names Josiah as one of three who did not "commit trespass." His ardent religious zeal was not a sudden transitory flash but a bright and steady flame.

Fifty years after Hezekiah's death, his great grandson, Josiah, made another and final attempt to bring the nation back to God, but his effort was almost fruitless. The king felt that the *precepts*, not the *purposes*, of God must be his rule of conduct. Thus, although he was assured by Huldah of the certainty of the destruction to come upon Jerusalem, Josiah did not in the least relax the energy of his efforts to reform it. He acted in the spirit of that important distinction, that "duty is ours; events are God's" (II Kings 22:16).

In the twelfth year of his reign, when he was 20 years of age, Josiah set about the purging of the land of the abominations which had polluted it. For 6 years he labored at his sacred task to overthrow pagan worship and rites. His work of reformation was not entrusted to others. Josiah himself went through the kingdom to see that his commands were executed.

Josiah's zealous exertions were not confined to his own particular domain of Judah. He exerted similar authority over the cities of Israel which were subject to Assyria. So he burned the bones of idolatrous priests upon Jeroboam's altar at Bethel. It is somewhat remarkable that it had been divinely predicted that he would accomplish this task some 350 years before (I Kings 13:2; II Kings 23:15, 20), and he could not have been ignorant of such a prophecy.

Josiah's work was not only negative, correcting irregularities, but positive in that he sought to establish real godliness in the nation. The Temple, neglected and profaned, was repaired and the public worship of God restored. It was while the repair of the Temple went on that Hilkiah, the high priest, found the Book of the Law, which was the most outstanding event in Josiah's reign of 31 years.

The history of the world proves that the acceptance and application of the great truths of the divine Word not only change man's opinions, but produce a total alteration of character, motives and conduct. Probably it was the original copy of Deuteronomy Hilkiah discovered, which had been secreted during the reigns of Manasseh and Amon. Evidently copies of the book were unknown or disregarded or scarce, seeing the king was not cognizant of it. The entrance of the Word, however, brought light. Through the Law, Josiah discovered how far the people had journeyed fom God, and to what terrible wrath they were exposed.

Huldah, the prophetess, pronounced her verdict on the book as being the Oracle of God, and declared that destruction would be poured out upon Jerusalem and its inhabitants for long, continuous idolatry but that Josiah, the pious king, would be mercifully removed before judgment fell.

As soon as Josiah understood the importance of the discovered book, he summoned his rulers and all the people of the city and went in solemn procession to the Temple and read in their ears the awful denunciations of the Law. His own repentance was deep, but one fears that the greater part of the people yielded a hypocritical compliance even though they ratified the vows the king offered. Nicholls' comment is:

> II Chronicles 34:32, 33 depicts a remarkable change from the state of wickedness into which they had previously plunged during the reign of Amon. But the description here given requires some qualification, for from Jeremiah 3:10, and other parts of the first twelve chapters of his prophecy, delivered during Josiah's reign, we learn that with regard to many it was but an external obedience, a restraint upon, not a change of disposition, and hypocrisy which threw off its mark as soon as Josiah died. These passages of Jeremiah also explain II Kings 23:26 where it is said that notwithstanding Josiah's piety, and the extent to which he carried the reformation, the Lord turned not from the fierceness of his great wrath.

A public celebration of the Passover, on a scale unheard of since the time of the Judges, was observed, just 100 years after the destruction of Samaria. Judah's amiable king steadfastly preserved in righteousness as his nation prospered. Some 13 years after his great work of revival Josiah went out to battle against Pharaoh-necho, king of Egypt, who was on his way to attack the Assyrians.

In the venture, Josiah revealed a lack of balance in his character. He was censured for undertaking such an expedition which probably was undertaken without due deliberation or consultation with the Lord and His prophets. God sometimes allows even godly men to follow foolish and evil counsels in order to punish those with whom they are convicted, as in Josiah's case.

Josiah received a mortal wound in battle and died as he was being conveyed from Megiddo to Jerusalem. It would seem as if God removed Josiah in mercy to himself so that he might not behold the approaching desolation of his country, which in spite of the king was hastening to disaster. Although he died in war, Josiah yet died in peace of mind and heart and was gathered to his grave in peace.

Josiah's death was a great national calamity. In his untimely death the fervent hopes of the godly remnant received a setback. His passing was widely lamented. Deepest sorrow prevailed. Jeremiah lamented for the king and mentions him in his Lamentations (4:20). As we think of the nation's sorrow over Josiah, the Latin proverb comes to mind, "The riches of kings are the hearts of their subjects."

Alas, Josiah's monumental reform was only outward, for after his death the people went back to their idolatries! Enthusiasm over a new-found faith waned, and God was forsaken.

JEHOAHAZ
(II Kings 23; II Chronicles 36; Jeremiah 27:10-12)

The King Who Reigned for Only Three Months

The career of Josiah's successor was too short to make any marked impression on the history of Judah. At 23 Jehoahaz came to the throne, but his reign only lasted for 3 months. Although brief it was bad and its end bitter. Jehoahaz, son of Josiah and of Hamutal, the daughter of Jeremish of Libnah, is called *Shallum*, which might have been his name before the untimely death of his father brought him to the throne.

Jehoiakim, an older brother of Jehoahaz, was in direct line for kingship, but was passed by the people of the land, doubtless because tyrannical tendencies had manifested themselves in him. Jehoahaz, the fourth son of Josiah, was chosen king probably because the people felt they had in him a more capable ruler for the emergencies of the time. But Jeremiah's account of him shows that their estimate was fallacious (22:10).

In his three-month reign, Jehoahaz persisted in the abominations of his forebears, Amon and Manasseh. "He did evil in the sight of the Lord." Ellicott observes that in Ezekiel's lamentation for the princes of Judah, Jehoahaz is called a young lion that "devoureth man," alluding to his oppressive rapacity and shameless abuse of power (14:1-4).

After Josiah's good reign, Judah began a melancholy change for the worst. Pharaoh-mechol, the Egyptian monarch, deemed it unsafe to leave the nation that had meddled in his designs unpunished. Judah was possessed and made a tributary province and heavily taxed. Jehoahaz was deposed and carried captive to Egypt where he died as foretold by Jeremiah (22:11, 12; 27:10-12). Still a youth when made a slave, Jehoahaz, who never saw his land again, must have been made to serve his foreign master with vigor.

JEHOIAKIM
(II Kings 23:35-24:7; II Chronicles 36:5-8; Jeremiah 22:18-21; 25-27; 36)

THE KING WHO WAS BURIED AS AN ASS

We could give this king another title — A *Fool of a King and His Penknife.* There is an old saying to the effect that a child and a fool should never be trusted with a penknife, for each of them will employ it either in whittling away things of value or in injuring themselves. Jehoiakim's penknife was used according to his folly.

When Jeremiah, the prophet, came to the king with the divinely inspired prophecy of the king's and his nation's coming catastrophe, the roll of parchment containing the prophecy was brought to the king in one of his palaces and read to him and to his courtiers. What a terrible indictment of the king's sins and of the coming inevitable consequences the roll contained.

The royal sinner did not like what he heard and, stopping the reading, asked for the roll to be passed to him. Revealing his contempt for God and the prophet, Jehoiakim took a scribe's knife, cut the roll in pieces, flung them into the fire and watched them until they were reduced to white ashes. But while the king destroyed that particular roll, he did not get rid of the solemn truths it contained, for they were re-written and added to.

Others have tried to use Jehoiakim's penknife. When the Bible was first printed in England, the Romish bishops and priests bought up all the Bibles they could find and made bonfires of them. The printers used the money to provide ten presses where there had been one, and the Bibles in the land increased tenfold, much to the chagrin of the priests who found that bonfires could not burn the indestructible Word of God. The impious act of Jehoiakim is being continued not by a scribe's knife but with the scribe's pen in the hands of modern, destructive critics.

When Jehoiakim showed the utmost contempt and defiance of God by destroying His message to his heart, a proof of the hardness of the hearts of the king's courtiers is seen in their lack of penitence. Garments were not rent — the Eastern mode of expressing sorrow or alarm. How unlike his father Josiah (II Kings 22:11)! Evidently the courtiers were less open to holy fear than the people were.

Nothing good is recorded of this godless king who indulged himself in the erection, by enforced and unpaid labor, of costly royal palaces. He manifested an utter disregard for the best interests of his subjects. In religion, he introduced still more strange heathenish rites from Egypt. Summarizing his character, Greenbough says of Jehoiakim:

> He was a poor, weak-brained, besotted simpleton, whom his flatterers and courtiers had persuaded to regard himself as a Solomon. A man steeped in vice, a coward and a braggart, with a vast stock of obstinacy and bravado, and a huge opinion of himself, but without a spark of real courage and manliness. He was committing one political blunder after another, leading the nation swiftly to destruction, and dragging it down with himself to the lowest stage of godlessness and immorality. He was like one sailing gaily toward a cataract, with the rapids all about him, and the final plunge not far off.

The phrase, "his abominations . . . which were found in him," is said to mean "found on him," referring to a belief that he was tattoed with idolatrous marks, or signs forbidden by the Mosaic Law (Leviticus 19:28; see Revelation 13:16-17, etc.). This we do know, he was not reformed by adversity. He was guilty of the vindictive murder of the prophet Uriah who prophesied in the spirit of Jeremiah and also attempted to kill Jeremiah for his declaration of truths he hated.

Jehoiakim was raised to the throne of Judah by Pharaoh-necho and made a vassal king in the place of his younger (half) brother, Jehoahaz, and reigned for 11 years. His original name was Eliakim, but Pharaoh-necho changed it to Jehoiakim to assert his authority and also his rejection of the people's choice of Jehoahaz.

Placed on the throne by the king of Egypt, Jehoiakim was deposed by the king of Babylon, Nebuchadnezzar, whose name first occurs here in Scripture. Jehoiakim was carried captive to Babylon along with Daniel. Jehoiakim's reign is not significant for any personal impress of his character but because it witnessed the beginning of the end of the nation. Politically the fourth year of Jehoiakim's reign, in which Nebuchadnezzar won his great victory over Pharaoh-necho at Carchemish on the Euphrates, was the turning point of the age. The prophecy of Habakkuk, as well as that of Jeremiah, should be read in this connection.

Jehoiakim's miserable death was foretold by Jeremiah, "buried with the burial of an ass," meaning, he had no burial, for asses had no burial then. Dragged in chains to captivity, probably he died on the journey and his corpse was left behind, unburied, as the army marched on. The king's body was "cast out in the day to the heat and in the night to the frost" (II Chronicles 36:30). What a contrast between the life and death of Josiah and Jehoiakim! For the latter, no mourning by relatives or subjects was made. How different were the lamentations for Josiah!

The phrase, "slept with his fathers," refers to the mere fact of death, not to the manner of his death and place of burial. The same phrase is used of godless Ahab who died in battle, and of every king of Judah whose death is recorded, and who is said to have been buried, except Jehoiakim who fittingly illustrates the Proverb —

"The name of the wicked shall rot" (10:7).

JEHOIAKIN
(II Kings 24:8-16; II Chronicles 36:9, 10; Jeremiah 22:24-30; Esther 2:6)

THE KING WHO WAS IN PRISON FOR 37 YEARS.

The son and successor of Jehoiakim reigned for only 3 months and 10 days, not long enough for his evil ways to make much of an impression upon the life of the nation. Also spoken of as Coniah and Jeconiah, Jehoiakin, whose mother was Nehushta, daughter of Elnathan of Jerusalem (see her name under section on Queens, was 18 years of age when he began to reign. The "eight years" of II Chronicles 36:9 is explained thus —

"The *eighteen* must include his co-regency, the *eight* to his reigning alone. This practice was common in Israel and Judah as well as in ancient contemporary kingdoms."

The eighth year of his reign represents the time his father entrusted him with regal authority. Jehoiakin's brief span as a free king was more of a historic landmark than a reign. The first wholesale deportation of Jewish captives to Babylon took place in Jehoiakin's time, with the king himself being taken captive along with all the royal household and the court. Jehoiakin's resistance to Nebuchadnezzar's siege of Jerusalem proved to be futile and with his surrender to the King of Babylon, 10,000 captives, including "all the better and sturdier elements of the people from prince to craftsman," were taken. The most valuable treasures of the Temple and the royal palace were taken as loot. The wicked King Jehoiakin remained a captive for 37 years. Through a misunderstanding of Jeremiah 22:24-28, Josephus speaks of Jehoiakin as "naturally good and just."

When Nebuchadnezzar first attacked Jerusalem in the reign of Jehoiakin, a company of hostages was carried away, including Daniel and his three friends. The second attack, in Jehoiakin's reign, saw Ezekiel and Mordecai taken prisoner. Jeremiah evaded capture and urged the exiles in Babylon to make themselves at home and to be good citizens (29:1-10).

Jeremiah predicted that Jehoiakin would never have a descendant on David's throne. He died "childless" as to the throne. Not one of his seven sons succeeded him as king (I Chronicles 3:17, 18). In him, the scepter departed from Judah. Zedekiah, who succeeded Jehoiakin, perished before him (Jeremiah 52:31). The scribes, keeping the royal register, named Jehoiakin as the last of his line.

After Jehoiakin's long captivity, a strange thing occurred. In the first year of Nebuchadnezzar's successor, Jehoiakin was released and raised to the dignity of king and ended his life in royal fashion (II Kings 25:27-30; Jeremiah 52:31-34). Good influence at the court must have prevailed on his behalf, and he was given precedence over other captive kings in Babylon. A higher chair of state in the royal hall was allotted him. It was thus that Cyrus kept Croesus, king of Lydia, at his court. The chivalrous behavior of the Black Prince toward his royal captive, John of France, affords a similar illustration. Ellicott remarks —

> The writer evidently dwells with pleasure on this faint gleam of light amid the darkness of the exile. It was a kind of foreshadowing of the pity which afterwards was to be extended to the captive people, when the divine purpose had been achieved, and the exile had done its work of chastisement and purification (Psalm 106:46; Ezra 9:9; Nehemiah 2:2).

We have no account of Jehoiakin's death and burial as in the case of other kings.

ZEDEKIAH
(II Kings 24, 25; Jeremiah 52)

The King Who Became a Blind Slave

How true were Tennyson's words of Zedekiah's reign of eleven years, "A doubtful throne is ice on summer seas"! The proverb has it, "A king's word should be his bond." Judah's last king perfidiously broke his oath to Nebuchadnezzar and hardened himself against the faithful ministry of Jeremiah and consequently reaped a sad harvest. Zedekiah rebelled against the King of Babylon although he was bound by an oath which he took when he was made vassal-king of Judah. He had to swear fealty by the God of his fathers.

The prophet Ezekiel makes this a point of a prophecy against Zedekiah and his grandees, "Mine oath that he hath despised" (17: 11-21). Jeremiah also exhorted the king to conform strictly to his oath, in opposition to all those lying teachers, who, with their pretended divinations, encouraged Zedekiah to throw off the yoke of subjection (Jeremiah 27, 28). Antagonism against Jeremiah, the servant of Jehovah, was strong, but he continued, notwithstanding contempt and violence, to declare the will of heaven.

Jeremiah maintained that it would be vain, as well as impious, to resist the Babylonian monarch, and that, upon their rebellion against him, they should be given up to utter desolation. Zedekiah, however, persisted in his determination to take the advice of his flattering counselors, and by his perfidy provoked Nebuchadnezzar to invade the land and beseige the city.

Indecisive Zedekiah (Jeremiah 38:19, 20) was not able to stand against the invading army. When Nebuchadnezzar took the best of the people, men of weight and character, under Jehoiakin, he left behind a people broken in resources and spirit so that they would not be moved to rebellion (Ezekiel 17:14). Zedekiah's people had neither property nor handicraft (Jeremiah 39:10). In his distress, the king sent for Jeremiah, a prophet for whom he had respect, and entreated his prayers on his behalf (32:1), but Zedekiah was too weak and timorous to follow the prophetic counsel in defiance of his princes who were intriguing Egypt. It would seem as if Zedekiah hoped for some miraculous deliverance similar to that of King Hezekiah from Sennacherib. Judah was carried away into captivity and thus ended the kingdom as Jeremiah had predicted (20:4). Feeling that the end was near and that God had forsaken the land (Ezekiel 8), Zedekiah made the nation to become a cesspool of idolatry and of uncouth temple rites. Ezekiel was the outstanding prophet in captivity.

Zedekiah, whose name was changed from Mattaniah, was the third son of Josiah and the full brother of Jehoahaz. Jehoiakin was childless at the time of his captivity. Zedekiah, after reigning for 11 years, was brought before the king of Babylon at Riblah, and had the anguish of seeing his sons and the nobles of Judah slain before his eyes. Zedekiah's own eyes were then gouged out.

The blinding of captive kings was quite usual among Assyrians and Chaldean rulers. Assur-banipal boasted that he placed a king of Arabia in chains, and bound him with the dogs, and caused him to be kept in one of the great gates of Nineveh. Darius is spoken of as taking a rebel king of Sagarita, and cutting off his nose and ears, keeping him chained at his door.

The LXX version translates "put him in prison" (Jeremiah 51:11) as "the house of the mill," as though Zedekiah, after he had been blinded, had been made to do slave-work like that of Samson (see Lamentations 5:13). How long Zedekiah remained in captivity and when he died we are not told. Jeremiah had prophesied that he would die in peace and have a state mourning (34:4, 5).

A remarkable illustration of how the obscurity and apparent contradiction of unfulfilled prophecy is removed by the event, is seen in comparing the prophecies of Jeremiah and Ezekiel concerning Zedekiah. Jeremiah had foretold that Zedekiah should behold the king of Babylon and go to Babylon (34:3); Ezekiel foretold that Zedekiah should not see Babylon (12:13). Zedekiah, Josephus informs us, thinking these prophecies contradictory, believed neither. But both were exactly fulfilled. Zedekiah did see the King of Babylon, not at Babylon, but at Riblah, whence, his eyes being put out, he was carried to Babylon and died there and Judean royalty ended.

Dr. W. Graham Scroggie reminds us that:

The Monarchy and the Dependency periods overlap for twenty years 606-586 B.C.), that is to say, though the last three kings were Jews, they had their throne by the will of foreign Powers, first Egypt, then Babylon. And it is important to see that in this score of years three prophesied events commenced:

The *Servitude*, 70 years, 606-536 B.C. (Jeremiah 29:10)
The *Exile*, 50 years, 586-536 B.C.
The *Desolation*, 70 years, 586-516 B.C. (Jeremiah 25:1-11)
Twenty years of what is commonly regarded as the Captivity, were, in fact, not in the period of the exile, but of the Servitude.

Summarizing the period covered by the kings of Judah we note these facts:

About half of the Judean sovereigns were good; hence the long continuance of the kingdom over that of Israel.

As a rule, the mothers of the Judean kings are specially named, but not so in the case of the kings of Israel.

Only one female sovereign is named among those of Judah, and not one among the sovereigns of Israel.

The fathers of the godly kings, Hezekiah and Josiah, were bad men, thus illustrating the sovereign goodness and choice of God.

It is also worthy of careful observation that according to the personal piety and faithfulness of the monarch, Judah was blessed, and the country enjoyed peace and prosperity.

The longest reign was that of Manasseh, 65 years, while the shortest was that of Jehoahaz, which lasted only 3 months.

The books of Chronicles specially detail the doings of the kings of Judah.

Judah was carried to Babylon some 468 years after David began to reign over it, 388 years after the falling off of the Ten Tribes, 134 years after the destruction of the kingdom of Israel. As with individuals so with nations, iniquity is their ruin (Psalm 9:17).

The preservation and continued pre-eminence of Judah and of the Davidic line shows remarkably the finger of providence preparing for the coming of the Messiah, as foretold by prophecy (Genesis 49:10; Isaiah 11:10). The preservation of the House of David is also remarkable when we remember the great wickedness of many of the family — Jehoram, Ahaziah, Ahaz and Amon.

THE KINGDOM OF ISRAEL 975-721 B.C.

The Kingdom of Israel, consisting of the Ten Tribes who revolted over Rehoboam's despotism, existed for nearly 260 years under 19 kings, Jeroboam to Hoshea, all of whom were idolaters. The kingdom was ultimately overthrown by the Assyrians under Shalmaneser and terminated with the Babylonian exile. The term, *Israel*, is sometimes used of the Jews as a whole, but in the records of the kings it is usually confined to the Ten Tribes.

The capital of the Northern Kingdom was first at Shechem, then at Samaria. Summarizing the histories of both the Southern and Northern Kingdoms, Dr. W. Graham Scroggie notes these facts —

In the Southern Kingdom there was but one dynasty, the Davidic, but in the Northern Kingdom there were nine dynasties.

In the South were nineteen kings and one queen; in the North were nineteen kings.

In the South some of the rulers were good, some unstable and some bad; but in the North, all were bad.

In the South were three religious revivals, in the reigns of Jehoshaphat, Hezekiah and Josiah, but in the North there were no revivals.

The tribes in the South were taken into Babylonian captivity by Nebuchadnezzar; and the tribes in the North, into Assyrian captivity by Shalmaneser.

The Foreign Powers that come into touch with the South or the North in this period were Assyria, Egypt, Babylon, and Syria.

The prophets to Israel were Jonah, Amos, Hosea and Micah. In recent years efforts have been made to identify the Ten Tribes. Spoken of as *The Lost Ten Tribes*, the British people are affirmed by some to be these tribes. After release from captivity they were dispersed abroad and were known by James to whom he addressed his Epistle (1:1). As such, they are known to God, and the promise is that all Twelve Tribes are to be bound together into one royal nation (Zechariah 11:7).

JEROBOAM I
(I Kings 11:26-40; 12-14:20;
II Chronicles 10-11:16; 12:15; 13:3-20)

THE KING WHO ESTABLISHED HIS KINGDOM ON IDOLATRY

Jeroboam, Israel's first king, was a religious apostate who gave his character to his kingdom and to succeeding kingdoms. His example was followed by every succeeding king. They all trod in the steps of the idolatry he established. Jeroboam's ancestry, character and ability, as well as reasons for assigning him the Ten Tribes, and the conditions on which his kingdom would be established, are given in detail in passages cited above.

Jeroboam, a name borne by two of Israel's kings, reigned for 22 years and was the son of Nebat, an Ephraimite and a servant of Solomon. His mother's name was Zeruch. The LXX version gives her name as Sariva and says that she was a harlot; and that Jeroboam's wife was Ano, an Egyptian princess.

It is clearly evident that Jeroboam was a gifted and courageous young man, and that because of his ability and strength of character, King Solomon chose him to oversee the fortifications and public works at Jerusalem. He was also placed over the levy of the House of Joseph — a term representing the whole of the Ten Tribes (Amos 5:6; 6:6). Jeroboam thus shared in the imposition of the grievous yoke and owing to his position had every opportunity of oppressing the people and creating discontent. The LXX says that he exalted himself to seek the kingdom and that Solomon sought to kill him. It would seem as if when the cleavage came, Jeroboam had the support of the people in his designs.

Burdensome taxation filled the people's hearts with bitterness and jealousy, and as a widow's son, Jeroboam knew from experience the gall of oppression. In his flight from Solomon he met Ahijah of Shiloh, whose approval Jeroboam had. By tearing his mantle into twelve pieces and giving ten to the fugitive, Ahijah the prophet confirmed him as King of the Northern Kingdom. Prophets often resorted to such symbolic acts.

Josephus says of Jeroboam that he was "a young man of warm temper, and ambitious of greatness and could not be quiet." His temper made him too hasty to get the government into his own hands. His plot failed and he fled to Egypt where he was kindly received by Shishak, the successor of Solomon's father-in-law. Because of his strong grip on those he had influenced, Jeroboam was not forgotten.

At the death of Solomon the rising tide of discontent created by his oppressive reign burst all restraints. At first, the northern tribes were at Shechem and solemnly promised to serve Solomon's son and successor, Rehoboam, if he would only lighten the burdens imposed upon the nation. Wrongly advised, Rehoboam, in a spirit of despotism, refused the request and decided to make the tasks of the people heavier. Such rough treatment resulted in the *Marseillaise* of the Ten Tribes —

> "What part have we in David?
> Neither have we interest in the son of Jesse:
> To your tents, O Israel!
> Now see to thine own house, David" (I Kings 12:10).

Jeroboam returned from his forced exile in Egypt and took up residence in his native Shechem. Quickly he was raised to the throne by the popular assembly. Alas, however, he failed to rise to the greatness of his opportunity and position! His kingdom degenerated into a mere military monarchy. Fortifying Shechem, Jeroboam made it his capital, which latterly was removed to Terzah.

There was continual war between Rehoboam and Jeroboam (I Kings 14:30). Then there was Jeroboam's inglorious war with Abijah of Judah. When Shishak invaded Judah he did not spare Israel, but took many of its towns. The king's failure in not setting his heart to seek the Lord was his undoing. He was determined to lean on his own understanding, rather than on divine wisdom (Proverbs 3:5).

Jeroboam was a religious apostate. Fearing a reaction in the favor of the House of David and the continuation of religious pilgrimages to Jerusalem, he established national sanctuaries in Israel. Making "two calves of gold" as symbols of the strength and creative power of Jehovah (Psalm 106:20), he set them up in sanctuaries at Bethel and Dan, much against the opposition of many of the priests to image-worship (I Chronicles 11:13). Jeroboam also founded a new, non-Levitical, vile priesthood, and introduced popular, pagan festivals on the model of the feasts at Jerusalem.

This was *the sin* wherewith the king made Israel to sin. In 21 cases where Jeroboam's name is mentioned, his apostasy is linked to it, "Who did sin, and made Israel to sin." The masses were not long in following the immoralities of heathenism, which hastened the destruction predicted by the prophet Ahijah. An anonymous prophet publicly denounced Jeroboam for his idolatrous worship and was angry when rebuked (I Kings 13:4).

A crisis compelled Jeroboam to seek the aid of Ahijah. His eldest son fell sick and he turned to the prophet, now old and blind, for help. He never troubled himself about prophets until he was in trouble, just as some people never pray unless they are in a jam. Jeroboam sent his queen, disguised, to learn whether their child would live or die. Warned of God of Jeroboam's effort, Ahijah bade the king's wife return and say that the House of Jeroboam would be destroyed root and branch and that his son would die — the reward of bequeathing to posterity "the reputation of an apostate and succession of endless revolutions."

It would seem as if Jeroboam himself had a miserable death, being stricken with a languishing disease. We read that "the Lord struck him, and he died" (II Chronicles 13:20). Powerless to injure his neighbor, his death was regarded in a judicial phrase as "the finger of God" just as Herod was smitten with a terrible death (Acts 12:23).

Thomas Grey, bard of the seventeenth century wrote —
            "Ruin seize thee, ruthless king!
            Confusion on thy banners wait!"

NADAB
(I Kings 14:20; 15:25-31)

THE KING WHO WAS SLAIN BY A USURPER

We are indebted to Longfellow for the lines —
"No action, whether foul or fair,
Is ever done, but it leaves somewhere
A record, written by fingers ghostly,
As a blessing or a curse, and mostly
In the greater weakness or greater strength
Of the acts which follow it."

Jeroboam's foul example lived on in his son and successor, Nadab, who followed his father's evil courses. The constantly-recurring phrase, "made Israel to sin," signifies perseverance in the filthy idolatries of Jeroboam's reign.

The second king of Israel occupies brief space in the royal annals of Holy Writ. He and all Israel laid a seige against Gibbethon, but Nadab was conspired against and assassinated by Baasha, a usurper. With Nadab's death, the utter destruction of the family of Jeroboam, as foretold by Ahijah (I Kings 14), took place. Such an event was typical of the entire history of the Northern Kingdom, which was one of revolutions and counter-revolutions.

BAASHA
(I Kings 15:27-16:7)

THE KING WHOSE REIGN WAS FILLED WITH WAR AND TREACHERY

Apart from his attempt on the independence of Judah, and its failure, we know little of Baasha, who reigned for 24 years in Israel. Scripture tells us that he was of common birth (I Kings 16:2) and sprang from an obscure tribe, undistinguished in its history. Ellicott comments —

> Baasha is the first of many military chiefs who by violence or assassination seized upon the throne of Israel. The constant succession of ephemeral dynasties stands in striking contrast with the unchanged royalty of the house of David, resting on the promise of God.

True to his name, meaning *wicked*, Baasha was a most wicked king, who persisted in the sins which he was raised up to destroy in the House of Jeroboam. To make his throne more secure, he massacred all the relatives of his predecessor, and by his barbarous actions, fulfilled the prophecy pronounced against Jeroboam (I Kings 14:1).

Baasha carried on long warfare with Asa, king of Judah, and was prevented by Ben-hadad, king of Syria, in the building of Ramah. Dr. R. K. Harrison reminds us that Baasha sent out a bribe of the Temple treasure to the Syrian king, but Ben-hadad drove Baasha back to his capital city, Tirzah, while Asa marched on Ramah and demolished it.

The prophet Jehu warned Baasha that because of his sinful reign he would suffer the same fate as that of Jeroboam (II Kings 9:9). "The curse of the Lord is in the house of the wicked" (Proverbs 3:33). Judgment, in the form of total and utter destruction, overtook Baasha and his house because of his evil ways and also because he had killed Nadab and his sons. "Sin which works out God's purpose is not the less truly sin."

ELAH
(I Kings 16:5-14)

THE KING WHO WAS MURDERED WHILE DRUNK

The sacred historian deemed a few lines quite enough to record the sordid story of the drunken sot known as Elah, Israel's fourth king, who reigned for two years. Shakespeare in *King Henry V* wrote of —

"Boundless intemperance
In nature is a tyranny, it has been
The untimely emptying of the happy throne
And fall of many kings."

While Elah's throne was far from happy, his "boundless intemperance" brought about his fall, even as it did in the case of another royal drunkard, King Belshazzar.

The son of Baasha was a bad king and conspicuous as a debauchee. While "drinking himself drunk," as the Bible puts it, he was conspired against and slain by Zimri, the ambitious military commander. Thus there came about as foretold by the prophet, the extirpation of the House of Baasha following the death of Elah. "The Baasha dynasty," says one commentator, "had its origin in a murder and it ended in a murder." The government had no stability. These revolutions illustrate the truth that, "they who take the sword shall perish by the sword."

The short-lived reign of Elah also recalls the ancient proverb, "As the whirlwind passes, so is the wicked no more" (Proverbs 10:25). When Zimri attacked Elah, the king was so drunk he never knew what hit him. Writing of the curse of drink Solomon says, "At the last it biteth like a serpent, and stingeth like an adder" (Proverbs 23:32).

ZIMRI
(I Kings 16:9-20)

THE KING WHO REIGNED FOR ONLY SEVEN DAYS

As captain of half the chariots under Elah, Zimri used his position to conspire against the king and was therefore a traitor and a usurper.

The record makes special mention of "the treason that he wrought." A proverb has it, "The king is not king by reigning, but by ruling according to law." Zimri recognized no law. A kingdom founded on treason and murder cannot possibly stand.

Zimri assumed the rule of Israel after his murder of Elah. Such a dastardly crime and conspiracy lacked the support of the people. As soon as news of the crime reached Gibbethon, the army raised Omri to the throne. In one short week this wicked king utterly destroyed the equally wicked house of Baasha. The phrase, "sins which he sinned," covers Zimri's whole life, not merely his 7 days' reign. Commenting on the constantly-recurring phrase, "walking in the way of Jeroboam," Ellicott observes that this indicates the historian's sense of the curse lying on the whole kingdom from its idolatry, which Zimri did not attempt to repudiate; unless, perhaps his conspiracy had clothed itself under pretense of a righteous zeal for the fulfillment of prophecy of Jehu (verses 3, 4), and had thrown off the religious pretense after the deed was done. For except in this way, he had no time for "walking in the way of Jeroboam."

In despair, Zimri set fire to his palace and perished in the flames his own hands had kindled, a desperate act having many parallels in history, the latest being the fire kindled by Adolph Hitler, the would-be world dictator in which he, and his newly-wed wife, were burned to ashes.

The ignominious end of Zimri's week-old reign remained as a blot even upon the blood-stained record of the deeds of violence ushering in the change of dynasties in the Northern Kingdom. Zimri's foul crime was abhorred even among arch plotters. With Zimri's death, the kingdom was split into two factions.

The name of Zimri passed into a proverb for unusual treachery. Jezebel called Jehu a second *Zimri*, meaning, a regicide like him who slew Baasha and likely to enjoy as brief a reign as he. "Had Zimri peace who slew his master?" asked Jezebel of Jehu (II Kings 9:31). Such a question inferred that success could not attend Jehu's enterprise: but Jehu had a divine warrant, Zimri had not. An express command from God alters the whole nature of the case and of the action.

OMRI
(I Kings 16:15-28; 20:34; Micah 6:16)

THE KING WHO EXCELLED IN SIN

Omri must have been a sinner extraordinary, seeing that the Bible gives him this reputation, "he did worse than all that were before him." One or two of the previous kings were bad enough, but here was one who was worse than the worst of them. This sixth king of

Israel does not occupy much space in the royal annals, but the little notice he has is not at all commendable.

As a popular captain of Zimri's hosts, Omri was unanimously chosen king by the army and became the founder of the third dynasty which continued for nearly 50 years. With the death of Zimri the nation was split into two factions. There was civil war between Omri and Tibri, lasting for 4 years, but on the latter's death Omri assumed the leadership of the whole nation. Bullinger remarks that "Omri began to reign *de jure* when he slew Zimri, in the 27th year of Asa; but only *de facto* on the death of Tibri, the usurper."

Omri stands out as one of the most important military kings of Israel. He manifested strength of character in his dealings with foreign powers and during his reign the country enjoyed a more settled government and prosperity than it had for 48 years. The renowned Moabite Stone, discovered in 1868, speaks of Omri's prowess as a commander:

"Omri, King of Israel . . . oppressed Moab many days because Chemosh was angry with his land. And his son succeeded him, and he who said, 'I will oppress Moab.'"

With a soldier's eye for a strategic position, Omri bought the hill of Samaria from Shemer and transferred his capital from Tirzah to Samaria, which continued as the capital of the nation until it was taken by Shalmaneser, when Israel was carried into captivity about 721 B.C. That the Northern Kingdom endured as long as it did was due largely to the strength of its capital. With the fall of Samaria, the nation fell.

Ben-hadad I besieged Samaria shortly after Omri built a city there and forced Omri to make "streets" in the city for the Syrians. Omri was the first king of Israel to pay tribute to the Assyrians under King Asur-nacirpal III. Down to the time of Sargon, Northern Israel was known to the Assyrians as "the land of the house of Omri."

What was looked upon as the wisest political move of the twelve-year reign of Omri, but which was one fraught with much evil for Israel, was the marriage of his son Ahab to Jezebel, daughter of Ethbaal of the Sidonians. Such an alliance was forged as a protection against the powers of the East.

Although Omri laid the foundation of a strong kingdom he failed to impart to it the vitalizing and rejuvenating force of a healthy spiritual religion. Micah speaks of the hopeless apostasy of Omri's reign that came about through the substitution of a foreign religion for the worship of Jehovah. If only with "his might that he shewed" there had been godliness of life, what a different record we would have had.

AHAB
(I Kings 16:29-22:40; II Chronicles 18)

THE KING WHO SOLD HIMSELF TO WORK WICKEDNESS

What a mixture of a man Ahab was! Some of the finer qualities were his — he was an able and prosperous monarch and no mean soldier, yet he deliberately sold himself to work wickedness. This most wicked of all the kings of Israel broke both the first and the second commandments, in teaching Israel to worship Baal instead of the Lord and in the establishment of an idol.

On the death of his father, Omri, Ahab, who reigned for 22 years, had the task of shaking off the Syrian yoke. In making Phoenician influence along with Baalism of prime importance in Israel, Ahab led the nation into those paths that hastened its downfall. This apostate monarch exceeded in wickedness and idolatry all the kings before him, and because of his evil ways brought about the total destruction of his house. Ahab's reign is given at length because of the important epoch in the *moral* history of the kingdom.

Ahab, the seventh king of Israel, was one of the strongest and at the same time one of the weakest of Israel's kings. Had he possessed a stronger nature he might have overcome some of the evils of his time. But "he failed to comprehend the greatness of Jehovah; he failed to stand for the highest justice and his sins are visited upon his posterity" (I Kings 22:19).

In the military field, Ahab had the opportunity of crushing the threatening power of Syria, but when Ben-hadad came to him in the garb of a suppliant, begging for mercy, Ahab received and treated him as a brother, a leniency for which the prophets denounced him. Doubtless Ahab thought that the king won as a friend, might be of greater service to Israel than a king slain. But what delusion awaited Ahab!

That Ahab was guilty of a short-sighted religious policy is seen in his alliance with Phoenicia. Jehoram married Ahab's daughter, Athaliah. Contact with Phoenicia resulted in Phoenician religion plaguing Israel. Baal, proud mistress of the seas and possessor of dazzling wealth, came to occupy an equal place with Jehovah, God of Israel. So a temple was built to Baal in Samaria. Strange though it may seem, Ahab continued to name his children after the true God.

Ahab's Phoenician wife, Jezebel, champion of foreign culture, a woman as imperious and able as she was vindictive and unscrupulous, was his undoing. The grand marriage with this clever and wealthy daughter of the king of Tyre, of the same great stock that founded Carthage, meant sorrow for the nation. The influence of a bad woman is the power "which destroyeth kings" (Proverbs 31:3). Infatuation for the royal harlot Cleopatra was the ruin of the mighty Roman general, Mark Antony, Shakespeare reminds us in the lines —

"O this false soul of Egypt!
Whose eye beck'd forth my wars, and call'd them home:
Whose bosom was crowned, my chief end —
Like a gipsy, hath, at fast and loose,
Beguiled me to the very heart of loss."

At the instigation of Jezebel, altars of Jehovah were torn down and false ones reared. She was also responsible for widespread religious persecution and hatred of the true prophets. Ahab connived in the determination of his unprincipled wife to destroy the religion of Jehovah, root and branch. Ahab himself outstripped his father's idolatry. In a later study, Jezebel has been dealt with in connection with the murder of Naboth. "Wrong religious principles have their counterpart in false ethical ideals and immoral civil acts."

Prominent in Ahab's reign is Elijah, who, like an accusing conscience, challenged the troubler of Israel. Three nameless prophets, as well as Michaiah, rebuked the king and pointed out his errors (I Kings 20:13, 26, 25). While Ahab humbled himself at the preaching of Elijah he yet returned to his idols (I Kings 22:6). He was made to realize that neither religious rights nor civil liberties can be trampled under foot without divine retribution, as the dramatic scene on Mount Carmel proves.

Not only was Ahab a splendor-loving monarch, he was a great military leader as well. He fortified the cities of Israel and defied the Syrian hosts, inflicting a triple defeat upon them. Lured by false prophets, but warned by the true prophet, Michaiah, Ahab took up the gauntlet against Syria, being joined by Jehoshaphat, king of Judah. This was the first time since David that all Israel and Judah stood united against a common foe. Although Ahab had previously spared Ben-hadad, yet it was in this battle that Ahab was killed by the Syrian king.

Ahab entered the battle in disguise but an arrow shot at random inflicted a mortal wound. With the fortitude of a hero he stayed in his chariot and died from his wound at sunset and, as prophesied, dogs licked up his blood. His body was taken to Samaria and buried there. As a false witness Ahab perished (Proverbs 21:28). Dr. James Cooper reminds us that —

God's dealings with Ahab illustrate His extreme unwillingness that any should perish (II Peter 3:9). He tried him every day, with warnings (I Kings 17:1); with an abnormal and predicted drought of three years and six months (18:5; James 5:17); by one of the most striking of all miracles (verse 38); by stern rebuke (21:19); by a gracious relaxation of His sentence on the first symptom of repentance (verse 29); and by a twofold military success of no ordinary kind (20). But divine overtures were of no avail, and the fear of the wicked came upon Ahab (Proverbs 10:24).

AHAZIAH
(I Kings 22:51; II Kings 1:18)

THE KING WHO PREFERRED BEELZEBUB TO GOD

The son of Ahab and Jezebel, eighth king of Israel, reigned about 2 years. Purposely he followed in the steps of his wicked parents and also emulated the older idolatry of Jeroboam. As to the character of this idolatrous king, he is represented as being weak and unfortunate. He belied the name he bore. *Ahaziah* means "God-sustained," but a good name does not insure a good character. He served and worshiped Baal and moved the God of Israel to anger.

Ahaziah followed three avenues of evil — his wicked father and equally-wicked mother, and the older idolatry of Jeroboam. In the second year of his reign the Moabites revolted against him and refused to pay the tribute which Ahab his father had extracted. "Moab rebelled against Israel after the death of Ahab." Ahaziah appears to have been too weak to offer resistance.

Ahaziah was dangerously injured by falling through the lattice in his upper apartment in Samaria. This accident resulted in a disease and a bed-ridden condition. The king sent messengers to Beelzebub, the god of Ekron, regarding his recovery. Elijah, divinely prompted, met the messengers and rebuked them for seeking information from an idol as if there were no God in Israel to contact. The prophet pronounced the doom of the king, which message was carried back to the infirm king, whose death speedily followed.

Ahaziah attempted to form an alliance with Jehoshaphat, King of Judah, to revive the ancient, maritime traffic between Ezion-Geber and Tarshish, but the ships were wrecked and the project failed (I Kings 22:48; II Chronicles 20:35-37). A comparison of these passages provides us with an illustration of the proverb, "If sinners entice thee, consent thou not" (Proverbs 1:10). Jehoshaphat built a new fleet, but Ahaziah refused to have any share in this second venture. Bitter experience had taught him the danger of evil communications (I Corinthians 13:33). If we partake of other men's sins, we shall also receive of their plagues. Affinity with the ungodly, however rich and great, is to be shunned (II Corinthians 6:14).

JORAM
(II Kings 1:17; 2; 6; 9)

THE KING WHO WAS KILLED BY AN ARROW THROUGH HIS HEART

As Ahaziah died childless, Joram, also called Jehoram, his brother, succeeded him as king of Israel. This next king in Israel's portrait gallery reigned for 11 years and continued to walk in the idolatrous course of Jeroboam and in the wicked ways of his evil parents. Although he put down, to some extent, the Baal worship his father Ahab so warmly sponsored, other forms of idolatry were practiced. Baal's status was removed but Baal worship outlived the half-hearted reform efforts of Jehoram.

This inconsistent king, who neglected the advice of Elisha, yet was curious to hear of his miracles (II Kings 3:1-3), never got away from the influence of his mother, Jezebel, who lived through his reign, and who remained as wholehearted in the worship of her false gods as her son was halfhearted in his desire for the true God. The removal of Baal's statue appears to have drawn Elisha the prophet to Jehoram, who deeply respected the warnings and miracles of the prophet. During Jehoram's reign the translation of Elijah took place, the healing of Naaman, the overthrow of the Syrian hosts, the terrible famine of Samaria when children were slain for food, and the raising of the Shunammite's son. The close alliance between Judah and Israel, begun by Ahab, continued through Jehoram's reign.

A crisis in Syria seemed a good time for Jehoram to achieve his father's ambition, namely, to recover Ramoth-gilead. Along with Ahaziah of Judah, Jehoram seized it, but in the conflict was wounded and retreated to Jezreel to recuperate. Jehu, his captain, was left at Ramoth-gilead to continue the war, but with characteristic haste, he set out for Jezreel and killed Jehoram on the very piece of land Ahab had taken by treachery from Naboth the Jezreelite, whose murder God had threatened to avenge on the family of Ahab (I Kings 21:19, 22).

The proverb about "whoso findeth a wife, findeth a good thing" did not hold good in the case of Jehoram, for his wife, the daughter of Ahab, wielded an influence on her husband in the wrong direction.

JEHU
(II Kings 9-10:36; Hosea 1:4)

The King Who Acted As a Bloody Executioner

During the 28 years of his reign, Jehu wallowed through a river of blood, and he proceeded with his bloody work as if he reveled in it. Scripture does not comment on the atrocities of Jehu, but appears to commend his zeal and to rejoice that what he began he accomplished. We cannot gloss over the ferocity of Israel's king, but view it in its right perspective. God, in the course of His providence, makes use of tyrants and wicked men as His instruments to execute His righteous judgments in the earth.

By divine commission, Elijah was instructed to anoint Jehu to be king over Israel. God, as the supreme king of Israel and the Lord of all souls, had the unquestionable right of choosing Jehu as His instrument of inflicting the threatened doom on the house of Ahab and the destruction of Baal worship. Elijah was translated before Jehu's anointing took place, so the duty devolved upon Elisha, who went to Ramoth-gilead and performed the sacred rite. It was God, however, and not Elisha who anointed Jehu as king. "Thus saith the Lord God of Israel, *I* have anointed thee king over the people of the Lord, even over Israel." The Ten Tribes, in spite of their corrupt and divided state, were still reckoned as the Lord's people (I King's 19: 1-8; II Kings 2:11; 19:1-10).

A furious driver, an index of his character, Jehu promptly devised measures to lend his sword to God. Alas, there is no trace of godly fear in the grim task of exterminating the enemies of the Lord! Jehu surrendered his sword to the Lord but not his heart, and in this represents those who are willing to fight for religion but not live by it. For his work of judgment, thoroughly fulfilled, Jehu received an earthly reward for his earthly service — his sons to the fourth generation sat upon the throne of Israel. His was the only dynasty to occupy the throne so long. But because of the lack of obedience to God, and the cruel fashion in which he carried out his bloody mission, Jehu became hateful to God and in the end was punished by God, who stripped him of his dominions eastward of Jordan.

Jehu, the son of Nimshi, first of all executed judgment on Ahab's house. At Naboth, he charged Joram with his gross iniquities and drawing his bow, which, as captain of the host he always carried with him, shot Joram through the heart. At Jehu's orders, the former king's body was thrown into the field of Naboth, taken so wickedly by Joram's father (II Kings 9:11-16).

Next, Jehu ordered Ahaziah to be slain, then drove hard to Jezreel to deal with Jezebel, as we have fully shown in our study of this female devil. Jehu then slew all Ahab's relations and friends, the great men of his court, and the false priests who were at Jezreel (II Kings 10:1-11). Departing for Samaria, about halfway Jehu met several members of the royal family of Judah, who because of their alliance with Ahab's kindred were pitilessly slaughtered.

As Jehu drove on he met a strange figure who possibly reminded the king of the great Elijah — it was Jonadab, the austere Arabian sectary, the son of Rechab, who imposed a rule of life on his descendants that they should drink no wine nor dwell in houses (Jeremiah 35). In him, Jehu's keen eye discovered a ready ally and so he said to him, "Come with me and see my zeal for the Lord." So together they entered Samaria, where Jehu at once ordered the execution of all the servants of his predecessor (II Kings 10:17; II Chronicles 22:8).

In his awful task of meting out judgment upon the House of Ahab, Jehu had carefully concealed his hostility to Baal-worship. Now, with deep craft, he professed his devotion to that form of idolatry and his zeal for it was more rigorous than that of Ahab (II Kings 10:19). He followed the sins of Jeroboam, yet proclaimed a solemn assembly for Baal, whose priests, prophets and worshipers were called to a great service in the vast temple reared for the idol by Ahab and Jezebel at Samaria. Jehu presided at the sacrifice, and at a given signal a band of soldiers entered and massacred the assembled host. "Thus he destroyed Baal out of Israel."

Reviewing the reign of Jehu we note how destitute of fear he was, fear of man or of God. His energy, promptitude, daring, unscrupulousness, and utter fearlessness enabled him to execute his rough work with relentless thoroughness. Gentler measures would have failed to eradicate Baal-worship from the nation. His professed "zeal for Jehovah" was largely a cloak for worldly ambition. Jehu "took no heed to walk in the law of the Lord God of Israel with all his heart." Any religious profession was a mere pretense, for he had no purity of worship in his heart.

Jehu, being stealthy, cruel and bloody, was unmerciful. Although called in the course of divine providence to execute God's righteous judgments among His enemies, Jehu, even as executioner, might have been merciful. A terrible parallel to Jehu's merciless attitude is given by Baird in *The Rise of the Huguenots*. In a letter written by the unhappy King Charles IX of France in 1572 to Pope Gregory XIII announcing the massacre of St. Bartholomew we read,

"Inflamed by a zeal for the Lord of Hosts . . . I have suddenly destroyed by a single slaughter all the heretics and enemies of my kingdom."

Though his act was approved by the pope, the whole Christian world now abhors the deed and refuses the apology.

The latter years of Jehu were clouded with misfortune, and the bloodshed in which his rule was founded provoked a reaction and the king's closing years were dark with trouble. Later on, Hosea pronounced the divine condemnation of Jehu's utter lack of mercy in his bloody work. "I will avenge the blood of Jezreel on the House of Jehu" (1:4). In cleaving to Jeroboam's sin, serving his own astute, political ends, being disobedient to the command of God, Jehu brought upon himself the judgment of God. It is a terrible thing to be the instrument of God in punishing or reproving others, if one's own heart and hands, by His grace, are not kept pure from sin.

JEHOAHAZ
(II Kings 13)

THE KING WHO, WHEN AFFLICTED, SOUGHT GOD

Too many people only pray when trouble overwhelms them. Forgotten in the good days, God is desperately sought when the shadows fall. And such is His grace that He responds to desperate prayers. Jehoahaz, another wicked king of Israel, who reigned for 17 years, was such an one who prayed when afflicted.

The king's story can be briefly told. When he succeeded his father, Jehu, Jehoahaz found a discouraged and humiliated people. Much territory had been lost in warfare to the Syrian king, Hazael (II Kings 10:32, 33). Israel also suffered from the continued hostility of Damascus (II Kings 13:3, 4). Added to this, Israel was up against the unfriendliness of the neighboring kingdom of Judah to any member of the House of Jehu.

During his reign, Jehoahaz was not only kept in subjugation to Hazael who forced him to reduce his armies and pay tribute, grievous oppression came from Ben-hadad, who made Israel "like dust in threshing." Added to these calamities was the sin of Jehoahaz himself, who brought on Israel Jehovah's anger more than in Jehu's time. Jehoahaz persevered in his father's idolatry, in calf-worship at Bethel and Dan. He also revived the cult of Asherah-worship around a sacred totem pole — a form of Canaanitish idolatry introduced by Ahab (I Kings 16:33).

As misfortunes overtook the king he "besought the Lord, and the Lord hearkened unto him." Prostrate before the Lord, Jehoahaz rent his garments, a sign of humiliation common in the Bible. The king's prayer under affliction was heard, God was moved to pity irrespective of Israel's merits and He promised them a "saviour" (II Kings 14:25, 26). But though the King's prayer did not meet with an immediate response, it was not ultimately ineffectual. Answer to prayer often comes when the petitioner is dead and gone. The promised "saviour" came in Joash, Jehoahaz' successor, who rescued the kingdom and re-established its affairs.

The lesson we learn from Jehoahaz is that the longer sin is indulged, the heavier the final reckoning — an accumulated entail of guilt descends (Exodus 20:5). Elisha, whose ministry extended through the reign of Jehoahaz, doubtless made his influence felt.

JEHOASH
(II Kings 13:10-25)
THE KING WHO BECAME A SAVIOUR

Although Jehoash, also called Joash, reigned for 16 years, the epitome of his reign is brief. He was raised to the throne of Israel during his father's lifetime. Two of his 16 years as king were in conjunction with his father. This brave yet wicked king was but one of the many who trod in the steps of evil Jeroboam, founder of the kingdom.

Yet this monarch's touching appeal to the dying Elisha is really beautiful and displayed the feelings of a heart not wholly turned aside from God. Somehow Jehoash favored the prophet whose long ministry of 66 years was now drawing to its close. Learning of the illness of the aged Elisha the young king hastened to Dothan and paid his respects to the great service the prophet had rendered. In a touching interview, the king affectionately exclaimed, "My father, my father, the chariots of Israel and the horsemen thereof," implying that Elisha himself had been in the place of chariots and horses to the kingdom.

The conversation about the three arrows illustrated the three deliverances Jehoash would accomplish for oppressed Israel. Thus the king became the "saviour" God had promised his father, Jehoahaz, for he recovered from Ben-hadad, king of Syria, all the cities which Hazael had taken from his father, and other parts usurped by Syrian monarchs. Wm. Shaw Caldicott says that —

> Jehoash did not long survive his crowning victory, but left a resuscitated state, and laid the foundation for a subsequent rule which raised Israel to the zenith of its power. Josephus gives Jehoash a high character for godliness, but, like each of his predecessors, he followed in the footsteps of Jeroboam I in permitting, if not encouraging, the worship of golden calves. Hence his conduct is pronounced as "evil" by the historian (II Kings 13:11).

At his death, Jehoash was deemed worthy of burial in the royal sepulchers of Israel's kings.

JEROBOAM II
(II Kings 14:23-29; Amos)

The King With a Tarnished Name

The sinister influence of Jeroboam, the son of Nebat, cast a lengthening shadow over the whole of the history of Israel. Successive kings were condemned for walking in the evil ways of the first Jeroboam, who fashioned the Ten Tribes into a kingdom. Evidently Jehoash, or Joash, had deep regard for the original Jeroboam, seeing he gave his son such a name.

A study of the king before us proves that often great political events are passed by. The reign of Jeroboam, covering over 40 years, longer than that of any other king of Israel, is compressed into a few sentences. On the other hand, details of private life are dwelt upon, because they display those things which are of most esteem in God's sight, and which it is most important for us to know (Ruth; I Kings 17).

Jeroboam II, son of Joash, was the thirteenth king of Israel and the fourth of Jehu's dynasty, who came into power on the crest of the wave of prosperity that followed the crushing of the supremacy of

Damascus by his father. Jeroboam, young and ambitious, resolved on a war of retaliation against Damascus, and on further conquests, and the condition of the eastern world, namely, the struggle of Assyria against Armenia, was in Jeroboam's favor. Thus, he was one of the "saviours" God promised Israel in the reign of Jehoahaz.

Not only did the king deliver Israel from Syria and take its capital (Amos 1:3-5; 6:14), he also fulfilled a further prophecy of Jonah regarding "the restoration of the coasts of Israel from the entering in of Hamath unto the sea of the plain" (14:23-29). Amos warned Israel not to be too elated over Hamath, "for that shall be the foe's starting point to afflict you." Under Jeroboam, the kingdom attained its greatest glory.

The long reign of Jeroboam gave him time to collect huge tributes from his greatly increased territory. Samaria now had full coffers enabling Jeroboam to turn hovels into "houses of hewn stone" (Amos 5:11). The king built both a winter and summer palace for himself. Amos gives us a vivid picture of the luxury the rich enjoyed (6:14-16). But plenty and penury existed side by side. The poor of the land suffered utmost distress, so much so that a man was sold into slavery for a pair of shoes (Amos 2:6; 8:6).

The lengthy period of prosperity and respite from Syrian hardships should have led Israel to repentance, but they repented not and a speedy and final judgment followed. Calf-worship, as an engine of state policy, still remained at Bethel. Amid such wealth and social organization, religion of a kind flourished but ritual substituted for righteousness. Amos denounced the substitution of the one for the other (5:21). Temples, with their false worship, flourished at Gilgal and Beersheba (Amos 4:6; 5:5; 8:14).

Toward the end of his reign Jeroboam decided to add greater splendor and dignity to the central shrine at Bethel consistent with the increased wealth of the nation. Amos was commissioned to go there and declare that the sanctuary would be laid waste and that God would raise a sword against the House of Jeroboam. Amaziah, the priest, exaggerated the prophecy of Amos regarding the king's punishment (Amos 7:9-13). Large extensions of territory acquired by Jeroboam were prophesied earlier by Jonah (II Kings 14:25).

Jeroboam died after reigning for 41 years and was buried in state and entombed with the other kings of Israel. He was succeeded by his weak son, Zachariah, after an interregnum of some 11 years. The expression of Amaziah, "the land is not able to bear all Amos' words," implies a critical state of the country which eventuated in actual anarchy for some time after Jeroboam's death, resulting in the rapid downfall of the kingdom.

Thinking of the added territory to Israel's domain which Jeroboam made possible, a Japanese proverb seems somewhat apt —
> "He that steals gold is put in prison;
> He that steals land is made a king."

ZACHARIAH
(II Kings 10:30; 14:29; 15:8-12)

The King Who Was Publicly Assassinated

Zachariah, or Zechariah, the son and successor of Jeroboam II, was the last in descent from Jehu. At his death, the House of Jehu became extinct as foretold. The king lived just long enough to fulfill God's promise to Jehu (II Kings 10:30; 13:8). R. K. Harrison says that "With the death of Zachariah, the dynasty of Jehu came to an end and ushered in a period of civil unrest and strife, similar to that which marked the beginning of the House of Jehu."

Zachariah, who reigned for only 6 months, succeeded to a magnificent inheritance, not only to the kingdom of the Ten Tribes, but of the Syrian state of Damascus which his father had subdued. Alas, in his unusual wealth and dignity of his position lay his peril! Not many hands are steady enough to carry a full cup.

The days of Zachariah must have been clouded by the remembrance that from prophecy he knew that he was the fourth generation of Jehu to sit on the throne of Israel and that Amos had declared that the sword would rise against the House of Jeroboam. Thus, after only 6 confused months on the throne for Zachariah, Shallum, a claimant to the throne, conspired against Zachariah and slew him in public. The people evidently sympathized with the crime. It was a symptom of the rapidly-increasing corruption of morals which allowed the people to look on with indifference as their king was murdered. Probably Hosea, who prophesied in Zachariah's time, alluded to this assassination when he referred to kings given and taken away (13:10, 11).

In his brief reign the king gave support to the illicit worship Jeroboam instituted. He upheld calf-worship, which had become the religion of the state. Another of the bad kings of Israel, Zachariah did evil in the sight of the Lord.

SHALLUM
(II Kings 15:13-15)

The King Who Was Murdered After a Month's Reign

Shallum, who ascended the throne by conspiracy and murder, was himself slain and illustrates the retribution law so prominent in Scripture (Matthew 26:52; Galatians 6:7). All we know of Shallum is that he was a son of Jabesh and that he reigned for a month of days, as the margin expresses it. When he murdered Zachariah and seized the kingdom he fulfilled the prophecy that Jehu's dynasty should last only to the fourth generation.

Shallum was killed by Menahem, a general of Zachariah's army quartered near to Samaria, who, when he heard of the murder of Zachariah, marched to the capital determined to seize the throne, which he did, crushing all opposition to his regime. How gory is the history of Israel, with its successive reigns founded on bloodshed!

MENAHEM
(II Kings 15:16-22)

THE KING WHO WAS BAD AND EXCEEDING CRUEL

Menahem was another wicked sovereign and terribly cruel. His character was destitute of true kingly qualities. This son of Gadi was the sixteenth king of Israel, reigned for 10 years, and was a strong and determined ruler, who with a firm hand, enforced his occupancy of the throne. "Whatever military ambitions he might have entertained were crushed by a resurgence of Assyrian power," says R. K. Harrison. Menahem deemed it wise to become a tributary to Tiglath-pileser III, in whose annals his victory is described thus —

"As for Menahem, terror overwhelmed him . . . he fled and submitted to me . . . silver, coloured woollen garments, linen garments . . . I received as his tribute."

Menahem was guilty of savage cruelty, for he smote and ripped up the women with child, copying the unscrupulous cruelty of the Syrian Hazael (II Kings 8:12). In religion he departed not from the sins of Jeroboam. Perhaps at the beginning of his reign he was guided by better principles (Zechariah 11:4-8). He attempted, however, no reform in national religion. Like all his predecessors he followed the worship of the golden calves, and like them incurred the heavy censure of the historian. Hosea and Amos depict Israel's demoralization at this time. Unlike two or three other kings, Menahem died in peace.

PEKAHIAH
(II Kings 15:23-26)

THE KING WHO WAS SLAIN BY A MILITARY GROUP

It was certainly true of many of the kings of Israel that heads wearing crowns were uneasy. Within two years of his accession, Pekahiah, son and successor of Menahem, was foully murdered by a military group. Thus he was the seventh king of Israel to meet death by violence. The others were Nadab, Elah, Tibni, Jehoram, Zachariah and Shallum.

Pekahiah was unable to appease the Assyrians as his father had done. When he came to the throne "he was enveloped in the danger which always accompanies the successor of an exceptionally strong ruler, in a country where there is not a settled law of succession." It is quite possible that Pekahiah preferred his father's policy of tributary vassalage to the plan of resistance to Assyrian power.

In the brief record of Pekahiah's short reign nothing is said of his personal character apart from the fact that like his predecessors he adhered to the system of false worship introduced by Jeroboam I. The chief conspirator against Pekahiah was Pekah, his adjutant, who, with 50 Gileadites penetrated into the palace and slew the king and his bodyguards, Argob and Arieh. Such an act of treachery and violence is in accordance with all the prophet Hosea tells us of the internal condition of Israel at that time. "They . . . devour their judges; all their kings are fallen" (7:7). Josephus accounts for the short two-year reign of Pekahiah because he imitated the cruelty of his father.

PEKAH
(II Kings 15:25, 27-38)

The King Who Was Humbled But Still Defiant

This eighteenth king of Israel, when he seized the reins of power by murdering his predecessor, endeavored to restore the political fortunes of Israel which had suffered much by civil wars and foreign exactions (II Kings 14:19-31) and joined forces with others against Assyria. Allied with Rezin of Damascus, Pekah moved against Jotham of Judah (II Kings 15:37, 38) and slew 120,000 in one day. But the King's plot with Rezin to set aside the line of David and raise a Syrian, "a son of Tabeal," to the throne of Judah was frustrated according to God's purpose and promise (Isaiah 7:1-16).

All the schemes of this son of Remaliah, who reigned for 20 years, met with disaster. Left with but a third of his kingdom, Pekah, unpopular with his subjects, was humbled but still defiant. A plot was formed to assassinate Pekah, and Hoshea, whom Tiglath-pileser had made a vassal, was the tool chosen to slay Pekah (II Kings 15:30). The following interesting record is found in the Assyrian annals —

"Paqaha (Pekah) their king I deposed and I placed Ausi (Hoshea) over them as king . . . talents of silver as tribute I received from them."

A noticeable absence from the biography of Pekah is any reference to the religious conduct of the king. Evidently he followed the wicked course of previous kings and the historian felt Pekah's influence was beneath notice. Isaiah, who ministered during the reign of Pekah, has several references to him (7:1-10:4).

HOSHEA
(II Kings 15:30; 17)
THE KING WHO WAS A WILY DIPLOMATIST

Hoshea, the son of Elah, and the nineteenth and last king of Israel, was actually a satrap of Assyria and only held his throne on good behavior. It was a time of social revolution and dynastic change, the last five kings being murdered, with Hoshea himself as one of the murderers. The kingdom Hoshea ruled over was only a shadow of its former self, seeing Tiglath-pileser had already carried into captivity several of the northern tribes. The prophet Hosea gives us a clear picture of the politics of the time and of the altered condition of things (4-14).

It was over a shrunken and weakened kingdom that Hoshea was placed as the viceroy of a foreign power. When Tiglath-pileser died and his son Shalmaneser V succeeded him, Hoshea, an intensely patriotic individual, sought to discontinue payment of tribute to Assyria and formed secret affiliations with Sabacho, King of Egypt. For this treasonable action Shalmaneser bound Hoshea in prison (II Kings 17:4-16), and beseiged Samaria for almost 3 years. Before it fell, Shalmaneser was succeeded by Sargon II, who overthrew the Israelite monarchy and carried the northern tribes to Assyria. With characteristic bombast Sargon said —

"I beseiged and captured Samaria, carrying 27,290 of the people who dwelt therein. Fifty chariots I gathered for myself and the rest of their wealth I let the soldiers take."

With his captivity Hoshea disappears from Biblical history.

The invasion of Samaria and banishment of the king are graphically described by Hosea. "Her king is cut off as foam from the water" (10:7). Isaiah also depicted the quick absorption of Samaria by Shalmaneser and Sargon, "As the hasty fruit before the summer, which when he that looked upon seeth, while it is yet in his hand, he eateth it up" (28:4).

Hoshea, a wily diplomatist who reigned for 9 years, is spoken of as doing "evil in the sight of the Lord, yet not as the kings of Israel that were before him." The qualified phrase does not mean that he was a high-principled man or of irreproachable character. It simply implies that he did not give official sanction and prominence to calf-worship as his 18 predecessors had done. Tiglath-pileser carried off the golden calf from Dan, and Shalmaneser the other from Beersheba, so that there was not the same temptation to this idolatrous form of worship (Hosea 10:6).

Says W. Shaw Caldicott, "Such was the ignominious end of a line of kings, not one of whom had, in all the vicissitudes of two and a quarter centuries, been in harmony with the theocratic spirit, or realized that the true welfare and dignity of the state lay in the un-alloyed worship of Jehovah." The historian dwells upon the moral causes of the catastrophic captivity (II Kings 17:7-41). God's claim to the full allegiance of the people was based upon the fact that He had emancipated them from the Egyptian bondage. But His re-deemed ones, particularly the Ten Tribes, had become guilty of two national sins —

1. Gross idolatry — the worship of other gods
2. A heathenish mode of the worship of God under the form of a bullock as originated by Jeroboam I.

With the captivity, the distinctive character of the nation was lost. While the land was not entirely depopulated of Jews, those remain-ing lost their distinctive existence through mixture with their heathen neighbors. A remnant from Judah and the Ten Tribes returned from captivity under Zerubbabel, Ezra and Nehemiah. The great, national restoration of all Jews is yet to be fulfilled. Since the termination of Jewish monarchies, the people have been "without a king" (Hosea 3:4).

Going back over the history of the Northern Kingdom we can enumerate the following facts:

While it is said that some of the kings of Judah "did right in the sight of the Lord," not once is this said of any King of Israel. Of only one, Jehoahaz, is it said that he "besought the Lord," and that under deep pressure and at a time of real distress.

Idolatry from first to last characterized the reigns of the kings of Israel. The oft-recurring expression, "walked in the ways of Jero-boam," proves how Israel's first king gave character to the kingdom during its entire history. Tracing the decline and fall of idolatrous Israel, a striking illustration is afforded of the fearful consequences of sin. Zachariah is killed by Shallum — Shallum is murdered by Menahem — Pekahiah is assassinated by Pekah.

The longest reign was that of Jeroboam II, and the shortest reign Zimri's — the former reigned 41 years, and the latter 7 days. It will be observed that two kings bore the name of *Jeroboam*. Other paral-lel names to be noted are —

The *fifth* king of Judah and the *ninth* king of Israel were both named *Jehoram;* the *sixth* king of Judah and the *eighth* king of Israel were named *Ahaziah;* the *seventeenth* king of Judah and the *eleventh* king of Israel were called *Jehoahaz;* the *eighth* king of Judah and the *twelfth* king of Israel were called *Jehoash.*

The books of Kings specially detail the history of the kings of Israel, made up of eight dynasties, the founders of which were Jero-boam, Baasha, Omri, Jehu, Shallum, Menahem, Pekah and Hoshea.

The kingdom of Israel, or that of the Ten Tribes, existed for about

250 years under 19 kings and came to an end with the destruction of its capital, Samaria, by the Assyrians about 722 B.C.

The overthrow of Judah took place about 130 years after the end of the Northern Kingdom. During this period two great efforts were made to turn the people from idolatry. Repentance, however, was not very deep and in spite of the ministry of the prophets, Isaiah and Jeremiah, the kingdom ran on to its doom. Samuel witnessed the outgoing of the theocracy *and* the incoming of the monarchy; Jeremiah saw the outgoing of the monarchy and the incoming of the dependency; and Paul saw the outgoing of Judaism and the incoming of Christianity.

While the kings of the latter period of the north and the south were Jews, they only held their throne by the will of foreign powers — Egypt and Babylon. The great heathen monarchs were Shalmaneser, Sennacherib, Merodach-baladan, Esar-haddon, Pharaoh-necho and Nebuchadnezzar, records of whom are to be found in the British Museum.

The following table given by Fausset in his *Bible Encyclopaedia* sets forth the contemporary reigns of the kings of the two kingdoms. Chronological difficulties of Scripture must be borne in mind in dealing with the length of these respective kingdoms.

DURATION OF REIGN IN YEARS	KINGS OF ISRAEL		DATE B.C. (USSHER)	KINGS OF JUDAH
22	I	⎧Jeroboam I	975	Rehoboam
			958	Abijah
			955	Asa
2		⎩Nadab	954	
24	II	⎧Baasha	953	
2		⎩Elah	930	
7 days	III	Zimri	929	
12	IV	⎧Omri	929	
22		Ahab	918	
			914	Jehoshaphat
2		Ahaziah	898	
12		Jehoram	896	
			892	Jehoram
			845	Ahaziah
28		⎧Jehu	884	
			878	Jehoash
17		⎩Jehoahaz	856	

16		Jehoash	841	
	V		839	Amaziah
41		Jeroboam II	825	
			810	Azariah or
6 mo.		Zachariah	773	Uzziah
1 mo.	VI {	Shallum	772	
10		Menahem	772	
	VII {	Pekahiah	761	
2				
20	VIII {	Pekah	759	
			758	Jotham
			742	Ahaz
9	IX {	Hoshea	730	
			726	Hezekiah

241 yrs.	Samaria }		
7 mo.	taken {	721	
7 da.		698	Manasseh

(Judah, from the first foundation of the kingdom, lasted 487 years. The discrepancy between the sum of the dates 254 and that of the reigns 241 odd (Clinton) is due probably to *round numbers being used by the writers for exact ones, not specifying the months.* Inter-reigns too must have taken place, *e.g.* eight years between Pekah and Hoshea.)

643	Amon
641	Josiah
610	Jehoahaz
610	Jehoiachim
599	Jehoiakin
599	Zedekiah
588]	Jerusalem
or	
587]	taken.

As Israel possessed Canaan as their Promised Land, it may prove helpful at this point briefly to survey what the Old Testament records of

CANAAN AND ITS KINGS

Canaan was about the center of the then known civilized world when God placed His people there, to whom He had committed His Oracles, that they might be in an advantageous position to give divine instruction to the world (Psalm 147:19, 20; Romans 3:2).

Canaan received its name from a son of Ham and brother of Migraim or Egypt (Genesis 10:6), and is the general designation of the nations inhabiting the country from the Mediterranean on the west to Jordan on the east, prior to Israel's occupation of the land. R. K. Harrison says, "The boundaries of Canaan suggested in Genesis (10:19) included all the territory which lay to the west of Jordan between Gaza and Sidon, although the Amarna letters thought of Canaan primarily in terms of the Phoenician coast." Canaanites are described as drinking by the sea and along the side of the Jordan (Numbers 13:29). *Canaan* is used in the Old Testament in an extended sense to denote the whole of Palestine west of Jordan (Genesis 12:5, etc.). Canaanites first settled in Palestine, in the reign of Tyre and Sidon. From there they spread throughout the land. Having Amorite and Hittite founders, it is stated to be "the land of the Canaanites" (Exodus 16:3), also as "the land of the Hittites" (Joshua 1:4). Isaiah speaks of Hebrew as "the language of Canaan" (19:18).

For a time Canaan was a province of Egypt and at another time, formed part of the Babylonian Empire. The word *Canaan*, means "a servant of servants," that is, the most abject slave (I Kings 19:20, 21). God said, "Cursed be Canaan," meaning his posterity (Genesis 9:25), for He foresaw their wickedness which began in their father Ham. Such a curse did not affect individuals so long as they continued righteous, for Melchizedek and Abimelech appear to have been Canaanites (Genesis 14:18-20; 15:16; 20:6).

The religious beliefs and deities of Babylon were linked to those of the primitive Canaanite. The gods and goddesses of Babylon permeated the land. People "served their gods upon the high mountains, hills and under every green tree" (Deuteronomy 12:2). "As the myths of ancient Ugarit indicate, the religion of the Canaanite peoples was a crude and debased form of ritual polytheism," says Harrison. "It was associated with sensuous fertility-cult worship of a particularly lewd and orgiastic kind, which proved to be more influential than any other nature-religion in the Near East. Sodom and Gomorroah were in the very midst of Canaan, a fact that aggravated the guilt of the Canaanites, who, in Joshua's time took no warning from their punishment to avoid their sins (Genesis 19:23-25; Leviticus 18:24, 25; Joshua 10:40)."

While Canaan was not an empire, it had its "kings" who were obliged to pay tribute to surrounding powerful nations like Babylonia. The territories over which these Canaanite kings ruled were small indeed, not much larger than villages. For example, Ai, where Joshua was defeated trying to take it and then conquered, was made up of only 12,000 (Joshua 8:25). Canaan was not much larger than Britain or a third of the state of Texas. Yet, although its kings were only pint-size, they deserve a place in our over-all study of Bible kings.

It is to the two historical books of Joshua and Judges that we are indebted for our information of the identification and destruction of the kings of Canaan, the majority of which must be placed in the list of the Bible's unnamed kings, of which they are many (see Revelation 17:10; 21:24, etc.). Let us have a look at these kings, as they appear in the books of Joshua and Judges.

Adoni-zedec, King of Jericho, (2:1; 10:1)

Disturbed by the report that Joshua's spies had searched his territory, this king, along with his people, trembled at the thought of an
Israelitish invasion. King and people were destroyed and the city
razed to the ground, and a curse pronounced upon any seeking to
rebuild it.

All the *kings of the Amorites* and the *kings of the Canaanites* are
grouped together (5:1), seeing that these two principal nations were
representatives of the rest. Then the *king of Ai* was hanged on a tree
until eventide, just as the *king of Jerusalem* died (8:2, 29; 10:1). Ellicott suggests that possibly "both were hanged on the same tree, and
were exhibited, each in turn, as the curse of God" (Deuteronomy
21:22, 23). But when we read of this treatment of the enemies of
Joshua, we cannot but be reminded of the greater Joshua, who fulfilled the curse of God in His own Person, and made a show of "the
principalities and powers" by triumphing over them in His Cross (see
Esther 9:10, 13).

*The kings of the Hittites, the Amorites, the Canaanites, the Periz-
zites, the Hivites* and *the Jebusites* are mentioned as uniting for the
last struggle with the victorious Joshua (9:1-12). Contrast their "one
accord" with that of the praying disciples (Acts 1:14). The alliance
of the five kings presents a dramatic episode (10:1-27). These kings
were:

Adoni-zedec, king of Jericho
Japhia, king of Lachish
Debir, king of Eglon
Hohan, king of Hebron
Paran, king of Jarmuth.

A hard and bloody battle was fought with this assemblage of kings,
but the miracle of the sun standing still aided Joshua in a complete
victory over his enemies. The combined forces of the kings were
wiped out and the five fleeing kings were caught hiding in a cave,
in which, after being hung on separate trees, they were entombed
(10:6-27).

The same day *the king of Makkedah* shared a similar fate (10:18).
The king of Libnal and *the king of Debir* also fell to Joshua (10:30,
39, 42). Horam, king of Gezer, who came to help Lachish was slain
(10:33). Then we come to another confederacy of kings in Joshua's
path of conquest —

Jabin, king of Hazor, also king of the Canaanites (11:1).

Some writers distinguish between the Jabin — a dynastic name like
Pharaoh, Herod — of Hazor, and of Canaan (Judges 4:2, 23, 24). In
both places we have a Jabin; in both there are subordinate kings

(11:29; Judges 5:19); in both, chariots are prominent; in both the general outline of circumstances is the same; and the same names occur in the list of conquered kings (11:21, 22). In the fight with Jabin of Canaan the going was hard, or "became heavier and heavier in its pressure." The battle at Kishon was the beginning of a complete deliverance of Israel from the yoke of the Canaanites. When Deborah sang in her song of triumph, "Hear, O ye kings" (Judges 5:5), she may have referred to the kings allied with Jabin. There were no kings or princes in Israel at that time. Thus the appeal might have been to "the kings of the earth" as in Psalm 2:10.

JOBAB, king of Madon, along with *the king of Shimron,* and *the king of Achshaph,* and the kings of the mountains, plains and valleys (Joshua 11:1-5), met together or "assembled by appointment," as the Hebrew expresses it, to plan a campaign against their common foe, Israel. But at the waters of Meron they were utterly defeated. Hazor, head of several kingdoms with their kings, experienced the worst punishment (Joshua 11:10-15). These little kings were taken and slain in a battle lasting for some seven years. Some of the kings who lost their possessions to Israel are named:

SIHON, king of the Amorites (see Deuteronomy 2:31, 37). He was king of the Amorites by birth, but king of Heshbon only by conquest (Judges 11:19; Joshua 12:1-7).

OG, king of Bashan (Deuteronomy 3:3-9; Joshua 13:31). These were the two kings of the Amorites whom God drove out of the land (Joshua 24:12).

In recording the territory he had conquered, Joshua enumerates 31 kings subjugated by Israel (12:8-34), with their order of conquest. Two kings are reckoned to Moses and 31 to Joshua, giving a total of 33 (Joshua 12:7, 24). The two slain by Moses are individually represented as far greater than any who are named in Joshua. In the Psalms, we have Sihon, king of the Amorites, and Og, king of Bashan (Joshua 24:12) expressed by name and the rest only summarized as "all the kingdom of Canaan" (Psalm 135:11, 12; 136:19, 20). Joshua's list of conquered kings reads —

The king of Jericho	The king of Libnah
The king of Ai	The king of Adullam
The king of Jerusalem	The king of Makkedah
The king of Hebron	The king of Bethel
The king of Jarmuth	The king of Tappuah
The king of Lachish	The king of Hepher
The king of Eglon	The king of Aphek
The king of Gezer	The king of Lasharon
The king of Debir	The king of Madon
The king of Geder	The king of Hazor
The king of Hormah	The king of Shimron-meron

The king of Arad
The king of Taanach
The king of Megiddo
The king of Kedesh
The king of Jokneam of Carmel

The king of Achshaph
The king of Dor in the coast of
Dor
The king of the nations of Gilgal
The king of Tirzah

This array of "thirty and one" unnamed kings must be added to other unknown sovereigns of the Bible. Scripture is silent on who they were and facts connected with their lives and respective reigns. Perhaps they did nothing worthy of being mentioned by name and so pass before us unknown, unsung, unhonored. It will be noted that the "dukes" (13:21) are the anointed leaders, called "kings" (Numbers 31:8).

Recounting the benefits and the victories God had made possible for Israel, Joshua speaks of the fate that had overtaken BALAK, king of Moab, when he warred against Israel (Joshua 24:9). Just when he led an army against Israel we are not told.

Coming to the book of Judges, a period when there was no king in Israel, every man doing what was right in his own eyes, we have the sad story of God's people given over to their enemies because of their departure from God. Yet when they were truly repentant, God raised them up judges, or saviours, to deliver them. Of kings, in this historical book, we have —

ADONI-BEZEK (1:5-7)

This is more of a title than a name, and means "Lord of Bezek," as *Adoni-zedek* means "Lord of Zedek" (Joshua 10:1). The punishment meted out to this cruel Canaanite king made him realize that a divine retribution had overtaken him. "The Lord God of recompenses shall surely requite thee" (see Jeremiah 51:56; I Samuel 15:33; Judges 15:11; Exodus 18:11; Proverbs 5:22; Matthew 7:2; Galatians 6:7; James 2:13; for further illustration of retribution).

The 70 kings Adoni-zedek mutilated (Josephus says there were 72) were possibly rulers of small towns the king had taken in the extension of the territory of Bezek. These were petty kings like those we have already mentioned. "The title, 'King,' was freely given to every petty Emir, and even to village Sheykhs." These conquered kings had been treated with cruel insolence, like dogs eating fragments thrown them (Matthew 15:27). Now Adoni-bezek suffers the same fate, and experienced that an

"Even-handed justice
Commends the ingredients of the poisoned chalice
To our own lips."

Ellicott gives us the suggestion that the cutting of the king's thumbs would prevent his ever again drawing a bow or wielding a sword, and the cutting of his toes would deprive him of that speed which was so essential for an ancient warrior. Further, any of these mutilations would be sufficient to rob the king of his throne since ancient races never tolerated a king who had any personal defects.

CHUSHAN-RISHATHAIM, king of Mesopotamia (Judges 3:8-11)

Many scholars give us *Cushan* for "Chushan," a derivation of "Cush," a son of Nimrod (Genesis 10:8). *Cushan* only occurs in Habakkuk 3:11, "I saw the tents of Cushan," or *Ethiopia*, as the margin puts it. The king's name may be more of a term of hatred than an actual name, seeing it means "Cushan of the double wickedness." The Spirit-anointed Othniel overcame the long oppression of the king of Mesopotamia and delivered Israel from its bondage. The LXX translates Mesopotamia as "Syria of the rivers," namely the rivers Euphrates and Tigris.

EGLON, king of Moab (Judges 3:12-30, see I Samuel 12:9)

We read that "the Lord strengthened" this heathen king against His own people for the reason that they had done evil in His sight. Eglon, successor of Balak and the king to whom Samuel refers (I Samuel 12:9), had a peculiar name. It means "fat bullock" (Psalm 22:12; Amos 4:1), and like "Cushan-Rishathaim," may be a term of hatred or scorn, rather than a name. This corpulent oriental monarch was treacherously slain by Ehud's left-handed dagger thrust. His death was exactly similar to that of Henry III of France, by the Dominican monk, Jacques Clement, who, in a deceitful fashion came before the king. Ellicott quotes the record of the foul deed from Guigot's *History of France.*

> On Tuesday, Aug. 1, at 8 a.m. the King was told that a monk desired to speak with him. The King ordered him to be admitted. The monk entered, having *in his sleeve a knife unsheathed.* He made a profound reverence to the King, who had just got up, and had nothing on but a dressing-gown, and presented him despatches from the Comte de Brienne, saying, that *he had further orders to tell the King privately something of importance.* Then the King ordered those who were present to retire, and began reading the letter. The monk, seeing his attention engaged, *drew his knife from his sleeve, and drove it right into the King's small gut below the naval,* so far that he left the knife in the hole.

Another *king of Moab* was the one David encountered when he took refuge in the Cave of Adullam (I Samuel 33:3, 4). It was natural for David to seek hospitality among his kinfolk in Moab. His grandmother, Ruth, was a Moabitess.

MESHA was also a king of Moab, who, being a sheepmaster, rendered to Jehoram the king of Israel, a tribute of 100,000 lambs, and 100,000 rams, with wool (II Kings 3:4, 26; see Isaiah 16:1).

Then a further *king of Moab* was among the group of five kings who were charged to subject themselves to Babylonia (Jeremiah 27:3).

ZEBAH and ZALMUNA are spoken of as kings of Midian. The historian, Josephus, refers to them as "leaders" and calls OREB and ZEEB, not "princes" but "kings" (Judges 8). The two Midian kings and their armies were routed by Gideon. It was in this connection that the warrior, Gideon, was likened unto a "king" (Judges 8:18), who added to his other gifts a tall, commanding presence which was always impressive in those times (I Samuel 10:24; 16:6, 7). Gideon refused the title of king, and even ruler (8:23).

"One so fair I never saw with my eyes, nor so stately, for he is like a King."

Iliad

Gideon was a king in all but name and was also guilty of polygamy as practiced by kings against the divine decree (Deuteronomy 17:19; see Judges 10:3; 12:9).

ABIMELECH, king of Shechem (Judges 9)

While we rightly call Saul the first *king* of the United Kingdom of Israel, Abimelech was the first Israelite to bear such a title. It is doubtful, however, whether his royalty was recognized beyond the limits of Ephraim. This son of Gideon, known as "The Bramble King," followed the customs of oriental despots of anticipating conspiracies among members of their own family and near relatives. Polygamous households were characterized by lack of affection and conspicuous jealousy. So Abimelech set a fatal precedent when he slew 70 of his father's house (see I Kings 15:29; II Kings 10:7; II Kings 11:1; 15). He killed them on a stone or rock and was himself brought down to death by a stone (20:53). "The murderer of his brothers" on one stone, after a reign of 3 years, "is slain by a stone flung on his head, and the treacherous idolaters are treacherously burnt in the temple of their idol."

Other monarchs bearing the name of Abimelech, which was more of a royal title than a personal name, are —

ABIMELECH, king of Philistia (Genesis 20) a contemporary of Abraham, who lied to the king about his wife Sarah and who was reproved by the heathen king.

ABIMELECH, king of the Philistines, probably the son of the former Abimelech who had relations with Isaac who followed his father, Abraham, in lying about his wife (Genesis 26) and who also was upbraided by the king.

ABIMELECH, king of Gath (I Samuel 21:10-22:1; Psalm 34). This king, also known by his personal name, Achish (I Samuel 27:2, 3), is the one with whom David sought refuge during his exile (I Samuel 27).

Jephthah sent messengers to *the king of Ammon* (11:14), to *the king of Edom,* (11:17), to *the king of Moab* (11:17), without much avail (see Numbers 20:14 for the letter of Moses to KADESH, king of Edom). NAHASH, another king of Ammon (I Samuel 12:12), mentioned by Samuel in his stern rebuke of Israel, was the barbarous king who attacked Jabesh-Gilead just after Saul's election as king of Israel (I Samuel 11:2). NAHASH, king of the Ammonites, who befriended David, was likely a son or grandson of the former Nahash (II Samuel 10:2) whom Saul conquered.

IX

The Earth and Its Perfect Monarch

During the history of the world mighty empires have arisen and vanished, leaving nothing save ruins. Emperors, kings and dictators have appeared, wise yet wicked, dynamic yet destructive, and have passed from the earthly scene, leaving for posterity nothing save a tarnished name. But a Potentate is coming who will be the perfection of all true kingly virtues. A few of the kings of earth have been noble, righteous and beneficent, but the Bible speaks of One who outshines them, and of whom we can truly say, "There has never been His like." The reign of earthly kings is short and circumscribed. The reign of God's King is to be universal and eternal.

No one with an honest and open mind can study the Christology of the Bible without being impressed with the revelation of the Kingship of the Lord Jesus Christ. His Messiahship is attested to by prophets and apostles. His prominent title as *Messiah* betokens His appearance on the earth as God's anointed King. While extreme modernists may deny the direct predictions of Christ as King, those who love and obey Him have no difficulty in accepting such predictions as ideal representations of Him as earth's ideal Sovereign, who is to reign in righteousness. The essence of Messianic belief was the coming of a personal Deliverer who would unite in Himself the Old Testament offices of Prophet, Priest and King, each of whom was raised up in Jewish history. In all three offices, Christ is manifested as their perfection, and all spring from His Person and His work. He is the *Prophet* who reveals — the *Priest* who offers and intercedes — the *King* who rules. And in Him all three offices commingle. He rules by His sacrifice and His teaching — He reveals by His Kingship and life.

As it was God's purpose to set up a kingdom, the question arose who was to be the king to administer its affairs, for there cannot be a kingdom without a king. Kingdoms there were, but the failure of earthly monarchies turned the thoughts of the devout to the Coming One, who as King would restore the glory of the Davidic throne. And, as we are to see, this conception of a divine king provides a

179

growing and glowing aspect of prophetic Scriptures. Premonitions of a continued and gracious royalty confront us at every turn.

Predicted As King

Abraham was singled out as the father of the race from which, according to the flesh, the divine King should come (Genesis 12:1-3). His dominion was prophesied by Jacob when he declared that Christ was to come to the tribe of Judah and that the scepter should not depart until Shiloh came (Genesis 49:8-10). Kingly dignity and dominion are suggested by the star and scepter in Balaam's prophecy (Numbers 24:15-17).

Up to this point, Israel was a *theocracy* with no king but God. When she became a *monarchy*, and visible kings were hers, prophecies of Christ as Messiah take on a regal tint and portray more vividly His Kingship. Thus, almost 500 years after Jacob's prediction, Nathan the prophet assured King David that his house and his kingdom were to be established for ever (II Samuel 7:16) — which promise was confirmed with an oath (Psalm 89:3, 4, 35-37).

Many of the Psalms speak of Christ being anointed as King of the earth (2:6-12, see Revelation 11:15; Psalms 10:16; 24; 45; 72; 89; 110). In ancient times kingship was acquired by conquest, by superior prowess. The word, "king," means *able man* or *the one who can*, which significance in the highest sense is true of Christ, as quotations from the Psalms prove. Christ establishes His right to reign by His matchless power, infinite love and the influence of His perfect character. All kings are dependent upon the heavenly King (Psalm 144:10).

Isaiah was another who saw Christ's day as King and rejoiced. To the prophet, the Babe to be born of a virgin was to be the Prince of Peace, from the throne of God, and the King who would reign in righteousness, whose kingdom would have no frontiers (Isaiah 2:1-4; 9:6-9; 11:1-10; 32:6).

Years after David's death the promise of the king's glorious Successor was re-affirmed to Jeremiah, the prophet of woe, who was enraptured over his vision of Christ as the coming Messiah, who, as the King, would reign and act wisely (23:5, 6; 30:18-24).

Ezekiel, taken up with his "wheels," symbol of God's over-ruling providence in the affairs of nations, wrote of Christ who would appear as King and reign, "Whose right it is" (21:27).

Daniel, who saw and spoke of the rise and fall of many mighty empires, could go beyond the thrones and crowns that perish to "Messiah the Prince," whose Kingdom would be an everlasting one (2:24; 9:24, 25; 7:13, 14).

Hosea, writing to a backsliding Israel, calls the nation to repentance and to a remembrance of the prophecy of the coming of One, the greater David, their King (3:5; 13:10).

Micah foretold the coming of Jesus out of Bethlehem, with strength and majesty, not only as a present Saviour from sin, but as the Ruler of Israel whose going forth had been of old even from a past eternity (5:2-4).

Zechariah, by the Spirit, predicted the Messianic Advent. He could rejoice over Christ's appearance as King, "Behold, thy King cometh unto thee." The prophet could also travel through gloom to glory and exultingly cry, "God shall be king over all the earth" (3; 9:9; 14:9).

Presented As King

If the Old Testament provides us with the *prophetic portrait* of the Kingship of Christ, the New Testament presents us with His *historic portrait as King*. Thus the outline in prophecy is complete in history, for the truth of His Kingship is woven into the texture of the New Testament. Matthew names Christ as King some 14 times; Mark, 6 times; Luke, 5 times; John, 14 times. It is impossible to miss Christ's present and prospective royalty in the teachings of Christ Himself and of His Apostles. Abundant proof is offered of our Lord returning as God's true King as the fulfillment of Old Testament prophecies. As for His Kingdom, it is described in plain words as being —

Spiritual in nature — Luke 17:20, 21
Universal in range — Matthew 8:11; 21:43
Emanating from life within — Mark 4:26-29
Victorious over all opposition — Matthew 21:44

The King's forerunner, John the Baptist, convinced that Jesus would appear as the Messiah, announced that the Kingdom, in the person of the King, was at hand (Matthew 3:1, 2).

In the kingly genealogy of Jesus, prominence is given to His royal lineage as the Son of David, who would occupy the throne of David and reign over the House of Judah (Matthew 1:1, 2; Luke 1:32, 33).

Confirming Old Testament Scriptures as to Christ's coming as King, and of His Kingdom as being everlasting, Gabriel announced to Mary that of her Son's reign there should be no end (Luke 1:26-33). The Son of David expresses Christ's title to the throne of David over Israel and Judah yet to be (Luke 1:32, 33).

Christ was *born* a King, and His Kingship was recognized by the Wise Men who in their offerings represented the first-fruits of the Gentile world. *Gold* is thought to mark His Kingship; *frankincense,* His priesthood; *myrrh,* His death and burial. But is there not something unique in the language of the question of the Wise Men? "Where is he that is *born* king of the Jews" (Matthew 2:2:). It is very rarely that one is born in a royal household as a king. Born as prince or princess, as the case may be, yes! But only becoming the king or queen on the death of the reigning monarch. An unusual exception to this fact was the late King Alfonso of Spain, who was born as king, for the reason that his mother was pregnant with him when his father died. Thus, king in the womb, he was king when born. Jesus, however, was born a King seeing he was a King before He was born, who lived before His birth at Bethlehem. He came as "the king eternal" (I Timothy 1:17).

Jesus never repudiated the title of *King*, when the scribes and early disciples recognized Him as the King of Israel who was the predicted Ruler (Micah 2:5, 6; John 1:49). They accepted the teaching about Him as coming to sit on the throne of His glory (Matthew 25:31-34). Godly Jews, nurtured in Old Testament prophecies, had no doubt as to Jesus being the promised Messiah and sought by force to make Him King (John 6:15). But He did not yield to the demand of the people. He could wait, for He knew that the day would come for Him to be universally accepted as King. Thomas Dekker, of the fifteenth century, wrote, "A patient man is a pattern for a king." With true kingly patience, Jesus awaits His crowning day.

Proclaimed As King

In many forcible ways, Christ proclaimed His Kingship. All claims to Messiahship imply His dominion. His miracles attest His power as the King to whom all regal power was given (Matthew 28:18-20). His teachings and parables likewise declare the Kingdom of God and the Kingdom of Heaven with Himself as the Administrator of their affairs. His word, as a King, was authoritative (Ecclesiastes 8:4. See Matthew 22:43-45; John 18:36, 37). He spoke of gathering out of the Kingdom all that was offensive, of those who can only enter the Kingdom by the King and who will shine as the sun, of the honor of the faithful to be seated with Him on the throne of His glory (John 14:6; Matthew 19:28). Under the guise of a nobleman absent in a far country, Christ is returning to receive a Kingdom (Luke 19:12-15).

His Kingdom is not to be an earthly dominion after the fashion of the world's kingdoms. His present, spiritual Kingdom, as well as His future Kingdom, are not of this world (John 18:36). Because of the unworldly origin of His Kingdom, His subjects do not fight or employ worldly means to further its interests. This is "the kingdom of his dear Son" into which all the saints have been translated (Colossians 1:13).

Christ accepted the declaration of others as to His Kingship. He never denied that He was a King and would have a Kingdom when the mother of James and John sought places of honor in His Kingdom for her sons (Matthew 20:21-23). He also accepted the hosannas and homage of the multitudes as they saw the predictions of Zechariah fulfilled before their very eyes (Matthew 21:1-16; Mark 11; Luke 19; John 12).

Protestations of Christ's Kingship were denied by the religious leaders of His time, who charged that He made Himself King. The proclamation over the cross in three languages — Hebrew, Greek and Latin — *The King of the Jews,* was not acknowledged of the priests. So they begged Pilate to alter it to, *"He said,* I am the King of the Jews," implying a bogus claim (John 19:3, 12, 21).

Pilate asked, "Art thou a king then?" and Jesus did not say, "No," but "Thou sayest I am a king. To this end was I born" (John 18:37) — born as a King, born to be King. How unlike a King He looked when Pilate cried, "Behold the Man!" Battered and bleeding and decked in mock robes, He was anything but kingly and there was little pity in the hearts of those who rejected His Kingship — "Crucify Him, Crucify Him!" And as their *King,* He was crucified, and the truth of His redeeming Gospel is that —

"The head that once was crowned with thorns,
Is crowned with glory now."

As He died in agony the taunt of the godless who failed to see in this blood be-spattered Man a King, was, "If he be the king of Israel let him come down from the cross" (Mark 15:22). Had He wished, He could have displayed His kingly power and descended from His cross of shame, but He stayed there and drained the cursed cup on our behalf.

As the King who was to sit on the right hand of majesty on high, He blesses and commends the dying thief, who was the first sinner to enter Paradise through the royal blood of the King who died on a cross (Luke 23:42). Ovid, the Latin philosopher, gave us the proverb, "It is a kingly action, believe me, to come to the help of those who have fallen." Browning reminds us that the last kind word Jesus uttered was spoken to a thief.

The Resurrection attested Christ's claims to kingship. He had overcome Satan and death, and seeing Him alive forevermore, the apostles became heralds of the King and fearlessly acknowledged His sway as such. The disciples hoped for a visible kingdom (Acts 1:6, 7). On the Day of Pentecost, Peter declared that the crucified, risen Christ now occupied a throne and as Lord, both of the dead and the living, must be worshiped and served. Here was "another king," One different from the Monarch of earth (Acts 7:18; Exodus 1:8). At last, the throne of David was re-established and given to Christ (Acts 15:13-18). This is why the Book of Acts carries strong expectations of restored royalty (16:6, 15).

Paul's teaching is rich in majesty, glory and power of Christ as King. By revelation he knew that Christ would rule over the Gentiles (Romans 15:12); would reign till He had put all His enemies under

His feet (I Corinthians 15:23); was at the right hand of God, above all rule, authority and dominion (Ephesians 1:21, 22); that every knee would bow to him (Philippians 2:9-11); that all who suffer for Him now would reign with Him when He appears (II Timothy 2:12; 4:1, 18); that His Kingdom is to be an eternal one (Hebrews 1:8; see II Peter 1:11); that He would be a King-Priest after the order of Melchizedek (Hebrews 7:14-17; Genesis 14:18).

Pre-eminent As King

The predominant aspect of Christ in the Book of Revelation is that of His kingship. Here, His claims as King are beyond all doubt. Upon His head many diadems are to rest. Walter Scott says that a distinction must be drawn between *crowns* and *diadems*. The former speak of constitutional monarchy and the latter of despotic power (Revelation 12:3; 13:1). The saints in heaven have *crowns* (4:4, 10), expression of their royal dignity as sharers of Christ's Throne, but *diadems* rest on His head, denoting His absolute and supreme authority. "Many" implies that upon the head of the conqueror Christ every form and kind of government rests. He will be supreme in every realm and reign without a rival.

Among the many titles John ascribes to Christ, none is so expressive as "The prince of the kings of the earth" (Revelation 1:5). All earthly kings at His appearance as the One "higher than the kings of earth" must do Him obeisance. The kingdoms of this world are His by right and title and must acknowledge His ownership. Thus, when He comes to reign, it will be as *Lord* of all who exercise authority and as King of all who reign.

Then He is referred to as the King of nations or of the ages (Revelation 15:3). The A.V. has "king of saints" but competent authorities assure us that it should read "king of nations." He is spoken of as the King of kings, King of the earth, King of Israel, but never as "king of saints." Poets and hymnists may describe Him thus, and it may be true of Him in a spiritual sense. The appropriateness of the title, "king of nations," is seen when we remember that all the nations comprising the Roman earth are to come under judgment (Jeremiah 10:7).

In the final act of the Beast and his allies (Revelation 17:14; 19:19-21), Christ as "the Lord of lords, and King of kings" is to overcome them. Victory is assured before the battle commences, seeing that Christ is the mighty all-victorious Conqueror-supreme in heaven and on earth (Matthew 28:18). Publicly, officially and intrinsically, Christ is "King of kings and Lord of lords," bearing upon His garment and Person the expression of His universal dominion (Revelation 19:16).

As to Christ's Kingdom, it will be world-kingdom, for He is to fashion the kingdoms of this world into His own Kingdom. As to the duration of His reign, it is stated to be "to the ages of ages" (Revelation 11:15, 16), that is, throughout all time, extending to eternity. His reign will never cease (Isaiah 9:6). "Beware," says Alexander Pope, "for dreadful is the wrath of kings." John speaks of the wrath of the Lamb-King, and after 1,000 years of His beneficent reign of universal peace and blessing, the multitudes are still determined to resist His claims. What is left for Him to do? Why, He destroys the rebellious of earth, and the earth itself with fire (Revelation 20:8-10; II Peter 3:7).

When Napoleon was confined to the rock of St. Helena it is said that he spent much time reading the Bible. It is recorded that on one occasion he turned to Count Montholon, a fellow prisoner, with the inquiry, "Can you tell me who Jesus Christ was?" When no answer was forthcoming, Napoleon said, "Well, then, I will tell you. Alexander, Caesar, Charlemagne and myself founded great Empires . . . upon force. Jesus alone founded His Empire upon love . . . I tell you all these were men: none else is like Him. Jesus Christ was more than man . . . He asks for the human heart. He demands it unconditionally, and forthwith His demand is granted."

> Let ev'ry creature rise and bring
> Peculiar honors to our King;
> Angels descend with songs again,
> And earth repeat the loud *Amen!*

X

Prophetic Kings in Bible History

Previous chapters have made it clear that royalty pervades the Bible. The title "king," is mentioned in its sacred pages some 2,500 times; "Prince," about 350 times; "kingdom," around 35 times; "queen," 57 times. Among the kings and queens of the Bible there are those of a prophetic or symbolic nature. *Symbolic* queens are referred to in our section dealing with Bible queens.

By *prophetic kings* we mean, first of all, those who although they were historical personages in the past, are yet associated in some way or another with the future, and who therefore have a prophetic significance as well as an historic part. Then there are those who have not yet appeared but whose role is decidedly future, being related to the consummation of Gentile civilization.

Conspicuous in the first list of *prophetic kings* is Melchizedek whom Scripture affirms was a prophecy or type of the predicted Christ. As a contemporary of Abraham, perhaps the mysterious King-Priest should have been placed in the section of our study dealing with "ancient kings" where historically he belongs. Seeing, however, that he is before us as "a figure of the true," we present our cameo of him at this late stage.

MELCHIZEDEK
(Genesis 14:18-20; Psalm 110:4; Hebrews 7:1-4)

THE KING OF MYSTERY AND PROPHECY

A word of caution is necessary as we come to consider the mysterious yet illustrious personage before us. In the study of Holy Scripture we shall be wise if we give heed to plain, practical instruction, rather than spend too much time over critical inquiries. Is it not folly to explore that which is designedly secret at the expense of a right understanding and a deep experience of the influence of those important truths expressly declared?

Those who read the Bible simply to gratify a vain and conceited curiosity will find enough within its sacred pages to perplex and confound them. How foolish it is to be lost in endless, profitless researches and overlook the lessons to be gathered from those aspects of truth readily understood! Humbly we should pray for "a right judgment in all things," and instead of striving to unravel difficulties, endeavor to reap spiritual advantage from every passage we read.

Surely such a caution is particularly suitable as we give our attention to the history of Melchizedek, the concise description of whom, and the mysterious terms used of him, have given rise to various fancies, conjectures and useless disputes. Are we not exhorted to avoid those matters "which minister questions rather than godly edifying, which is in faith"? Henry Thorne rightly remarks:

> A veil of mystery shrouds the brief biography of Melchizedek. This old-world priest still remains as mystical as the handwriting at Belshazzar's feast, or the phantomed spectre that predicted the doom of Saul. The record is, however, suggestive because of its mystery. There are clouds, but they are the dust of the Saviour's feet. No type of the Redeemer could be perfect that was destitute of the element of mystery. Think of the mystery of His birth, of His cross, of His vacated tomb.

Just who was Melchizedek? A Hebrew tradition says that he was Shem, who was still alive in the days of Abraham, and as far as is known, the oldest living man at that time. But he could not have been Shem, for we are distinctly informed that he was "without father, without mother" (Hebrews 7:3), that is, he had no recorded parentage or genealogy. We do know who Shem's father was.

Others have identified Melchizedek as Christ in one of His theophanic appearings. But this supposition is not Scriptural for Melchizedek was "made like unto the Son of God," and that Christ's priesthood is "after the similitude of Melchizedek" (Hebrews 7:3, 15), language that would not have been used of Melchizedek had he been Christ Himself.

The king-priest has also been referred to as a mysterious celestial being, but the Bible expressly calls him a "man" (Hebrews 7:4). The brief and simple narration involves no considerable difficulty. Melchizedek was one of the kings of Canaan, with Salem or Jerusalem, as the city of his government. He was a king and a priest, blessed Abraham and God, and received tithes from Abraham's war spoils, as he returned from his conquest over four confederate kings.

From the short account before us then, it would seem as if Melchizedek was one of the kings of Canaan preserved from the prevalent idolatry and wickedness of his country. As a devout worshiper of the true God, and holy in life, he was qualified to preside over solemn rites and offices as "the priest of the most high God." Doubtless there were others among the accursed race of the Canaanites who were faithful to God and who abhorred idols (see I Kings 19:10-18).

A city bearing his name was situated on the S.E.Hill, protected on all sides by valleys, with a wall round the entire hill. Probably the place where Melchizedek and Abraham met was in the Kedron Valley near the Gihon Spring.

Three times over in Bible history is Melchizedek mentioned — in history (Genesis 14:18-20): in prophecy (Psalm 110:10): in fulfillment (Hebrews 7:1-4). His name, occurring some eleven times, is entitled to the highest place among the sacramental names of the Bible. Melchizedek means *king of righteousness,* or, *the righteous king,* a title belonging in its supreme and perfect sense to the Son of God alone, who is the King "righteous in all His ways and holy in all His works."

We are told that in his official capacity, Melchizedek was "without father, without mother." In the Aaronic priesthood, priestly appointments depended upon parentage. Melchizedek's priesthood was not after this order. Thus, we have no historical accounts of his parents, which, of course, he had. Well over one hundred years ago Thomas Robinson, of Cambridge, wrote:

> It is not to be concluded that Melchizedek was, like Adam, immediately created, or that he had no human extraction; but only that his genealogy is not recorded, and that sacred history has purposely concealed his ancestry. . . . Where or when he was born, or what the time and manner of his death, from whom he derived his office, or who succeeded him in it, we are not told. The very silence of Scripture is instructive for it raises our thoughts to Him who was "in the beginning" and "before all things."

From an old Palestinian tablet we read a letter from *Ebed-Tob,* the supposed successor of Melchizedek. Three times over he says: "not my father, not my mother installed me in this office but the Mighty King."

Melchizedek was both a king and a priest. Under the Law there was an impassable barrier between royalty and priesthood, but because Melchizedek was a type of Christ he combined both offices and is presented as a king of righteousness and of peace, and as a priest of the most high God. And the duties of the priesthood were not incompatible with the dignity of kingship. Taking no part in war with other kings, Melchizedek is a fitting type of Christ's peace-loving character (Isaiah 32:17, 18).

Priestly functions included the ministry of encouragement for the man who had fought God's battles. The bread and wine provided hospitable refreshment for the weary soldier and suggest another bringing forth of bread and wine (Luke 22:19), memorials of sacrifice. Then there was the bestowal of a benediction, "He blessed Abraham," and also the utterance of praise, "He blessed the most high God."

Abraham acknowledged the superiority of Melchizedek by paying him tithes of his battle-spoils. From this act Paul argues that the

Mosaic dispensation was intended to be subservient to the Gospel (Hebrews 7:2).

It is somewhat remarkable how much Christ is kept in view in the historical parts of the Old Testament (Genesis 14:18 with Hebrews 7:2). In his person, name, office, residence and government, Melchizedek is an eminent type of Christ. The death of the King of Salem is not recorded, which is suggestive of the endlessness of Christ's priesthood (Hebrews 7:23, 24). Beyond the ancient record, an unexpected luster breaks upon us — Jesus the Son of God stands revealed in all His glory.

He came as the King (Matthew 2:2).

What dominion is His, now, as "the head over all things to the Church," at His return to earth, as "the Prince of the kings of the earth."

He is "the King of righteousness"

Perfection of holiness is His, and He judges His people righteously. His laws are "holy, just and good."

He is "the King of peace."

Christ is peace personified. "He is our peace." By His finished work, He repaired the breach between God and sinners. Now we have peace with Him through Christ (Romans 5:1).

He is our Great High Priest.

A prophet may teach, but a priest may only sacrifice, and Jesus gave Himself for us, an offering and a sacrifice to God for a sweet-smelling savor (Ephesians 5:2). As the Priest, He intercedes for and blesses His people. Jesus "appears in the presence of God for us." He bears upon His heart before God the names of all His blood-washed ones. Abraham gave to Melchizedek "a tenth part of all." To Christ, we owe our all. May grace be ours to "honour Him with our substance, and with the first-fruits of all our increase"!

During His millennial reign, Christ will combine His kingly and priestly offices, and make possible for our blood-soaked earth the full benefits of His cross. Then in a perfect way, mercy and truth will join hands and righteousness and peace kiss each other (Psalm 85:10).

JESUS CHRIST THE LORD

The next King whose Biblical record is historic yet prophetic, is our blessed Lord Himself. Already, in the chapter dealing with His "kingship," we have indicated some aspects of His future ministry. At this juncture, we are simply grouping together several related passages declaring that He is the King to come — that was to appear, did appear, and will yet appear (Hebrews 9:28). He was the most illustrious of the kings to come out of the loins of Abraham and Sarah, seeing He is the Son of Abraham (Genesis 17:6, 17; Matthew 1:1, 2), and the One with power to remove or raise up kings (Daniel 2:21; Hosea 8:4).

The Psalms are eloquent with the truth of Christ as God's coming King. The most perfect Ruler the earth has ever had is on His way to inaugurate His reign. He is, and will be, higher than the kings of the earth (89:27). During His Millennial Kingdom, kings are to bring their gifts unto Him and praise, worship and serve Him (68:29; 72:10, 11; 102:15; 138:4; Isaiah 49:7; Zechariah 14:16, 17). He has, and will yet rebuke kings for the sake of His anointed (105:14; 149:8). His people are to drain the wealth of kings (Isaiah 60:16). Kings are to walk in His dawning radiance (Isaiah 60:3; 62:2).

During Christ's millennial reign, the kings of the earth are to bask in His splendor. The throne of the Lord in the heavens over the earth in majesty and greatness will surpass anything ever before seen or heard of in royal circles. Kings and nations are to contribute of their wealth and glory to earth's perfect King, as the last reference to "kings" in the Bible declares (Revelation 21:24-26). "The vice-regent of the King of kings, a lineal descendant of the royal David will sit on the actual throne and enter the actual temple then set up (Ezekiel 44, 46)."

Presently, Christ is our absent King and we should be found speaking a good word about bringing Him back (II Samuel 9:10, 11, 43). How guilty of lethargy about Christ's return we are, as David's followers were of his absence. Christ is the King we should long to see in all His beauty (Isaiah 33:17). Horatius Bonar has taught us to sing —

> Great King of kings, why dost Thou stay?
> Why tarriest Thou upon Thy way?
> Why lingers the expected Day?
> > Thy Kingdom come!

THE KINGS OF THE EAST

The verse containing a reference to "the kings of the East" (Revelation 16:12) has suffered much at the hands of many interpreters. Some commentators neglect the verse altogether. Among explanations of the identification of these particular kings, mention can be made of the following —

These kings are the Parthians who at one time threatened Rome at the Euphrates. They refer to the Jews' return from all parts of the earth in their final regathering, in harmony with Isaiah 49:12. They are the "ten kings" of Revelation 17:12. They are the apostles and evangelists of the four angels of Revelation 9:14, 15. They may be identified as rulers like Vitringa, Constantine the Great, and Flavian. They may be Gog and Magog of Ezekiel 38. They may represent saints in general. They may represent the forces of rude and open evil which have been long restrained, similar to the four barbarian and tyrant kings from the East in Abraham's days (Genesis 14:1-24). So there you are — take your pick!

The most simple, sensible and logical interpretation of the passage is just what it says, Professor J. F. Walvoord reminds us. The kings not *of* the East, suggesting their origin there, but *from* the East, that is the eastern side of the Euphrates. By the *East* is meant "the rising of the sun," a beautiful Oriental and poetical expression signifying the East. Dr. A. C. Gaebelein says, "The term, 'Kings of the Sunrise,' may even mean the far Asiatic nations, like China and Japan." Dr. H. A. Ironside, commenting on the verse, wrote, "Is it only a coincidence that, for a millennium at least, Japan has been known as the 'Kingdom of the rising sun'?"

The drying up of the Euphrates River, making possible the transit of these eastern kings, has likewise been subject to various interpretations such as the lessening of the power of the old Turkish Empire, the decline of the Roman Catholic Church, the fall of Babylon as given in Daniel 5. As for ourselves, we take the passage to mean the literal Euphrates River which is mentioned twice in the Book of Revelation (9:14; 16:12), and in both cases the epithet, "great," is used to describe its size, 1780 miles long, and by far the longest and most important river of Western Asia, and famous in Bible history and prophecy.

The drying up of this river bearing the same relationship to Southwestern Asia as the Mississippi bears to North America, will remove a geographical barrier to the tremendous military invasion of the Promised Land from the Orient. The miraculous removal of this barrier is an act of judgment, so that the eastern nations can the more readily pour their armies into Canaan. The Golden Bowl (16:12-16) is emptied out on the great river, drying up its vast expanse of water. A somewhat similar judgment is associated with the West (Isaiah 11:15), for "both the Nile and the Euphrates are dealt with," says Walter Scott, "the western and the eastern boundaries of the land of Palestine. There used to be no difficulty in accepting the statement in this paragraph in its full and literal sense."

THE KINGS OF THE EARTH

The kings of the earth are not to be confused with "the Ten Kings" (Revelation 17:2). The former (17:18; 18:3, 9; 19:18, 19) signify the rulers and leaders of an apostate Christendom generally, while the latter kings are associated with the revived Roman Empire. The kings of the earth are a specific class and number, guilty of fornication with Babylon and lament its fate. The ten kings are to be prime movers in Babylon's political downfall (17:16).

In the dirge of Babylon's fall, the kings of the East being most intimate with her, and feeling her loss more than others, lead in the general lament. The merchants of the earth sorrow over Babylon because of the loss of their trade and wealth. The kings of the earth mourn over Babylon because of the loss of the luxury it provided. Then these kings of the earth are included in the most gigantic confederacy of kings and peoples ever beheld (19:19-21).

The Ten Kings

These vassal kings and the Beast they serve are to be God's instruments for the destruction of both religious and political Babylon (Daniel 7:24; Revelation 17:13; Acts 4:26). Prophecy reveals that all things will be centralized and ready for the mastermind to seize upon and dominate. The Antichrist, with the ten European kings giving him their power and owning his allegiance, will take the reins of government. Who will be like unto the Beast (Revelation 13), when he has an invincible European army and navy made up of the men and ships of the ten great powers?

These ten kings are to give their kingdom to the Beast, meaning, that there is absolute subjection to him. "Unable to maintain separate and independent kings, the ten kings voluntarily place themselves and their kingdoms under the rule of the Beast, and from henceforth he becomes their master, who allows them but the shadow of royalty." Real power is the Beast's (13:2-7), and what the kings possess is traced to God as the source (13:13, 17).

"The Ten Horns" (17:12) represent the same royal personages or their Kingdoms, existing not as *separate* kingdoms or nationalities but co-existent with the reign of the Beast who grants them their authority as kings. John makes it clear that the Beast and confederate kings continue to exist after Babylon's destruction (17:16, 17) and in their war with the Lamb, Heaven's Lord and King, suffer a deserved extermination (Revelation 17:14; 19:19-21). "The ten kingdoms shall be *contemporaneous* in contradiction to the seven heads, which were *successive*."

The Seven Kings

As the "seven kings" (Revelation 17:1-11) are an integral part of "the seven heads which are seven mountains whereon the woman sits," it is essential to consider the double application of the symbol of "the seven heads." John uses in his description of Babylon and the Beast —

1. The Seven Heads as Mountains

Without doubt, these "mountains" are the seven hills on which Rome rests, namely, Palestine, Nierinah, Aventine, Caelian, Virninal, Esquitine and Janiculan. "The seven-hilled city" is a term used of Rome even in its earliest ages. Roman historians and poets seemed proud to designate their famed city in this way. Wordsworth reminds us that, "The unanimous voice of Roman poetry during more than five hundred years, beginning with the age of John, proclaimed Rome as *the seven-hilled city.* . . . On the imperial medals, which are preserved, we see Rome figured as a woman on seven hills, precisely as she is represented in the Apocalypse."

The papacy has been located and has flourished, more or less, for over 1500 years in Rome and because Roman Catholicism is so closely interwoven with the city of Rome, to separate them would be to deal the Romish Church a blow from which she could hardly recover. Thus, as the seat and center of the Woman's almost universal authority and influence, just judgment is to overtake her and the apostate religious system she represents.

2. The Seven Heads as Kings

The Seven Heads also symbolize and signify the various and successive forms of government from the rise of the Roman Empire on through its history to the end of "the times of the Gentiles." These seven heads or kings are divided up in this way —

Five Are Fallen

Walter Scott, one of the safest and sanest expositors of the Book of Revelation says that these five fallen heads are "kings, consuls, dictators, decemvirs, and military tribunes, and have been applied to Egypt, Assyria, Babylonia, Greece and Persia. Others consider the reference to Augustus, Tiberius, Caligula, Claudius and Nero." Scott himself believes that they each and all represent *one* head or form of government, namely, the imperial.

By "fallen" or "fell" we are to understand the ruin or destruction of a system or a kingdom (14:8; 16:19). "Death of an individual ruler would not be so spoken of. Hence the term, "kings," in our passage signifies the ruling authority for the time being. The four beasts of Daniel 7:17 are said to be four kings. Thus the term, *kings,* must not be confined in its application to royal personages. The context in each case must determine —

One is

The present tense here implies the imperial form of rule instituted by Augustus Caesar existing in John's time, when he wrote his book.

This is the sixth head. The previous five forms of rule had ceased. "Augustus absorbed the power and authority covered by the old names under which Rome had been governed and commenced the long and imperial line which became extinct in the year 476 A.D."

The other is not yet come

This seventh head continues for a brief season, seeing that the eighth and last phase of the empire is *the* point of interest. Between the breaking up of the Roman Empire and its yet future revived appearance, many centuries have elapsed.

The eighth, and is of the seven

Although referred to as the eighth, this king, Satan's masterpiece out of the abyss, is yet "of the seven" (17:11), meaning that the character of the brief form of government under the seventh head is continued. Policies are accentuated but in no way changed. The last monarch will stamp his own character upon the empire before it ends in destruction. "The first five heads fell in succession. Then the sixth came to a violent end; the seventh is merged in the eighth, which suffers a judgment more awful than history records."

The Four Kings

The four kings arising out of the earth are not personal rulers, but kingdoms (Daniel 7:18), frequently represented by their heads or founders. This is why kings and kingdoms are occasionally used synonymously (8:21). Daniel is interpreting his vision of the four universal empires, Babylonia, Persia, Greece and Rome (see Revelation 13:2).

In the account of the overthrow of Persia by the king of Grecia we have mention of another "four kings" (Daniel 11:2) but who they actually were is hard to say. As Cyrus was on the throne at the time, the passage may refer to Cyrus, Cambyses, Darius and Xerxes, the latter being the fourth king because the reckoning dates from Cyrus, and the short reign of Pseudo Smerdis, are not taken into account. The four kings Daniel speaks of were selected because their influence was most prominent in its bearing upon Israel.

The Three Kings

We now come to three specific kings Daniel mentions in his prophecy (chapter 11), who, although they have an historic record are yet prophetic of a coming world conflict.

THE LITTLE KING

The references to this august ruler, sometimes identified as "the little horn" (Daniel 7:8; 11:3) prefigure the *one* ruler over the Beast's empire (Revelation 13:1), the Roman prince who is to make a covenant with the apostate nations for seven years (Daniel 9:17) and break it in the middle of the period, and who finally perishes at the hands of the coming Lord (Revelation 19:20). This personal head of the United Nations of Europe, this little king, subdues the ten kings so completely that the separate identity of each is destroyed. Arising, possibly out of Greece or Syria, he will be friendly with the Jews, but will break with them and turn upon them in fury.

THE KING OF THE NORTH

This despot, leader of the northern armies (Ezekiel 38:1-4, 6), is the "overflowing scourge" (Isaiah 28; 30:27-30) and the "Assyrian" (Isaiah 10:14, 25; 31:8; Micah 5). Some writers identify him as the previous "little horn"; others as Antiochus the Great (Daniel 11:6, 13, 15, 40). Clarence Larkin's comment reads: "This vision of the 'King of the North' (Syria) and of the 'King of the South' (Egypt), in which the 'King of the North' prevailed, revealed to Daniel that Antichrist would arise in the 'Syrian' division of Alexander's Kingdom, for the description of the 'Little Horn' and that of the 'King of the North' correspond."

This "king of fierce countenance" (Daniel 8:23), is not to reign in his own right, although a mighty and powerful monarch. He is a subordinate of Gog acting for him in Southern Asia. This Assyrian is termed the king of the *North*, as indicating the geographical position of his kingdom toward Palestine.

THE KING OF THE SOUTH

Historically this southern king is identified as Ptolemy, a Macedonian, who ruled Egypt 322-305 B.C. whose chief leader was Seleneus who founded the Seleucid Dynasty. *Prophetically*, he represents Egypt, an ally of the western power, opposed, as in the days of Moses, to Israel. He plays a comparatively unimportant part compared with his brother monarch in the north (Daniel 11:5, 9, 11, 15, 40). An ally of the Beast, he will be opposed to his northern neighbor, the Assyrian. Eventually this "King of the South" is overcome by the sweeping assault of "the King of the North" (Daniel 11:42, 43; Revelation 13).

THE KING IN PALESTINE

Whoever this king was who is abruptly introduced into Biblical history (Daniel 11:36), he was one who raised himself not only above heathen deities but above the true God. Ellicott says, "Though there can be no doubt that the northern king is still spoken of, it must be remarked that the features of Antiochus are gradually fading away from the portrait. In no sense can Antiochus be called an atheist, whose main object was to Hellenize the Jewish religion, and to force the Greek gods upon the Jews. The character of the northern king, on the contrary, finds a parallel in Paul's description of Antichrist (II Thessalonians 2:4), who precedes the reign of the true Messiah."

Prophetically, then, this is the one who is to reign as king in Palestine during part of the period between the translation of the Church (I Thessalonians 4:17) and the appearing (Revelation 19:11). Walter Scott says of him that, "He is accepted by the restored nation on his own credentials as their prophet-king (John 5:43). His arrogancy and blasphemous pretentions know no bounds. He takes God's place in the Temple (II Thessalonians 2:4), and works miracles in the wider domain of Christendom (Revelation 13:13). He and the distinguished political chief of the empire work together; they wreak their vengeance on godly Jews and Gentiles who witness against their wickedness, and perish together eternally (Revelation 19:20; 20:10, 11)." The Bible clearly depicts the final judgment of all godless kings (Matthew 18:22; 22:3-13; 25:35-40; Revelation 16:11; Isaiah 49:23; Ezekiel 43:7).

John was commissioned to prophesy against "many kings" (Revelation 10:8-11). Such a prophecy was sweet as honey in his mouth but as bitter as gall in his belly. Prophecy is both sweet and bitter — it gladdens ·and saddens. The saint rejoices over God's ultimate triumph over all wrong, but such a triumph spells woe to those who suffer judgment. For other instances of a true witness before Kings see Matthew 10:18; Mark 13:9; Acts 9:15.

XI

Symbolic Kings in Bible History

The Bible is rich in its suggestive symbolism. One critic has said that man cannot exist, at least intellectually, without symbols and signs of various sorts. To all lovers of Holy Writ, its symbols and signs offer an avenue of profitable meditation, leading them to agree with Charles Kingsley's observation that, "This earthly world which we do see is an exact picture and pattern of the spiritual and heavenly world which we do not see."

If, as Thomas Carlyle puts it, "All visible things are emblems," then, certainly, some of the kings and queens of the Bible are emblematic of spiritual things. For the symbolic use the Bible makes of the royal title, "queen," the reader is referred to the section of this volume dealing with *Bible Queens*. The following are instances of kingly symbolism. Crowns and thrones are also employed symbolically.

Living on the King's Bounty (II Samuel 9:6-13)

King David's tender consideration of Mephibosheth is a striking evidence of his magnanimity. Shakespeare in *Hamlet* has the couplet,

"Such thanks
As fits a king's remembrance."

David had sworn to Jonathan before God to care for his family (I Samuel 20:14, 17; 23:18) but Mephibosheth, lame in both feet as the result of a fall (I Samuel 4:4), did not know of David's oath and feared revenge. Further, to have a no-kin cripple daily at a royal palace was something unheard of. A German proverb has it, "Neck or nothing, for the king loves no cripples."

David, however, was a king and loved the crippled son of his dear friend, and cared for him in generous fashion, and therefore symbolizes the grace of a greater King than David. All of us are cripples, spiritually and morally. We have sinned and come short of God's glory. Lame in both feet, we strayed from the pathway of righteousness, yet, through divine kindness, we have been brought into the King's banqueting house and made to sit at His table.

197

He daily spreads a glorious feast,
And at His table dine
The whole creation, man and beast,
And He's a Friend of mine.

Waiting for the King's Scepter (Esther 4:10, 11; 5:2-5)

None could have audience with the mighty King Ahasuerus unless he gave the sign of the extended scepter in their direction. In this way, anything distressing was barred from the range of royalty. Queen Esther, distressed over the threatened destruction of her race, was urged by Mordecai to seek the king's aid, and seeing her in the court, he extended toward her his golden scepter.

How different it is with the distressed and needy children of God, who do not have to wait for the waving of a scepter ere those needs can be presented! Access is ever open into the presence of our heavenly King. Because we are of His royal court we have immediate entry, none daring to bar us or make us afraid. With boldness we enter the holiest of all by the blood of Jesus, and, coming to a King, we large petitions bring.

A King and His Army (Job 29:25)

Job's reference to kings proves that he must have lived in the times of ancient kings.

In this chapter made up of Job's pathetic lamentation over the prosperous days that were gone, the words, "I," "king" and "me" are prominent. The patriarch had been as a mighty prince taking his seat in the place of justice. He had sat as a king among friends and foes alike, dispensing joy and justice, and had promised himself a long life and a peaceful death. Now Job mourns over his loss and lot, and thus symbolizes "one who had worn the poet's crown of sorrow in the remembrance of happier things in time of sorrow."

It is thus that Job serves as a type and representative of all who suffer, and who await a full release from all their trials through Him, who, Himself the Redeemer, endured the sorrows and sins of a sinful and unredeemed humanity.

The King Over Sons of Pride (Job 41:34)

The massive "leviathan" of this chapter is reckoned to be the Egyptian crocodile, an animal of superhuman strength, king over all proud beasts. The God who made the crocodile is here speaking and rebuking human pride, one of the great concerns of the Book of Job. The patriarch, moved by the divine speech, was humbled and completely divested of his pride and his misunderstanding of God, who hates fleshly pride and rewards true humility.

The Limit of Kingly Power (Psalm 33:16)

Napoleon is credited with the saying, "God is with the greatest battalions." But Scripture and history disprove such a sentiment. Often God delights in conquering majorities by minorities. He uses the weak things of the world to confound the mighty. "There is no king saved by the multitude of an host." Depending upon what we have, rather than upon what God is in Himself, we court disaster.

All through the Bible we are warned against confidence in the flesh. Kings and nations depend upon their weapons of defense for safety; and we depend upon our own wisdom, wealth and works, forgetting Him who is the unfailing Source of safety. It is thus fitting that this Psalm of "The New Song" ends with words expressive of dependence upon God: hope, wait, fruit. The last five verses of the Psalm contrast the safety and serenity of those who wait on and for God, with the helplessness and hopelessness of those who trust in human strength and resources.

> "The arm of flesh will fail you,
> Ye dare not trust your own."

The Traits of the Ideal King (Proverbs 16:12-15)

It was quite natural for Solomon, one of Israel's most illustrious kings, to discourse upon the virtues and vices of a king, and to symbolize aspects of kingly power and pleasure. In the portion before us, Solomon paints a fourfold portrait of an ideal king.

1. He loves righteousness (16:12)

As God hates all that is deceitful (16:11) so the kings He sets up should deem it an abomination to be guilty of wickedness or unrighteousness. Because He is just, rulers and subjects should reflect His character.

2. He delights in righteous lips (16:13)

Many of Israel's kings did not delight in righteous lips nor love those whose speech was right. Had Zedekiah been a lover of righteous lips he would not have struck the godly prophet, Micaiah, on the cheek (II Chronicles 18:23).

3. He curbs his anger (16:14; 19:12)

Royal anger has been responsible for the slaughter of multitudes. Herod's anger and jealousy over the birth of Christ as King of the Jews resulted in the death of innocent babes. When we control our temper we are mightier than kings who keep a city.

4. His countenance is life (16:15; 19:12)

If a king's wrath is to be feared, his favor is as dew upon the grass. The severity and goodness of God are opposite sides of the divine character of which we must never lose sight. Suffice it to say that ideal kingship can only be realized in Him who is the King of kings whose countenance of light is life.

Standing Before Kings (Proverbs 22:29)

Joseph is a fitting illustration of this proverb. Righteous, wise and diligent, he became second to Pharaoh (Genesis 41:46). Not all who work diligently at an honest business are invited to attend upon royalty. The underlying thought of the proverb is that diligence enables one to succeed and ultimately move in a higher circle.

The Glory of a King (Proverbs 25:2, 3)

"The lucidity of human law honors man, but the inscrutability of Divine law honors God, whose glory is seen in the marvels of the Universe and in Creation. These are beyond human comprehension, Job 36-39," is the exposition of *The Student's Commentary* on this passage. All the remarkable discoveries of science are but the unraveling of the secrets of nature, concealed there by God, who has so ordered things that man may not presume to measure himself with his Maker, but recognize his own insignificance (Romans 11:33).

The honor of kings is to search out a matter. They try to see their way through political difficulties and national perils. If good and true, they also unmask hidden crime and fraud. Often the hearts of kings — and of ordinary folk — are unsearchable. We must not presume upon their favor and think that we know all that is in their minds (see Proverbs 23:1, 2).

Old and Foolish Kings (Ecclesiastes 4:13, 14)

The tragedy is that the king who wrote this verse became foolish as he came to the closing years of his reign, and refused to obey when admonished of the Lord (I Kings 3:14; 9:3-9). Those who are poor in contrast to the wealth of kings may yet be wise. To quote *The Student's Commentary* again, "Jeroboam was the poor but clever youth who came out of prison and was made king: and whilst Rehoboam, the second youth, reigned in his father's stead, and for a time was accepted of all the people, yet they did not continue 'to rejoice in him,' but followed Jeroboam. Thus Rehoboam, though born to the kingdom and wealth of his father, became poor, for the King of Egypt took his wealth and Jeroboam took his kingdom." Blessed is the nation when its sovereign or ruler is wise, whether young or old!

The King Is Served by the Field (Ecclesiastes 5:9)

This verse is to be connected, not with what goes before, but after it, and contains "a consideration intended to mitigate the difficulty felt at the sight of riches acquired by oppression, namely, that riches add little to the real happiness of the possessors." Often poor subjects are happier than kings (Ecclesiastes 5:10-12).

Kings and others are bidden to remember that "the profit of the land should be for the benefit of all the members of the province who cooperate to produce the profit." In the past, private ownership of land, a system God never intended, for the earth is His, has been a basic cause of poverty.

The Chambers of the King (Song of Solomon 1:4)

Seeing this love idyll was written by King Solomon (1:1), it was but fitting for him to use the title of "king" to illustrate the union and communion existing between Christ and His Church. It is not hard to connect the King who invites us into His chambers with the glorious King of Psalm 2, and the One David speaks of in Psalm 55.

Stuart in his suggestive exposition of *The Song of Solomon* has this comment on the Royal Chambers, "The King withdrawing into the glorious chambers of His majesty and grace, has left without the soul that seeketh Him; in approach to Him the soul seems to itself to have lost rather than gained but therefore stirs itself all the more to prayer, resolution and hope; and from remembrance describes the chambers of the King into which it ardently desires now to be admitted."

While it is true that Christ will yet be seen and served as King, do we recognize His Kingship in the spiritual realm? Having Him as our Saviour, do we honor Him as our Sovereign? Have we given Him His coronation, crowning Him Lord of all? Does He reign supreme over the empires of thought, love and desire? If so, then fellowship in His chambers will be sweet.

The King at His Table (Song of Solomon 1:12)

The table, in Scripture, is the symbol of provision and fellowship. At His sacramental supper, the King still sits with His people and freely confers on them His royal favors. They in turn rejoice in such a privileged, close friendship, and His grace and presence draw forth the fragrant spikenard of praise, worship and love. While the King sat at His table, the house was filled with the odor of Mary's spikenard (John 12:1-3).

The King in His Galleries (Song of Solomon 7:5)

This interesting symbol seems to have a special reference to "the purple hair," the ancient locks of consecration by which the prince's daughter (7:1) had the strength of Samson's locks before they were cut by his treacherous wife, binding the king to herself. The flowing tresses of the beautiful maidens, portrayed in this chapter, were so long and attractively silken that a monarch would be caught and held by them, as expressed in the poetic couplet —

"When I lie tangled in her hair,
And fettered in her eye."

At present we are, as it were, in the open courts of His Palace, but
when He appears, He will translate His daughter, His Church (Psalm
45:9-15), into the secret of His pavilion.

The Soft Clothing of Kings (Matthew 11:8)

John the Baptist forfeited many pleasures and privileges when he
retired from society and lived in desert places to herald the coming of
the King. For His sake John became poor. Ellicott indicates that this
passage has a more pointed reference than at first sight appears and
cites a fact culled from Jewish historians.

> In the early days of Herod the Great a section of the Scribes had at-
> tached themselves to his policy and party, and in doing so had laid
> aside the sombre garments of their order, and had appeared in the gor-
> geous raiment worn by Herod's other courtiers.

But with John it was different, for he was not a man of party or
policy. He refused to share in the luxuries of a palace, or court the
favor of princes. For him it was not soft clothing, or as Luke puts
it "gorgeously apparelled," but the rough, hairy mantle of the prophet.
He did not live delicately, but subsisted on the desert food of locusts
and wild honey.

The Saints As Kings (Revelation 1:6; 5:10)

Made kings and priests to reign over the earth! What a stupendous
privilege is to be ours! What a glorious position awaits us! As
cleansed sinners we are brought into a dual relationship of royal
dignity and priestly nearness, as the outcome of the finished work of
Him who was crowned with thorns.

"Thine were the sharp thorns, and mine the golden crown;
Mine the life won, and Thine the life laid down."

We are "kings" and "priests," *kings* first, for we must reign in life
by Christ Jesus ere we can function as *priests*, interceding and serving
in holy things. Our heavenly King-Priest first gives us kingship,
sovereignty over ourselves, "the first, the best, the most philanthropic
of all kingship." Then comes a kingship among men with power to
establish and extend divine righteousness among others. In this kingship we represent God to men. In our priesthood we represent men
before God.

KINGS

The tense used is in the present. We reign with and in Christ,
here and now. Paul deals with law and grace as opposing monarchs
— "death, sin, reigned" (Romans 5:14, 21). "Grace reigned" (Romans
5:17, 21). Sovereignty is ours over human sin, fears and sufferings.

There is also the future aspect of this kingship, for we are to reign not *on* but *over* the earth. During the millennial reign of Christ, the saints are not subjects of His earthly Kingdom. Reigning with Christ, they exercise royal functions (20:4), which take their pattern from Him who unites in Himself royal authority and priestly grace. "He shall be a *priest* upon his *throne*" (Zechariah 6:13).

PRIESTS

This description of saints indicates their consecration to the will and work of the Great High Priest, even to the offering up of themselves unto death (Revelation 2:10). How little we exercise this priestly service on behalf of others! Every child of God has been made a priest and should recognize and use his or her privilege as such. May grace be ours never to forget, nor in practice sink below, our exalted dual position! Constant remembrance of the same will impart dignity of character and power in witness (Ephesians 2:6).

The Locusts and Their King (Revelation 9:11)

King Solomon, that keen observer of nature, says that the "locusts have no king" (Proverbs 3:27, 28), but John affirms that they *do* have a king. What is behind this apparent contradiction? Solomon's *locusts* were *natural* ones — John's locusts are *symbolic. Abaddon* or *Apollyon,* terms used to designate Satan, is the king of a vast host of evil agents exercising a malignant influence. The angel of the abyss or prince of the infernal regions, directly and indirectly, works havoc on the earth. Thus, as Walter Scott expresses it, "The locust army is a symbolical representation of judgment of a superhuman kind. The duration of the satanic scourge is limited to five months (9:5) — May to September — the time of natural locust life."

The claim to royal authority by these satanically controlled hosts is spurious. They ape the crown of gold adorning the head of the Son of man (14:14), and also the crowns of the triumphant elders or redeemed (4:4). But these hellish invaders are not crowned with gold. Their crowns are make-believe, crowns *like* gold.

Here we are, at the end of our absorbing and profitable study of the kings of the Bible, and the author would fain believe that, under divine guidance, he has prepared a volume that Bible lovers everywhere will find of service in their quest for truth. Our last word would be that we must ever remember that whether our rulers are good or bad, we are commanded to honor them (Proverbs 24:21; 25:6; Ecclesiastes 8:2; 10:20; Romans 13:1-5; I Peter 2:13, 17), and also to pray for them (I Timothy 2:1). May grace be ours to be as "kind as kings upon their coronation day," as Dryden expressed it!

Part Two
Bible Queens

INTRODUCTION

Not many queens adorn the portrait gallery of royalty in Scripture. Kings are in abundance, but queens are scarce, as is evidenced by the fact that the word, *king*, occurs over 2,000 times in the Scripture, but its parallel term, *queen*, only some 50 times. Egyptologists have unearthed monuments and mummies of a few ancient queens such as: *Nefert-ari, Ansera, Netem-Maut, Thyi,* and *Hatshepsut,* whom some writers identify as Pharaoh's daughter who rescued and adopted Moses, but Scripture is silent as to the majority of queens of succeeding dynasties.

Kings come before us with all their pomp and glory, but for the most part not even the names of their wives and the influence they exerted are recorded, although names of their children are. Most of the Bible queens are only referred to incidentally.

Among reasons advanced for this omission is the inferior position of women thousands of years ago. In Old Testament times, woman had not come into the rights and equality she presently possesses. Education, agitation and constant demand, and above all the dissemination of Scripture ideals as standards for women, have won for them the freedom and recognition they now enjoy. Women owe more to Christianity than men, as the cries of heathen womanhood prove. When God is dethroned in a nation the women are the first to pay the price.

Although the ancient Jews regarded women with much greater reverence than other nations, they never looked upon them as being fitted for leadership. Throughout Israelitish history only two cases are recorded of women exercising any of the functions of the ruler. There are, of course, instances of the influence of a woman behind a man as in the case of Jezebel and Ahab.

First, we have the exceptional case of Deborah — one of the most remarkable women in the Bible — prophet, judge, ruler, warrior, poetess (Judges 4:5). Boldly she could say —

> "The rulers ceased in Israel, they ceased
> Until that I Deborah arose,
> That I arose a mother in Israel."

Genius and talent found her able and ready to meet her nation's emergency and peril. So she became the first woman leader of men, the first public woman of the Bible with a passionate patriotism achieving such a victory for Israel that the land had rest from war for forty years.

Second, we have the record of Athaliah, about whom we shall have more to say, who reigned over Israel for six years. A usurper and a most odious woman, she grasped the reins of government and ruled as queen of the realm. With this single exception, there is no case in Jewish or Old Testament history in which a woman is "queen" in the sense of one who reigns. Even the wife of the reigning king is never directly spoken of as queen. Jezebel and Maacah are called queens, but in each case it is as queen-mother (the mother of the reigning king), and not as wife or ruler (II Kings 10:13; I Kings 15:13).

Concubinage and polygamy were among the customs and traditions of the old world, and the actions and attitudes toward women of ancient rulers were not wrong, according to their moral and conventional codes, and must not be judged and condemned by our more enlightened standards. David "took concubines and wives out of Jerusalem," and Solomon "loved many strange women . . . had 700 wives, princesses and 300 concubines." Today in our country, it is against the law and contrary to our moral code for a man to have more than one wife. If convicted of bigamy, he is sent to prison.

Polygamy then, lessened the influences and position of the king's wives whose hold on his affections was shared by others. Kings and rulers kept large harems, as do some Oriental princes today. Usually there was a chief wife who held precedence over other wives but at best her lot was precarious. Among Solomon's numerous wives and "sixty queens" all nameless even as his first wife, Pharaoh's daughter, a favorite is singled out — *but one* (Song of Solomon 6:8, 9). Who was the privileged woman who had the pre-eminence in the king's affections? Whoever she was such flattery was enough to turn her heart.

Ellicott observes, "Among the Persians it was customary that one wife of the sovereign should be supreme over the rest, and her we sometimes find exercising an authority which contrasts strangely with the degraded position of women generally. Such a one was Atossa, the mother of Xerxes. Vashti, too, was evidently *the* queen *par excellence.*"

Other women, apart from the chief wife, felt no degradation in their position. More or less slaves, they had no legal status and could be disposed of at will. Any of them counted it an honor to "find favor in the eyes of her lord." Children of such became part of the harem.

Many of the Pharaohs married, in a purely formal way, their sister or even their daughters, in order to keep royal property and treasures in the family line. "Affinity was no bar to marriage in Ancient Egypt," says Leonard Cottrell. "Queens often married their brothers, and sometimes kings their daughters as in the cases of Snofru, Rameses II and Amenophis IV." Cleopatra first married her eldest brother, whose right to the throne was thus established. When he died, Cleopatra married her younger brother who ruled by right of this marriage.

I

Gentile Queens in Bible History

In these days when the word, "queen," is bandied about and we have all kinds of fictitious queens — Cotton Queens, Carnival Queens, Milk Queens, "Queen for a Day," etc., it is necessary to state what we mean by a "queen." The dictionary describes her as the wife or consort of a king. In the ordinary English sense the term, "queen," means one who reigns in her own right, or the wife of the reigning monarch. The Queen of Sheba is the first to receive the appelation in Bible history.

Among the Jews, the queen mother enjoyed a fixed position of dignity and received special recognition and honor, as seen with Bathsheba (I Kings 2:19) and Maachah (I Kings 15:13). Hastings remarks, "The queen as the wife of a monarch in Israel held a position of comparatively little importance, whereas that of a dowager queen (queen mother) commanded great influence."

NICAULI (Sheba)
(I Kings 10:1-13; II Chronicles 8:17; 9:1-12; Matthew 12:42)

The Queen With a Quest

While the name of this queen of the South, who came to Solomon, is not recorded, Josephus says that it was *Nikauli*. Among the Arabs she was known as *Balkis* or *Makeda*. The Abyssinians believe that Solomon married the Queen from Sheba and traced their lineage of kings from such a union.

Sheba, meaning *repose*, a province between the Red Sea and the Indian Ocean and famous for its spices, gems and gold (Psalm 72:10; Isaiah 60:6), was named after Sheba, grandson of Cush, who settled in Ethiopia (Genesis 10:7). Thus the Queen of Sheba was of the Semitic race and not wholly alien from the stock of Abraham. Queens were not unusual in her region (Acts 8:27). Legend has it that she was a ruler of the great kingdom of South Arabia and that she was renowned for her beauty, wealth and magnificence.

Through commercial intercourse the queen came to learn of the wisdom and wealth of Solomon and was determined to find out for herself the truth of all she had heard. So we have seven steps in her quest, for she *heard, came, communed, saw, said, gave* and *returned.* A legend states that the Hoopoe, a strange and wondrous bird long celebrated in literature, told Solomon of the queen, and described how she sat upon a throne of gold, silver, pearl, rubies and chrysolite. Solomon was so charmed by the story that he commanded his magic power, the wind, and instantly translated himself to her country where he saw the queen and her people worshiping the sun. He then gave the Hoopoe a letter for the queen, bidding her worship God. Greatly impressed, she visited Solomon in his world-renowned capital.

The queen came to Solomon, we are told, to ask him "concerning the name of the Lord" and to "prove him with hard questions." Such was no idle curiosity, which can be a good master as well as a bad one. In the queen's case, curiosity was the stepping stone to revelation and higher wisdom. She undertook a long journey, for those times, and at fabulous cost, to sit before Solomon and learn of his wisdom. She felt that no effort was too great or price too high for an introduction to the king's superb wisdom. She did not come on a visit of state or to enter into some kind of treaty, or even to behold Solomon's magnificence. Her quest was for wisdom and for a fuller knowledge of Solomon's God (Isaiah 60:3, 6, 19, 20). Commenting on the queen's inquiry "concerning the name of the Lord," Dr. Alexander Maclaren says, "The most natural interpretation of the passage is that Solomon's reputation as knowing, and able to teach, the name or the manifested character of Jehovah, had reached her in her distant kingdom, and thus she came to him."

Among the many tests by which tradition says the queen tried to prove Solomon's wisdom, was to hold in her hand two bouquets of flowers, the one composed of natural, the other of artificial flowers, and without moving from his throne the king was requested to distinguish between them. Without hesitation he ordered the window to be opened, and the bees that were buzzing outside came in and settled upon the flowers of the garden.

There is no evidence that the queen recognized the God of Israel, yet doubtless she heard from Solomon that "the fear of the Lord is the *beginning* of wisdom." Leaving the king she gave him a benediction, "Blessed be the Lord thy God (not *her* or *their* God, but Solomon's) which delighted in thee to set thee on the throne of Israel." Isaac D'Israeli's epithet of the queen, "a trifling woman," is wholly unjustifiable. At the end of her visit to Solomon "there was no more spirit in her." Mind and feelings were deeply affected.

Our Lord paid the queen a tribute of admiration when, in dealing with the deserved judgment upon His generation, He called her "the queen of the south" (Matthew 12:42). Dr. James Denny says, "The praise of Jesus is the highest certificate that can be bestowed on any one, and wherever we find it we may be sure there is something peculiarly worthy of admiration."

With all the pomp and pageantry, culture and commerce the queen's country represented, she had no need to curry even Solomon's favor. She sought the widening of her mental and spiritual horizon.

> "Great souls by instinct to each other turn,
> Demand alliance, and in friendship burn."
>
> *Addison*

Does not this queen represent those young women of today with a thirst for higher knowledge and culture, all that is artistically beautiful, and for the poetry of religion? Receptive to wisdom, they become wise. Their lives are enriched by contact with intellectual superiority, reading and questioning. Would that more could be found following the Queen of Sheba in her quest!

A greater than Solomon is ours in Christ, of whom it is said that, "no man ever spake like this man." He came as the personification of the wisdom of God, and it was from Him that Solomon's wisdom was derived. "To him shall be given the gold of Sheba" (Psalm 72: 15). When He comes into His recognized Messiahship (Isaiah 60:3, 6, 19) then —

> "Kings shall fall down before Him
> And gold and incense bring."

We have all read and heard of the matchless glories of our Redeemer, who was made unto us WISDOM, but when we gaze upon His magnificence in heaven, ours will be the confession of the Queen of Sheba —

> "The half was not told me:
> Thy wisdom and prosperity exceedeth the fame which
>   I have heard."

VASHTI
(Esther 1, 2)

THE QUEEN WHO DARED TO REFUSE

While it is generally supposed that Queen Esther is the heroine of the book bearing her name, Queen Vashti has my vote as the moral heroine in this dramatic record. Vashti, queen of Ahasuerus or Xerxes, King of the Persians, and ruler "from India even unto Ethiopia, over an hundred and seven and twenty provinces" was the wife of this mighty monarch before his accession.

By birth Vashti was a Persian princess. Bullinger says that she was the daughter of Alyattes, King of Lydia, married by Cyaxares to his son Astyages after the battle of Halys. Other writers identify her as Amestris, the queen consort through Xerxes' reign and queen mother of his son and successor. Vashti is also a name of an Elamite heathen deity.

The noble yet tragic story of Vashti is told in a few lines. She was the queen who dared to disobey her drunken husband and was deposed for refusing to exhibit her loveliness to satisfy the lustful eyes of drink-sodden lords. In the third year of his reign, Ahasuerus planned a great celebration to which he invited the lords and princes from his vast domain. It was an impressive festivity with a feast, the splendor of which is still without an equal.

The drunken debauch lasted for a week, and the king inflamed with wine and pride, sent for his wife, the queen, to appear before his guests. "For seven days he had displayed the glories of his wealth and power," says Mary Hallet, "for seven days the princes had poured flattery into his willing ears. Now should come the climax! All of his magnificent possessions had been seen and admired except one — Queen Vashti, probably the loveliest woman in the whole kingdom." But Vashti did not oblige!

The name *Vashti* means "beautiful," and the king wanted his drunken, jubilant lords to "feast their eyes on her," who was as beautiful as her name suggests. Had the king been sober he would not have asked his wife to expose herself at the banquet. Had Vashti been a vain and wanton woman, she would have acceded to the request of the king. But Vashti, one of the nobler women of humanity, naturally refused the unseemly request. No woman, possessed of a particle of feminine pride could, she felt, obey such a summons to surrender honor. The king's request was even more revolting to Vashti's sense of propriety, seeing Persian queens never appeared publicly at a banquet. This was why Vashti had her own feast. She was a queen who thought more of her queenly dignity than the glamor of her social position.

Thus it came about that Vashti was deposed and repudiated lest a precedent should be given for insubordination of wives to husbands. Fausset remarks —

Plutarch in agreement with Herodotus says that the Persian kings had their legitimate wives to sit at table, but when they chose to drink and revel they sent away their wives and called in the concubines. It was when his "heart was merry with wine," that he sent for Vashti as a concubine; but she, looking on herself as a legitimate wife, would not come.

What ultimately happened to this courageous queen we do not know. Possibly her husband when sobered up, regretted his impulsive anger and was troubled when he realized what had been decreed against his wife. We like to think with Mary Hallet that "Vashti continued to live in the king's household, stripped of the insignia of royalty, but with her own integrity clothed in purple." To her it was no disgrace to "accept disgrace and dishonor rather than lower the white banner of her modesty and pride."

As we think of this honorable queen, and of her great refusal, the words of John Milton seem apt:

> "Virtue may be assailed, but never hurt;
> Surprised by unjust force, but not enthralled;
> Yea, even that which mischief meant most harm
> Shall, in the happy trial, prove most glory."

A parallel to Vashti's dethronement as not too great a price to pay for unblemished womanhood and virtuous self-respect is that given us by Walter Scott in *Kenilworth*. Amy (the secret but beautiful wife of the Earl of Leicester, who commanded her to practice "duplicity and tergiversation" in order to further his dishonorable designs with regard to Queen Elizabeth) is made to say with great energy and firmness: "I cannot put your commands, my lord, in the balance with those of honor and conscience. I will *not*, in this instance, obey you. You may achieve your own dishonor, to which these crooked policies naturally tend, but I will do nought else can blemish mine." Amy was never more worthy of "the proudest name in England" than at that moment.

Was it not thus with Vashti who was never more of a queen than when she forfeited her crown and set her face toward degradation and desertion? Her prized womanly modesty saved her from a greater loss than the loss of the crown royal. Better far to perish than to lose the queenly grace of modesty and self-reverence. Vashti preserved her queenliness of character, the rarest coronet and the most royal diadem any woman can wear. Tennyson greeted the lamented Queen Victoria in his patriotic ode *To the Queen* —

> "O, loyal to the royal in thyself!"

Vashti was "loyal" to the inborn quality of royalty and will remain as long as the world lasts, a *queen*, indeed, because she followed right because it was *right*.

> Self-reverence, self-knowledge, self-control —
> These three alone lead life to sovereign power.
> Yet not for power (power by herself
> Would come uncalled for), but to live by law,
> Acting the law we live without fear;
> And, because right is right, to follow right
> Were wisdom in the scorn of consequence.
>
> *Tennyson*

TAHPENES
(I Kings 11:19, 20)

THE QUEEN WITH GENEROUS INSTINCTS

The name of this queen is not mentioned in profane history or on any Egyptian monument. An alternative rendering of Tahpenes is *Tachpenes,* and with a slight variation became Tahpanhes, an Egyptian city. The name was also given to a female deity of Egypt. Ancient royal families in the orient frequently incorporated the names of God with their own. Dryden gave us the lines:

> Victorious names who made the world obey:
> Who, while they lived, in deeds of arms excelled,
> And after death for deities were held.

All we know of this queen is told in two verses. Tahpenes is only important because of her association with Hadad, a son of the king of Edom, who, as a child was carried by his father's servants into the land of Midian, and then into Egypt, when the males of Edom were massacred by David's captain, Joab.

A special providence favored the child. The king of Egypt gave him house and lands, and ultimately the sister of his own queen, Tahpenes, to wife. A son was born to them, named Genubath, whom Tahpenes weaned, no doubt with the customary festival (Genesis 20:18). This indicated his admission into the royal family, and living in Pharaoh's palace, he would be brought up and educated as a prince of Egypt.

The Pharaoh to whom Tahpenes was married ruled at the close of David's reign and at the beginning of Solomon's reign. He was of the weak twenty-first dynasty and does not appear to have been specially strong or powerful. What we do know of this royal couple affords an interesting bit of ancient history for which we are grateful.

Both Pharaoh and his queen appear to have had generous instincts, and the sketchy portrait we have of them suggests they had a family life at once instructive and pleasing. Although Hadad was no relative, they did for him what Mordecai did for Esther the orphan. This glimpse of Egyptian court life and manners helps to make the ancient and ageless Bible the living, human Book that it is. There is much that we can read between the lines of the adoption of the fugitive prince, his training and marriage, the upbringing of his own son, the interest Queen Tahpenes takes in her little nephew, the reluctance of Pharaoh, now advanced in years, to let them leave the royal house, all so instinctive of a happy home-life. How eloquent are some of the silences of Scripture!

HERODIAS
(Matthew 14:1-12; Mark 6:17)

THE QUEEN GUILTY OF ADULTERY

The ambitious and wicked Herodias, the Jezebel of the New Testament, was the daughter of Aristobulus and Bernice, sister to Herod Antipas and granddaughter to Herod the Great. Partly Jewish in blood, she married her own uncle, Herod Philip, by whom she had Salome. She was the niece of the Herod she married.

Passion and pride prompted her to leave her first husband and live in adulterous intercourse with Herod Antipas. Such an unlawful marriage, and one which by the Mosaic Law was doubly incestuous, shocked the conscience and sensibilities of strict Jewish leaders and brought upon Herod and Herodias the just censure of John the Baptist, preacher of righteousness and repentance, whose condemnation of their wantonness brought him within the range of the vindictive bitterness of the queen. *Queen,* how unworthy of such a royal title was Herodias!

Herod, whose first wife was the daughter of Aretas, King of Arabia Petraea, was described by our Lord as a "fox" (Matthew 14:1; Luke 3:19; 9:7), a designation describing his character, for he was a man of craft rather than strength. His cunning must have served him well, for he kept his throne for many years.

Herod's passion blinded his mind to the gross wickedness of his conduct. The corroding immorality of his dynasty revealed itself in his marriage with Herodias, his brother's wife, and such lust proved his undoing. Josephus says Herod was a Sadducee, which would make his remarks concerning John the Baptist a striking instance of the power of conscience overcoming against a man's own will, the sophistries of infidelity (Luke 9:7). In his rage he imprisoned John, then to gratify the malice of his wife, he beheaded the greatest of all prophets to satisfy the wish of the woman who hated to hear the truth.

Crafty Herodias waited for "a convenient day" to "get back" on the prophet and the occasion came with Herod's birthday as a ruler. Knowing Herod's weakness as well as Madame du Barry knew that of Louis XV of France, she sought to bend him to her will, even though it meant the sacrifice of her daughter's modesty. Thus Salome danced in a filmy garment that half concealed her form in a dance of an impure and voluptuous nature, common enough both at Eastern and Roman banquets. What a reckless disregard of maidenly modesty! How different was the noble refusal of Vashti!

The Bible does not say that the daughter of Herodias was *Salome* but simply "the damsel." Josephus, the Jewish historian, tells us that Herodias had a daughter named Salome by her first husband, Herod's brother, Philip. Salome first married her first cousin and step-brother and afterwards became the wife of Aristobulus, king of Chalcia. The Salome present at the cross was the wife of Zebedee and the mother of the apostles James and John and therefore a different woman in character from Herodias' daughter.

Flushed with wine, and with passions roused, Herod promised Salome anything for which she cared to ask. Out she went from the banquet-hall and asked her wicked mother what use she was to make of the tetrarch's promise. Immediately Herodias seized upon the opportunity and instructed her daughter to ask for the head of John. Herod, like most weak men, feared to be thought weak and commanded John to be beheaded in the prison at Fort Machaerus. Thus an innocent life was surrendered and "there passed from earth one of her greatest sons."

How gruesome an act was the presentation of the bloody head on a plate to Salome and Herodias! A tradition relates that Salome's death was retributive in its outward form. She fell upon the ice and in her fall her head was severed from her body. "With what measure ye mete, it shall be measured unto you."

Herodias, the source of Herod's sin, also became the source of his shame, for at her instigation he went to Rome, A.D. 38, to sue the Emperor Caligula for the *title* of king, just conferred on his nephew Herod Agrippa. But as Fausset reminds us, instead of elevation, he lost his kingdom and was banished to Lyons, then to Spain, where he died. "The one faithful (humanly speaking) act of her life was her preferring to share Herod's exile rather than stay at home in her own country." Surely sinners "eat of the fruit of their own ways, and are filled with their own devices" (Proverbs 1:31; Jeremiah 2:19).

Had Herodias known Shakespeare she might have said with the queen the bard depicts in *King Henry VIII* —

"I swear again, I would not be a queen
For all the world."

CANDACE
(Acts 8:27, 28)

THE QUEEN WITH A BLACK SKIN

The name, *Candace,* meaning "forgiveness," and pronounced, Kan-day-see, has a pleasant rhythm about it. Candace is not a proper name but the title of the dark-skinned queen of Ethiopia, just as *Pharaoh* was a dynastic name or title. Women, usually the dowager-queen, had right of succession to the throne, and the name of Candace was common to them all. Pliny testifies that the government of Ethiopia was in the hands of women, who, for several successions, assumed the name of Candace. Egyptian monuments also confirm the prominence given to females as queens and potentates. Strabo mentions a queen of Merod in Ethiopia bearing the name of the Ethiopian queen we are considering. In the British Museum can be seen the lid of a stone sarcophagus bearing the name of one of the Candace queens.

The narrative before us is taken up with Philip the evangelist's ministry in Samaria and how he was divinely called to the desert to meet an influential member of the queen's staff, her imperial officer or treasurer, returning to Ethiopia after a religious pilgrimage to Jerusalem. From the reading and exposition of Isaiah 53, the "eunuch of great authority" was led to embrace Christ as his personal Saviour, was initiated into Christianity in a baptism performed by Philip at the wayside.

The eunuch thus transformed could have gone back to a dark and benighted people and kept the knowledge of the Saviour's love and sacrifice to himself, but the news was all too wonderful to keep locked up in his heart. Eusebius, the early church historian, speaks of the convert returning to his native country, there "preaching the knowledge of the God of the Universe and the life-giving abode of the Saviour with men." There is an Ethiopian tradition naming the eunuch as *Judiah* and representing him as propagating the Gospel in Arabia Felix and Ethiopia and of bringing Queen Candace herself to the faith.

Perhaps the eunuch had undertaken a special secret commission from the queen, who, with inward longings and a deeply religious nature, commissioned her important officer of the state to find out more about Jerusalem-worship. It is supposed that at this time a certain form of Judaism prevailed in Ethiopia, and that the queen as well as the eunuch were acquainted with the Messianic idea and of the uprising of one Jesus and desired full knowledge.

To any further knowledge of Christ the eunuch gathered in Jerusalem there was added the experience of His power to save from all iniquity, as he journeyed home. How readily and joyously must the queen have received the glad news of the wonderful work of grace in the soul of her trusted officer! And when he explained to his queen the inner meaning of the sublime chapter Philip had read to him, we can imagine how her heart would burn and her faith rise up as she came to understand the Gospel of redeeming grace.

> "He was wounded for *my* transgressions
> He was bruised for *my* iniquities;
> The chastisement of *my* peace was upon Him;
> And with His stripes *we* are healed."

BERNICE
(Acts 25:13, 23; 26:30)

THE QUEEN OF UNBRIDLED PASSIONS

For voluptuousness, Bernice is well classed with Cleopatra. Bernice or Berenice, is a Macedonian corruption of *Pherenice*, meaning "victorious" or "carrying off victory." It occurs in previous history as the name of the wife of Ptolemy, one of Alexander's generals, who had become king of Egypt and founder of an illustrious dynasty. The one thing Bernice was not victorious over was her lust or passion. It would seem as if she was one of the most wanton and fascinating women of her age. Drusilla, "which was Jewess," was her sister.

The story of Bernice reads like a horrible romance, or a page from the chronicles of the Borgias. From the pages of profane history we gather that she was the eldest daughter of Herod Agrippa I, and was married at an early age to her uncle, the king of Chalcis. On his death Bernice remained for some years a widow, but dark rumors began to spread that her brother Agrippa, who had succeeded to the principality of Chalcis, and who gave her, as in the instance before us, something like queenly honors, was living with her in a yet darker form of incest, and was reproducing in Judea the vices of which his father's friend, Caligula, had set so terrible an example.

In Scripture, Bernice is always mentioned as being with the King Agrippa II, before whom Paul appeared, and who closed the line of the Herodian house. Her relations with Agrippa her brother were the occasion of much suspicion. It was with him that she visited Festus and listened to Paul's defense. We wonder whether her conscience was stricken as she sat in pomp and heard the passionate appeal of the apostle! Because of their incest and depravity, Agrippa and Bernice were objects of satire to Juvenal, the Roman poet.

The ill-fated marriage with Polemon, king of Cilicia, could not and did not prosper. The queen's unbridled passions once more gained the mastery. She left her husband, who quickly abandoned her and her conception of Judaism she had forced upon him. "But Bernice's powers of fascination were still great," Ellicott observes, "and she knew how to profit by them in the hour of her country's ruin. Vespasian was attracted by her queenly dignity, and yet more by the magnificence of her queenly gifts. His son Titus took his place in her long list of lovers. She came as his mistress to Rome, and it was said that he had promised her marriage. This, however, was more than even the Senate of the Empire could tolerate, and Titus was compelled by pressure of public opinion to dismiss Bernice, but his grief in doing so was a matter of notoriety."

What a sordid story! How Bernice disgraced the name of queen! If only as she listened to Paul's story of a changed life she, too, had become "obedient to the heavenly vision," and experienced a complete transformation of life, what a mighty trophy of grace she would have been. We wonder, was she, with Agrippa, almost persuaded to become a Christian? It would seem as if these companions in sin and lust smothered any uprising of conscience and died in their shame.

There were, of course, multitudes of Gentile queens in the period represented by Old Testament history, but as the scope of our meditations restricts us to those specifically mentioned in the inspired record, the study of those queens belonging to succeeding dynasties must be left to the reader's search of literature outside the Bible.

II

Jewish Queens in Bible History

As a whole, royalty in the Jewish nation is far from being exemplary. What a mixed group its kings and queens are! History and experience prove that a woman may be the consort of a king, the sovereign of a kingdom, or even queen-mother, without possessing that sweet and beautiful trait of queenliness.

Is it not also true that a woman may be queenly, even if she is not the wife of a king? There is "royalty" in every woman, and the woman, whatever her environment or station in life, who is "loyal" to this inborn quality, sits upon one of the thrones of the world's life as *queen*, beloved, honored and reverenced by all around. Beauty of character is an accomplishment that neither blood nor station can achieve. May every woman be —

> "One of the queens of the world,
> Great in her simple love."

And whether clothed in royal crimson or in peasant garb, when she comes to die may she be affectionately remembered as

> "One has gone to crowned of God,
> 'Mid the holy ones above."

Alexander Pope gave us the lines:
> "Men, some to quiet, some to public strife;
> But every lady would be queen for life."

The best Bible queens, although few, inspire all women to manifest all the virtues of noble womanhood. The worst Bible queens, and they are numerous, serve to mark the dangerous shoals, quicksands and rocks of life, where their lives were wrecked.

Vallance C. Cook truly focuses the observations of Bible queens in this telling fashion: "The queens have a message for each sex, and especially for every youth and maiden. The degradation of the other, and *vice versa*, the exaltation of the one is the exaltation of the other. Both stand or fall together. To those who are rejoicing in the glory of youthful exhilaration and in the joyous hope of golden days to come, light and guidance, strength and warning can be gathered from a study of the kings and queens of the Bible."

Dr. Joseph Parker once wrote that "The Bible is full of ideal characters, and it is not afraid to show actual character in some of its completest humiliations. The two pictures are bound in the sacred volume. We have moral loftiness that is apparently unapproachable, we have the degradation that shocks the very first sensations of morality; we have exhortations that encourage the weakest of us to attempt the greatest things that have ever taxed human energies."

Studying the kings and queens of the Bible we have in the ideal what we may become; and in the actual we see what we have to avoid. Thus all Scripture is written for our edification.

MICHAL
(I Samuel 18:17-30; 19:11-17; II Samuel 3:14-16; 6:12, 13)
The Queen Whose Love Turned to Scorn

Among the named and unnamed women in the life of King David are a trio who played equally important roles as his consorts, namely Michal, Abigail and Bathsheba. Plurality of wives, as we have already indicated, was not deemed a sin nor crime for a monarch in David's time. The ancient law of God and the development of Christianity built up strong barriers against polygamy. Many Old Testament saints, however, appear not to have been conscience-stricken over the possession of many wives. But in most cases jealousy, contention, sorrow and tragedy came as the result of such a practice.

While we are to look at David's trinity of wives separately, it may prove illuminating if we (first of all) group them together and discover how each brought their impact to bear upon the life of David, Israel's illustrious king.

Michal was a princess, the daughter of Saul, Israel's first king, and spent her early life in her father's palace under the restraints of convention Saul created for his household. Perhaps it was this fact that made her somewhat haughty and led her to despise David for losing his dignity when he participated in the people's celebration at the return of the Ark.

By marrying her, David became the king's son-in-law and for the first time knew what it was to bask in a young woman's love and adulation. With Michal it was love at first sight. Twice over we read that she "loved David," but what his heart reactions were we are not told. Anyhow, such a union raised the shepherd youth to royal status.

Abigail was the wife of a rich farmer and had beauty and brains. She must have been a woman of rare patience to have lived so long with her churlish husband, Nabal, who was a fool by name and nature. When David married her after Nabal's death, he achieved the social status of a powerful sheik and had the benefit of a wise woman's counsel in the care of Nabal's herds.

Abigail, a Hebrew woman, restricted by the customs of her time, only gave advice in a period of emergency. Hers was a disciplined will. Life with a beast like Nabal made it so. It was thus that in all humility she sought out David and by her calm winsome manner subdued David's urges and saved the life (but not for long) of her worthless, drunken husband.

Bathsheba, the wife of a soldier in David's army, does not appear to have the qualities of character Abigail possessed. Doubtless she found it difficult to employ her hours of solitude while her husband, Uriah, was at the front helping to fight the nation's battles. Did this make her a willing party in the mad infatuation David displayed for her?

Because of Bathsheba, David became guilty of adultery, deceit and murder, even though it was by Bathsheba that he was to have a son to succeed him as king of Israel. If Bathsheba had possessed the self-respect of Vashti and the wisdom of Abigail, the pages of David's great and glorious life would not have been blotted with the dark crime costing him his influence as a father and as a king.

As we look at the portrait of David's first wife, Michal, we must observe that although the Bible does not specifically call any of David's wives *queens,* nevertheless, because of their union with him they became his consorts. While we are not told how many wives and concubines David had, eight of his wives are mentioned by name — Michal, Bathsheba, Abigail, Ahinoam, Maacah, Haggith, Abital and Eglah (II Samuel 3:1-5).

Let us begin with Michal, the younger of two daughters born to Saul by Ahinoam. Actually, Michal was Saul's substitute wife for David, who should have had Merab, the elder daughter, as the result of his prowess as a fighter. But Merab was given to Adriel.

Michal's name is a contraction of the archangel Michael, which means "Who Is Like God." Deeply impressed with the poet-warrior who killed the giant Goliath, Michal made no attempt to conceal her love for this handsome young man. She must have been a woman of unusual strength of mind to declare her love in that age.

When Saul learned of Michal's love for David, there was murder in his heart. He offered to give Michal to David and deceitfully had the message conveyed to him through his servants, "The king hath delight in thee and all his servants love thee, now therefore be the king's son-in-law." Saul then made a despicable demand. He required no dowry of David. All he asked David to do was to strip 100 Philistines of their foreskins. David, realizing the honor of being the king's son-in-law, slew 200 Philistines and gave Saul a double supply of what he requested. Saul never thought David would come out of that encounter alive. But God preserved David, and Saul had to fulfill his part of the bargain and give him Michal to wife.

In spite of the evident divine preservation of David, Saul was bent on his death, and so we come to that episode when Michal risked her own life to save the husband she loved. Her love was put to the test, and quick to discern her husband's danger, she outwitted the messengers sent to slay David, whose escape she aided. When the messengers came they found they had been tricked by the image in the bed. Pretending that David had threatened to kill her if she did not aid him in his escape, Michal soothed her father's jealous mood. Although a Jewess, professing faith in the covenant God of Israel, Michal must have had some association with idols as the "image" she provided proves.

The next glimpse we have of Michal is when David ascended the throne of Israel. Forced to be a fugitive because of Saul's jealousy, Saul took Michal from David and gave her to Phaltiel. Saul and Jonathan were killed at Mount Gilboa, and David's first act as king was to make Jerusalem his capital and place there the sacred ark of the covenant, symbol of God's presence. As king, David demanded the return of his wife, Michal, which Abner arranged. Such a demand seems to indicate that David still had a deep regard for his first wife.

We are told that Phaltiel wept when Michal was forced to leave him, but she shed no tears. She was returning as a queen. Quickly, however, any love that may have lingered in her heart for David through the years of separation, turned to scorn. Taking off his royal robes of gold and purple, and left with only simple under-garments, David danced before the Lord in joy over the Ark's return, and the haughty queen, misinterpreting David's enthusiastic display, "despised him in her heart."

Unfortunately, she could not keep her scorn to herself but that night cut David deep with the lash of her biting sarcasm, "How shamelessly did the king uncover himself to-day!" Perhaps Michal resented being thrown from one husband to another. Back as David's wife she wanted a position as queen. But David did not yield to her whim to increase her queenly splendor. In no uncertain terms, he rebuked Michal for interpreting his humility as vileness and for her failure to recognize the essential significance of his religious acts. That all close relationship between them was severed is implied in the statement that Michal "had no child unto the day of her death."

Personal pride and love of prestige, so foreign to tears, appear to have been Michal's faults. Mackintosh Mackay speaks of a threefold pride connected with either *rank*, *wealth* or *intellect* and uses three Bible types.

"*Michal*, the wife of David — the type of pride or rank:
Salome, the mother of Zebedee's children — pride of wealth:
Miriam, the sister of Moses — pride of intellect."

How apt are the words of Alexander Pope when applied to Michal's pride of position —

> "Of all the causes which conspire to blind
> Man's erring judgment, and misguide the mind,
> What the weak head with straight bias rules,
> Is *Pride*."

ABIGAIL
(I Samuel 25:14-42; 27:3; 36:5-18; II Samuel 3:3)

THE QUEEN WHO WAS WINSOME AND WISE

In an age like ours when many so-called "beauties" appear to be minus brains, it is refreshing to turn to the story of Abigail, which owes part of its charm to its unexpectedness in the sacred record. Here is a woman, the more beautiful and noble because of her dark and unpleasant surroundings, a lily among thorns. Queenliness of character ultimately made her the ideal married woman of the Old Testament, and she teaches womanhood the value of prudence.

Her name, which was also the name of David's sister or step-sister (II Samuel 17:25) is suggestive, for *Abigail* means "whose father rejoiceth," and is understood as commemorating the joy of the father on the birth of a daughter. Surely a father is proud to have a daughter like Abigail, so charming and tactful. The mystery is, how could such a lovely woman become the wife of such a drunken, stupid brute as Nabal? Being the lady she was, she could never have married a man so opposite to her qualities for his possessions. Some women are ready to marry any kind of man if only he has plenty of sheep on the hills and goats in the stalls. In Abigail's day, marriage was often contracted without personal choice. Jacob had no choice in taking Leah instead of Rachel. Nabal and Abigail were a mis-mated couple. Apart from his wealth, Nabal had nothing to recommend him. He was most unbecoming and repulsive, while Abigail embodied many fine qualities.

Let us now trace the story of Abigail, who is described as "of a good understanding, and a beautiful countenance." Nabal, her husband, was a conceited, successful farmer, whose domain contained two villages and 3000 sheep and 1000 goats. His name means, *a fool*, a fact Abigail, as we shall see, used with telling effect. Apart from being purse-proud, Nabal had an ungovernable temper allied to his stupidity. By contrast, Abigail had features and form as comely as her mind was clever. When drunk, all Nabal's bad qualities came to the surface. What a churlish husband for a lady like Abigail to have!

As a soldier, David had never infringed on Nabal's rights. He had protected and cared for his herds, and now in need of food for his army, David had a right to a portion of Nabal's good harvest. Contemptuously Nabal declined to help David in any way and David, infuriated, threatened Nabal and his house with disaster and death. Abigail, learning of her unworthy husband's treatment of David and of his determination to slay Nabal "made haste" to dissuade David from avenging himself on the surly farmer.

The phrase, "made haste," emphasizes Abigail's thought and care, as well as rapidity of action. With a load of provisions she set out to meet an enraged man, and her wise method of approach is worthy of note. She did not check a ruffled spirit by argument, but won it by tact.

First of all, Abigail met David on her knees. She fell prostrate before him and took the blame of Nabal's churlish action. "Upon me, my lord, let this iniquity be." She did not argue whether Nabal was right or wrong. Mixing, most skillfully, humor with sorrow, she pled with David to pay no heed to her husband. "As is his name, so is he. Nabal is his name, and folly is with him." She was not disloyal when she told the truth. Abigail manifested great prudence as well as promptitude in trying to avert the wrath of David occasioned by her husband's insulting behavior.

Striking as she advanced, Abigail tactfully did not directly ask for anything. She took it for granted that what she desired had already been given by David's generous heart. The present tense of her statement is clever — "The Lord *hath* withholden you from the shedding of blood." She had heard of David's prowess even if her husband had pretended he had not, and she deprecated the shedding of blood in vengeance as David proposed. Abigail prophesied that God would yet avenge David of all his foes.

Abigail's soft answer turned away wrath (Proverbs 15:1). She had persuaded David that vengeance was God's and that He would repay (Romans 12:19). She also had implicit faith that God had destined David to become king of Israel, although it was far from her thoughts that she would be his queen. The woman who could say, "The soul of my lord shall be bound in the bundle of life with the Lord thy God," must herself have been bound in the same bundle.

David, enamored of Abigail, responded to her gracious eloquence and blessed her whose house he had threatened to destroy. Hearkening to Abigail's plea and accepting her person, David rejoiced at being deterred by her counsel from robbing God of His prerogative of vengeance. Hers was the harmonious combination of "the tact of a wise wife and the religious principles of a good woman." As Mary Hallet expresses it —

"Abigail's common sense, self-control, winsomeness, and vision gave her boundless influences over a really great man, and marked her as a really great woman."

Returning to her husband, Abigail found him in a drunken stupor, and wisely suffered him to "sleep it off." When he had sobered up, she told Nabal of David's hurt and threat which shook this brute of a man, so much so that he died from shock ten days later. When the days of mourning were past, David took Abigail, the beautiful Carmelitess, to wife. Michal, his first wife, had been given to another man. About the same time, David also took Ahinoam of Jezreel to wife (I Samuel 25:43). At Hebron a son was born to David and Abigail whom they named *Chileab* which some writers say means, "God is my judge" —an apparent allusion to divine judgment upon Nabal.

Both Ahinoam and Abigail accompanied David in his perilous journeys through Gath and Ziklag. Courage must have been theirs to follow the outlaw and his loyal army of men. David's wives were taken captive but gallantly he delivered them. Because of her nobility of character, Abigail (who is always called the wife of Nabal by way of explanation) must have exercised considerable influence over David. When the fugitive became king, Abigail must have been in the background with counsel, practical and wise.

John Ruskin, in *Sesame and Lilies*, reminds us that "in old times a knight's armour was often buckled on by his lady's hand. That which was only a romantic fashion may enshrine an eternal truth. The soul's armour is often set to its breast by a woman's hand, and it is only when she braces it loosely that the honour of manhood falls."

BATHSHEBA
(II Samuel 11-12; 25; I Kings 1:2; I Chronicles 3:5).

THE QUEEN WHOSE SIN WAS FORGIVEN

Bathsheba, who became another of David's queens, and mother of four of his sons, after the death of the child of adultery, has been referred to as the king's favorite consort who maintained her hold on David "long after her youthful charms had vanished." This we do know, the over-exposure of her body, while bathing, was the means of the darkest blot on David's illustrious career. It is not surprising that the tragic and romantic story of Bathsheba has offered full scope to the dramatist and that Hollywood found in it good box-office appeal.

Bathsheba — a Canaanite name (Genesis 38:2, 12) meaning "the seventh daughter" or "daughter of an oath," had a godly heritage as the daughter of Eliam or Ammiel. The other name given her is Bathshua, meaning "daughter of opulence." She appears in the human genealogy of Jesus as the former wife of Uriah and as the mother of Solomon by David (Matthew 1:6). A woman of considerable beauty, Bathsheba was married to Uriah, one of David's thirty chief heroes, and a brave and noble-minded soldier, who had the welfare of his country at heart.

The story of David and Bathsheba is built up with consummate art in the sacred narrative. It began with David tarrying at Jerusalem when he should have been accompanying the kings going forth to battle. As a younger man, David was always to be found in the thickest of the fight. Now he rested on his laurels and success and it was his undoing, for it had the tendency to make him soft and self-indulgent. The risks of battle no longer stirred his blood. Had he been at the front leading his forces, he would not have laid himself open to attack. Idleness is ever the devil's tool.

In the cool, early evening air, with time on his hands, David strolled around the flat roof of his palace and saw a beautiful, half-naked woman washing herself, and passions were at once aroused which led to David's shocking sin. Acting on sudden impulse, and not according to his essential character, David sent for Bathsheba and the beauty of the woman before him forced him to commit adultery. The king should have known better for as Mary Hallet says:

> He was a slender stripling when Michal first saw him in her father's court, his fingers weaving upon a golden harp and his quiet voice luring Saul from black despondency. He was not a great deal older when Abigail sped toward him to stay his hand from murder. But he was a *mature man*, veteran of many wars, ruler over Israel for a dozen years, when Bathsheba's beauty tempted him to sin which cast its sinister shadow over the rest of his life.

When Bathsheba told David of her menstruous condition, she revealed that she was more punctilious about the ceremonial Law than the moral Law. As a Jewess she must have known that the Law demanded death for adultery (Leviticus 20:10). Being guilty of capital crime against her husband and of high offense against God, did not seem to trouble Bethsheba as she became fit for David's advances.

Learning of Bathsheba's pregnant condition, David's sin became blacker, as he devised a way to cover up his crime. He sent for the valiant warrior-husband of Bathsheba, Uriah, and offered him leave from the battle-front, thinking that time spent with his wife might make the child begotten in adultery not his but Uriah's child. But Uriah refused to indulge himself when the rest of his comrades and the Ark were in danger.

David then made the brave, sacrificial, generous-hearted soldier drunk; yet even then his resolve not to spend a night of indulgence with his wife was greater than his irresponsible, half-drunken condition. Well, there was only one other thing to do. Uriah must die, and he became the bearer of his own death warrant. Uriah was slain and others with him. Thus a larger degree of blood-guiltiness fell upon David, now guilty of passionate desire, adultery, deceit and murder.

The question is, How far was Bathsheba David's accomplice in his terrible sin? Must the whole responsibility for the crime against Uriah be laid at the door of the king? Did he use his authority and power to steal another man's wife? Was Bathsheba in no position to repel the advances and desire of her royal lover? The evidence, we feel, makes Bathsheba a willing partner in David's sin. The glamor of being desired by the king turned her head and made her an easy conquest.

In the first place, Bathsheba should not have been so reckless as to take a bath where men could see her. She must have known she could be seen by those on adjacent roofs. Then, when sent for by David and learning of his desire, Vashti-like, she should have wrestled to death against the king's adulterous passion, as in similar circumstances Joseph did. Further, after the act, when her husband returned, there is no mention of Bathsheba's eagerness to see him and charge the king with his sin and confess her own guilt in the matter. Even though formal in her mourning for Uriah, it was not long before she went to the palace to supplement David's wives. No, the accusing finger points to Bathsheba as well as to David.

As we all know Bathsheba's baby was born without disgrace but died within a week and both David and Bathsheba suffered immeasurable grief and agony. Even kings and queens must learn that they are not above the laws of God. To sin is to suffer, to transgress is to be smitten. As Donald Davidson expresses it —

> Though Bathsheba was now exalted to the highest rank, all the honor that had come to her could not compensate for the loss of that baby boy. Death is a cruel thing at any time, but never more so than in the case of a little child. And when we remember that David and Bathsheba were profoundly conscious that the death of their son was a divine judgment on their sin, their agony of soul is not easy to imagine.

Through Nathan's ministry David was made conscious of his dark crime and of its consequences. "The sword shall never depart from thine house." He was disgraced by one son (II Samuel 13:14), banished by another (15:19), revolted against by a third (I Kings 2), betrayed by his friends, bereaved of his children. David's grief was deep. As a penitent, he "lay all night upon the earth," with Psalm 51 as his prayer, and while nothing is said of Bathsheba, she, too, must have repented and been assured of divine forgiveness. Out of this sordid tangle of illicit love and monstrous crimes shines the truth that God is a pardoning God, full of infinite forgiveness.

The assurance of divine forgiveness came with the birth of Solomon, who was to become Israel's most illustrious king. In after days, Solomon specially recognized Bathsheba's royal estate (I Kings

2:19) and paid her all deference as the queen-mother. Her strength of intellect and kindness and influence over David and Solomon appear in I Kings 1:11-31; 2:13-21. Tradition has it that it was Bath-sheba who composed Proverbs 31 as an admonition to Solomon on his marriage to Pharaoh's daughter. Yet another tradition says that Solomon wrote the chapter in memory of his mother.

Bathsheba's position in court was graced by dignity and queenli-ness. Hers was a commanding influence. Supported by Nathan, she successfully combatted Adonijah's attempt to secure the throne. Acting as Adonijah's intercessor in the matter of marriage to Abishag, she was most respectfully received by King Solomon, but her unwise request was refused.

The parting lesson we learn as we look back on the story of David and Bathsheba is not to let one sin ruin one's whole life. Sin can be forgiven, even though its effect may remain. Genuinely repented of, mistakes should act as guides to future conduct. God can restore the years the locusts have eaten. Augustine said that the fall of David should put upon their guard those who have not fallen and save from despair those who have.

MAACAH
(I Kings 14:21; 15:1-2; 15; II Chronicles 15:16)

THE QUEEN WHO WAS DEPOSED

Maacah, a favorite name in Jewish history, is used of both men and women, as the conclusion of this section indicates. The bearer of the name concerning us in this cameo is the one specifically mentioned as being "queen" or "queen-mother," as the margin states. We are told of her that she was the daughter of Abishalon (I Kings 15:2), the wife of Rehoboam, King of Judah (14:21), and mother of Abijam who succeeded to the throne (15:1, 2). Perhaps she was called Maacah after one of David's wives, the mother of Absalom.

Maacah is also listed as Michaiah (II Chronicles 11:20; 13:2). Bullinger suggests *Michaiah*, meaning, "Who is like Jehovah," was used of her as the queen-mother; but that she is called *Maacah*, meaning "oppression," when speaking of her idolatry (15:16). She comes before us as the favorite wife of King Rehoboam, no small distinction, for he had 78 official and unofficial wives. Among them there must have been keen competition for the king's favors.

Maacah must have been a woman of outstanding beauty and strong personality to have captured the chief place in the affections of such a fickle husband as Rehoboam. Her power as the head wife must have been felt throughout the king's harem, and having the ear of the king on most matters, must have been the power behind the throne. We can imagine how dependent he became upon this assertive consort of his.

That her word became law is seen in the fact that although Rehoboam had 28 sons and 60 daughters, by his almost four-score wives, he made Abijah, Maacah's son, to be the chief and ruler among his brethren, grooming him thereby as his successor. During Asa's (her grandson's) minority, Maacah may have acted as regent. The tragedy is that in her sphere as queen, this singularly clever and attractive woman used her influence in the wrong direction. How different the life of the court and of the nation would have been if Maacah's dominating power had been exercised on the side of God and righteousness!

When righteous, God-fearing Asa was of age and came to the throne, one of his first acts was to have the queen-mother expelled from the court because of her stubborn attachment to the idolatry derived from her ancestors of Geshur. Asa was most probably Maacah's grandson, mother being used in the sense of grandmother, as queen is used to designate queen-mother — a position Maacah retained until Asa's reign, but from which he deposed her.

Maacah's honored position as a king's wife and a king's mother never brought her any escape from Asa's task of reformation. Maacah had become hardened in her idolatry and blind to its consequence. As with Pharaoh, so with Maacah, the divine manifestations of mercy and of judgment were of no avail, and a ruthless act was necessary to purge the stream at its fountain-head. Thus Maacah was disgraced for her act of peculiar infamy (I Kings 15:13).

A woman of great strength of character and decision of purpose, Maacah's influence was yet bad and her deposition was a real benediction to the people of Judah. A depraved woman can corrupt her household and the neighborhood around her. Queens, however, like Maacah, Jezebel and Athaliah, corrupt entire nations. Sanctified womanhood is the most beautiful, potent thing in the world, but a vitiated and sinful womanhood is the most vicious and hideous spectacle of all. The British people revere their beloved queen, and her dear mother, the beloved queen-mother, for their sterling qualities of truth, graciousness and godliness. What shining examples they are of female royalty at its best!

Other Bible women with the name of Maacah are:

1. The daughter of Nahor, born to him by Reumah (Genesis 22:24).

2. The wife of David, taken in battle, who was of royal rank, the daughter of Talmai, King of Geshur, who became the mother of Absalom (II Samuel 3:3; I Chronicles 3:2).

3. A concubine of Caleb, son of Hezron (I Chronicles 2:48).

4. The sister of Huppim and Shuppim, the Benjamites, who be-

came the wife of Machir the Marassite, the "father" of Gilead (I Chronicles 7:12-15).

5. The wife of Jeiel, the father of Gibin, an ancestress of King Saul (I Chronicles 8:29; 9:35).

The three men bearing the name of *Maacah* are to be found in I Samuel 27:2; I Chronicles 11:43; 27:16.

Maacah is also the name of a small kingdom.

RIZPAH
(II Samuel 3:7; 21:8-14)

The Queen With a Mother's Heart

There is no episode in the realm of literature so touching as the sacrificial love of Rizpah in caring for her dead. Her gruesome vigil inspired Turner to paint his masterpiece and Tennyson to give to the world his *Rizpah*. A Hivite (Genesis 36:14), Rizpah, meaning "stretched out," was the daughter of Aiah and mother of Saul's two sons, Arboni and Mephibosheth. Foreigners were generally chosen as inferior wives by kings, but Rizpah, although classified as Saul's concubine, was no inferior woman.

After Saul's death, Ishbosheth suspected Abner of intercouse with Rizpah at Mahanaim, which in Eastern ideas was tantamount to aspiring to succeed to Saul's throne (II Samuel 3:7). Abner, who possibly loved Rizpah, was slain by the treacherous hand of Joab, so the poor woman was left doubly bereaved, and we have no further mention of her until some thirty years later when she suddenly emerges from her widow's seclusion with the full blaze of national publicity and imperishable honor as a woman of rare love and devotion.

Donald Davidson has this forceful comment:

If proof were wanted that the punishment meted out to the sons of Saul was not of God, it was evident in the open flaunting of the divine law in leaving the bodies to hang unburied. For had it not been plainly decreed that any felon hanged upon a tree must be buried before sunset of the same day? But the seven bodies swaying in the breeze was a pleasant sight to the vindictive Gibeonites. Vengeance was sweet, and the sweetness lingered with every glance at that hill-top with its seven gallows-trees standing out stark against the sky.

Rizpah's famous act was her vigil against bird and beast of prey waiting to devour the corpses of her two sons and five kinsmen on the sacred hill of Gibeah with which Saul, her husband, had been so closely associated (I Samuel 11:4). Rizpah had cared for her sons in life, and now in death she would not forsake them. So she who had worn queenly garments in Saul's court now donned the coarse robe of sorrow, to give the world an exhibition of a mother's sacrificial love.

Without tent to screen her from the scorching sun all day and the saturating dew at night, and with only her black widow's sackcloth to rest upon to keep her from the rocky ground, Rizpah watched her precious dead till the anger of Jehovah relented and the rain came. There she remained at her grim task scaring away the carrion from the naked corpses. How she must have fought against sleep during those anxious days and long, dreadful nights! The foul stench of the rotting bodies assailed her nostrils but love provided a perfume and also a determination to disturb approaching vultures. Those bodies were protected at great sacrifice without any thought of reward.

What a striking illustration of motherly devotion, strong as death, clinging at all costs with desperate temerity even to the lifeless remains of loved ones, Rizpah presents (Song of Solomon 8:1; Isaiah 49:15)! No wonder David was moved by the story of her tender care of the dead and willing to show that he cherished no enmity against the house of Saul, buried honorably the remains of Saul's descendants. How relieved and rewarded Rizpah must have been as she witnessed the decent burial of the bodies she had guarded so sacrificially!

It is not hard to trace a parallel between Rizpah's grief and that of Mary's great sorrow when the sword pierced through her own soul (Luke 3:35). To quote Donald Davidson again —

Does not Rizpah, keeping vigil over her beloved dead, slain innocently for the sins of another, not remind us of Mary, keeping her tearful watch close to that tree where He, who after the flesh was the fruit of her own body, was put to death for the sin of the world?

How much these two women have in common! To both is given the bitterest cup a mother could be asked to drink. But to both is given the joy of knowing that their suffering was not in vain. Rizpah showed that love was stronger than hate, and friendship was born again in hearts from which it had been driven out by the demons of anger and fear.

Centuries afterwards that other death upon a hill-top in Palestine was to teach the world the same truth — that man can never offer a full atonement for sin. It was only when God gave Himself in the person of His beloved Son, the righteous for the unrighteous, that love made its supreme sacrifice, and justice on high above all human ken was satisfied for ever.

JEZEBEL
(I Kings 16:31; 18:4-19; 21:5-28; II Kings 9)

THE QUEEN WHO WAS A SHE-DEVIL

Jezebel, a devil incarnate, comes before us as the most infamous queen in history. She was the female counterpart of Adolph Hitler who, in hell, is forever tortured by the cries of the millions he maimed and massacred. Thinking of the cruel crimes she committed, we recall another resourceful and wicked queen. Shakespeare portrays

the frightened man of Macbeth when he came to murder the king,
Duncan. But Lady Macbeth chided him —

> "Infirm of purpose!
> Give me the dagger. The sleeping and the dead
> Are but as pictures; 'tis the eye of childhood
> That fears a painted devil."

The character of Jezebel is all dark without a single light spot.
She is the Biblical and historical example of woman at her lowest
— woman under the domination of every evil passion and villainous
emotion. Nothing beautiful can be said of her. Yet, as one of the
Bible queens, she claims our attention, wicked though she was. Hers
was, and is, *the fascination of repulsion.*

Smith, in his *History of the Bible* says of her,

> Jezebel was a woman in whom, with the reckless and licentious habits
> of an oriental queen inherent in the Phoenician people. . . . The wild
> licence of her life became a proverb in the nation (II Kings 9:22). Long
> afterward her name lived as a by-word for all that was execrable, and
> in the Apocalypse it is given to a church or individual in Asia Minor,
> combining in like manner fanaticism and profligacy (Revelation 2:20).
> She is the greatest and the wickedest of the queens of the Bible.

Shakespeare has a fitting portrayal we can apply to Jezebel —

> "A strong adversary, an inhuman wretch,
> Incapable of pity, void and empty
> From every drachm of pity."

Suggestions as to the significance of her name vary. Some scholars
say that *Jezebel* means, "dunghill," which certainly fits in with her
character. Although she moved among princes, she was destitute of
true queenliness. She was as corrupt as she was cruel. Others tell
us that her name signifies "chaste," "free from carnal connection."
If this be so, then Jezebel belied the name she bore, for she was bad,
root and branch.

Jezebel, whose name occurs some 23 times in the Bible, was the
daughter of a regicide and a fratricide. Ethbaal, king of the Zi-
donians, her father, was also a priest of the Phoenician goddess,
Astarte. The Syrian princess married Ahab, King of Northern Israel,
which unequal yoke was a sin (I Kings 16:31). In Jezebel's Baalism
human sacrifices were offered and licentious acts indulged. Her
religion catered to the lowest and basest instincts in human nature,
and as conduct is the outcome of creed, Jezebel's behavior corre-
sponded to her belief.

As an unashamed idolater, Jezebel supported a vast number of the
priests of Baal and of Astarte and other heathen deities. "450 prophets
of Baal ate at her table." This woman was no weakling. Leaving her
land of idols, she could have followed the true religion of her
adopted land, as Ruth had done before her (1:16). But Jezebel not

only brought her idolatry with her, but because of her great influence over her husband, Ahab, he too became guilty of terrible idolatry. He not only sanctioned her iniquities, but became a partner in all the vile abominations in which she and her people reveled. What a curse Jezebel was to Israel!

As soon as Jezebel became queen, with absolute power, she set about destroying the worship and the witness of Jehovah, while protecting her own idols and lords. She attempted the utter destruction of the prophets of the Lord, and with them, as a necessary consequence, the Sacred Books. Hers was the defiance of God and His Law and the first record of the use of civil power against true religion by a woman.

Self-centered, Jezebel sought no advice and gave none. She was ruthless in her murderous ambition, and Ahab was under her complete domination and was as a catspaw in her hands. Ahab was king in name, but Jezebel *ruled* — she ruled the king, the home, and the nation, and at once a great blight spread its pall over the land, and, as Tennyson expresses it:

> "Which sicken'd every living bloom,
> And blurr'd the splendour of the sun."

Jezebel was the evil genius behind Ahab, without whom she was a serpent without fangs.

The fly in Jezebel's ointment was the rugged prophet, Elijah, faithful in his reproofs, who made no compromise with sin. Fire from heaven vindicated Elijah's condemnation of Jezebel's idolatry, and the slaughter of the prophets of Baal was like the cutting away of a rotten cancer from the life of the nation. The good of Israel lay in fidelity to God alone.

Strong and courageous as he was in his denunciation of the idolatry with which Jezebel had plagued the land, he yet was cowed before her threatenings. Unmoved by the slaughter of her prophets, she swore to have Elijah put to death, for she hated him for his prophetic ministry and delegated divine power. Elijah, however, found shelter from his bitterest enemy in her own country, Zidon. Thus signally did God's providence protect His faithful servant.

We now come to the dastardly crime making Jezebel the she-devil we have shown her to be, namely, the cold-blooded murder of godly Naboth. Not content with his own rich possessions, Ahab coveted the well-cultivated vineyard of Naboth bordering on his palace in Jezreel. As a spoiled brat, born and reared in an irreligious environment, and used to a life of selfishness, indolence, luxury and sensuality, Ahab felt that what he wanted he could have.

Naboth, however, refused to part with his family inheritance though offered either its value in money or a better vineyard in exchange. Ahab should have known that Naboth was a Jew and that his religion prohibited him selling or surrendering his inheritance. Ahab became angry and sullen over Naboth's refusal and as Clarence E. Macartney forcibly expresses it:

> Naboth's refusal was the introduction to one of the strangest, most powerful, and most terrible dramas of the Bible; a drama, on one side, of innocence, courage, independence, and the fear of God: on the other side, of covetousness, avarice, cruelty, perjury, death, and the terrible retribution.

Returning to his palace and meeting Jezebel, Ahab was asked the cause of his melancholy feelings. Jezebel, mocking him for his sulkiness, sarcastically asked if he was not king, implying that as king, his wishes should be immediately granted by his subjects. Then the crafty woman determined to secure Naboth's vineyard for her husband, and in her scheme she revealed her true diabolical nature.

Jezebel sent letters in Ahab's name to the elders of Naboth's township and commanded them to arrange a public fast and to seat Naboth at the head of the people. Two witnesses, sufficient for the purpose, were drilled to accuse Naboth of blasphemy and treason. Naboth was found guilty and stoned to death and thus died for a crime he never committed. Augustine is credited with the saying, "Abolish justice and what are kingdoms but great robberies."

Jezebel saw to it that Naboth's property was confiscated and given to Ahab. When Elijah heard of the foul act, he hurried to Ahab and Jezebel and threatened them with divine vengeance. Dogs would lick Ahab's dead body and a similar judgment would overtake Jezebel, seeing the sins of Ahab were attributed to Jezebel's influences. Had she not used every occasion to bend Ahab to her will? Ahab humbled himself under the preaching of Elijah yet returned to his idolatry.

The record of Naboth is not only a drama of faith in God and of magnificent loyalty to conscience and righteousness, but also a reminder of swift and terrible retribution. It is eloquent with the fact that sin finds us out and that crime never pays. Thus the dogs licked Ahab's blood in the very place where they had licked Naboth's blood. Ahab went out to meet the Syrian king, and thinking to escape his doom, shed his royal robes, going out to war disguised as one of his soldiers. A certain man drew a bow at a venture and smote Ahab. God knew, although the marksman did not, that the target was Ahab. So "the unknown soldier was the bowman of divine retribution."

What about Jezebel's doom? After Ahab's death she lived on for some 14 years, doubtless retaining much of her physical attractiveness. Mary Hallet says of her striking personality —

> Probably she had a dark Phoenician beauty, a regal bearing, and a certain physical allure; and we can picture a mobile mouth that easily

changed from smiling sweetness to sneering cruelty, and lovely eyes behind which something sinister forever lurked.

This we do know, that as queen-mother she still exercised an evil influence over those around her, especially in the courts of her sons Ahaziah and Joram of Israel, and in that of her daughter Athaliah's husband, Jehoram (II Chronicles 21:6; 22:2).

After the slaughter of Jehoram, Jehu, the furious driver, sped back to Jezreel. Already word had reached the palace that the king was slain but even the death of her own flesh and blood did not move the queen-mother. Although cognizant of Elijah's grim prophecy, her spirit remained composed, and completing her elaborate toilet, she exhibited, not mourning for the slain, but all her attractive seductiveness. She "painted her face and tired her head." The *tire* was a form of Persian *"tira."* Jezebel was determined to die as queen decked in all her royal apparel. We can compare the similar behavior of Cleopatra as set forth in *Antony and Cleopatra,* act V, scene 2 —

> Show me, my women, like a queen. Go fetch
> My best attire. I am again for Cydnus.
> To meet Marc Antony. . . . Bring our crown, and all.
>   *   *   *   *   *
> Give me my robe, put on my crown; I have
> Immortal longings in me.

Presenting herself at the window of the palace, Jezebel, seeing Jehu, hurled defiance at him. "Had Zimri peace who slew his master?" The inference was that success could not attend Jehu's efforts. But he had a divine warrant. Zimri had no express command from God which altered the whole nature of the case and of action.

Jehu shouted up to the city walls, "Who is on my side?" and servants near at hand, recognizing Jehu's star was now in the ascendancy, obeyed his command, seizing the queen and hurling her over the battlements. Quickly the horsemen rode callously over the mangled body, and pariah dogs soon tore Jezebel's rotten flesh from her bones, and thus she died as ignominiously as her husband had. Nothing "remained of her but the monuments of infamy." She had no dying bed and knew nothing of "love's last tender ministry," or "the dear familiar touch."

Later Jehu relented. Jezebel, with all her crimes, was a king's daughter, a queen, and mother of kings. Messengers were sent to collect her remains, but the dogs only left her skull and the bones of her hands and feet, which were given a decent burial. Surely such an act on Jehu's part teaches us to deal graciously and tenderly with the debased and fallen.

W. O. E. Oesterley in Hasting's *Dictionary* aptly summarizes the stained record thus:

In her strength of character, her lust for power, her unshrinking and resolute activity, her remorseless brushing aside of anything and everything that interfered with the carrying out of her designs, she was the veritable prototype of Catherine de Medici.

Although dead, the pernicious influence of Ahab and Jezebel lived on. The children following them were just as corrupt as their parents, for father and mother cursed the lives of their offspring. Think of this evil brood —

Ahaziah, who became king of Israel, worshiped his mother's idols and was rebuked by Elijah for his impiety. After a reign of two years, he died from serious injuries from a fall through a lattice at his palace.

Joram or *Jehoram*, king of Israel, also worshiped Baal and was slain by his own army, which revolted under Jehu on the very ground where Naboth's vineyard had been.

Athaliah, the daughter, as we shall see in our next portrait, introduced the worship of Baal into Judah and followed the example of her unrighteous mother, and also perished by the sword.

In the Apocalypse the name, *Jezebel*, is given to an idolatrous religious system leagued with apostate civil power (Revelation 2:20). Jezebel is here used in a figurative sense as a symbol of idolatrous seduction. What a telling illustration of the proverb, "The name of the wicked shall rot" (Proverbs 10:7), Jezebel is!

What's in a name? A good deal. To call any woman "a Jezebel" would be the equivalent of insulting her. George Stimpson in his interesting volume, *A Book About the Bible,* tells us that the term, "*Painted Jezebel,*" came into being during the sixteenth century when painting the face was accepted as *prima facie* evidence that a woman was loose in morals and bold in spirit.

ATHALIAH
(II Kings 11; II Chronicles 22, 23)

THE QUEEN WHO MURDERED THE PRINCES

Athaliah, the only woman who reigned in either of the two kingdoms of Israel, is referred to as "that wicked woman" (II Chronicles 24:7), a phrase summarizing the chief defect of her character. Athaliah was a replica of her mother Jezebel. "Like mother, like daughter." In idolatry she bore the hideous likeness of her mother, for as Kuyper expresses it: "Jezebel had brought poison from Sidon and injected it into the veins of Israel. Now Athaliah was to transfuse some of that same poison into Jerusalem's veins."

Athaliah, the daughter of Omri, king of Samaria, the only woman to sit on the throne of David, married Joram, or Jehoram, the son of Jehoshaphat, king of Judah. In Athaliah's youth the political relations of the two kingdoms of Judah and Israel had, after years of strife, become friendly (II Kings 8:18). But the union of Athaliah and Jehoram, Jehoshaphat's eldest son, was one of political expediency and is a blot on Jehoshaphat's memory. It was an arranged marriage, fatal to the cause of piety in Judah, a cause which godly Jehoshaphat had at heart.

Athaliah exercised an evil influence over her husband and son, as Jezebel did over Ahab and her children. Her character was far stronger than Jehoram's, who was 32 years of age when he came to the throne. Unscrupulous and wicked, she killed all who stood in the way of her ambition, as her mother before her did. While Jehu was destroying her house in the north, Athaliah sought to destroy the house of David into which she had married. Fanatically devoted to the worship of Baal, she demolished the Temple and built a house to Baal. Doubtless Athaliah was the instigator of her husband's murder of the six brothers who followed the ancient faith of Jehovah.

On the death of her husband, Athaliah usurped the throne, and proof of her energy and ability is seen in the fact that in spite of her sex, she was able to reign for eight years. On the accession of her son, Ahaziah, at the age of 22 years, Athaliah was still the power behind the throne, supreme in the councils of the nation as well as in the royal palace. She counseled her son in wickedness and was second to him in power and influence. When Ahaziah was slain by Jehu, Athaliah could not bring herself to take an inferior position and seized the throne, and tried to make her position secure by murdering all the male members of the house of David within her reach. Thus under the inspiration of this inhuman creature, the most horrible deeds were perpetrated.

We now come to one of the most dramatic episodes in Hebrew history, namely, the preservation of one of the young princes from Athaliah's massacre of her grandchildren. At this critical moment, God's word (Genesis 3:15) appears to be at stake. Those of the royal seed are becoming fewer and fewer. In fact, the light was almost quenched, for Athaliah "arose and destroyed all the seed royal of the house of Judah." What followed? "*But* Jehosheba, the daughter of the king, took Joash the son of Ahaziah and stole him . . . and hid him from Athaliah . . . so that she slew him not."

How much depended upon the preservation of Joash, whom Athaliah thought dead with the rest! Had he been killed, Judah's light and hope would have been completely extinguished, for Christ had been prophesied to come from the tribe of Judah and the house of David. Jehosheba, noble princess, half-sister of Athaliah, deserves a niche in the gallery of the noble because through her Satan's attempt to destroy *all* the seed royal was foiled. Joash was hid for seven years and at the opportune moment brought out of secrecy and placed upon the throne by the high-priest Jehoiada who had carefully planned such a sudden *coup d'ètat.*

The presentation and coronation of young Joash worked with astonishing ease and success, proving how carefully the surprise had been conceived. The guards had been secretly won over and arranged for the boy king to be brought to the Temple on the Sabbath Day and crowned the lawful monarch amid the joyous acclamation of great crowds. Aroused by the unusual noise of the people, and full of suspicion, Athaliah hastened to the Temple and, taking the situation in at a glance, rent her clothes, and hoping to rally the populace to her aid cried, "Treason!"

Athaliah's plea, however, came too late. The fiat had gone forth and there was Joash on a raised platform, the Book of the Law in his hand and a crown on his brow. The guards were ordered to remove Athaliah from the precincts of the Temple lest it should be polluted by her blood, and at "the horses' entry to the king's house," she was smitten by the guards and died as did her mother, ignominiously and tragically, unwept, unhonored and unsung. Like her husband, she "departed without being desired."

A queen for eight years, and queen-mother for one year, her diabolical schemes failed. Athaliah loved blood, and her blood flowed at the door of her palace. Having lived like her mother, Jezebel, she died like her, slain at her own walls and trampled under the hoofs of horses. Her miserable career of murder ended in her own (see Revelation 16:5, 6). Scholars are divided as to the real meaning of Athaliah's name. Some say it signifies, *"Whom God has afflicted."* If this is so, then how prophetic such a sacred name was. Others say Athaliah means "afflicting by removal," suggesting some bereavement at the time of birth. This we know, Athaliah is a striking illustration of the ancient proverb, "When the wicked perisheth there is shouting" (II Kings 11:13, 20). After her death, the altar of Jehovah was restored.

It remains to be noted that two men bear the name of the notorious *Athaliah* (I Chronicles 8:26, 28; Ezra 8:7).

NEHUSHTA
(II Kings 24:8-16; Jeremiah 13:18; 29:2)

THE QUEEN WHO WAS EXILED

While we have no Biblical record of the virtues of Nehushta, she deserves a small cameo of her own, since she is one of the few Israelitish women in the Bible to bear the title, "queen." In the above passages, it is more as "queen-mother" that she comes before us. Nehushta was the daughter of Elnathan of Jerusalem, one of Jehoiakim's princes, the wife of King Jehoiakin, and mother of Jehoiachin, his son, who began to reign when 18 years of age. Evidently she shared the throne during her son's minority.

Nehushta, which may mean *bronzed,* and possibly refers to her complexion, was taken into captivity along with her son and all the chief men of the land, and as far as we know died in Babylonian exile. Efforts have been made to connect *Nehushta,* "a proper name derived from the name of a metal," to a similar name *Nehushtan,* meaning a piece of brass, or the brazen thing, which name was given to the brazen serpent which Moses set up in the wilderness, and which he smashed in pieces (II Kings 18:4).

It is evident from Jeremiah's description that Nehushta, as queen-mother, wore a crown or tiara like that of the kings, and was thus invested with royal distinction. Apart from her captivity nothing is known of Nehushta, yet one can read between the lines. Judah had courted the Chaldean nobles as her lover-guides and friends, but her captivity brought an end to this alliance in which she had trusted. Jehoiakim, Nehushta's husband, was not a God-fearing man, and when he died he was buried "with the burial of an ass, drawn and cast forth beyond the gates of Jerusalem" (Jeremiah 22:18, 19). Jehoiakin his son followed the evil practices of his father. *Jehoiachin* means, "Jehovah will confirm," a foreshadow of the prophesied fate awaiting this king.

The question arises, How far did Nehushta influence both her husband and son? Did she aid and abet them in their evil ways and works, and was her captivity along with the rest deserved? Somehow we feel that if she had made a courageous effort to stand out against the tragic drift from God, the Bible, never silent when inner convictions are obeyed, irrespective of cost, would have lauded this queen. Thinking of the king and queen-mother and those of the court and people, languishing in captivity in Babylon we recall Shelley's words:

"Kings are like stars — they rise, they set, they have
The worship of the world, but no repose."

J. M. Barrie in *Margaret Ogilvy* has the arrestive paragraph: "For when you looked into my mother's eyes, you knew, as if He had told you, why God sent her into the world — it was to open the minds of all who looked to beautiful thoughts." If only Athaliah had had a mother like that, what different stories we would have of Jezebel and her wicked daughter.

ESTHER
(Book of Esther)

THE QUEEN WHO WAS ONCE A POOR ORPHAN

We find ourselves in hearty agreement with the sentiment that in the book of Esther "we have one example in the Bible of a story of which the whole scenery and imagery breathes the atmosphere of an Oriental court as completely and almost exclusively as *The Arabian Nights.*" Here is the romantic record of a poor orphan girl who rose to be the queen of one of the world's greatest empires, and who, as queen, was willing to sacrifice all for a great cause.

Esther was a Jewess of Benjamin and the daughter of Abihail and a descendant of the captives carried to Babylon with Jeconiah or Jehoiachin. She was thus born abroad of a family choosing to remain in Persia instead of returning to Jerusalem. Her name occurs about 58 times. Esther and Ruth are the only two Bible women with books named after them.

The double name of the queen is worthy of note. Her original Hebrew name was, *Hadanah,* meaning, "a myrtle," possibly because from her infancy she was distinguished for her loveliness of "form and countenance." The myrtle was a plant of sweet-scented and luxuriant beauty. *Esther* became her Persian name when she was chosen as queen. This name has the meaning of the similar Greek word, *Aster,* meaning, "a star." Some writers say it indicates the star of the planet Venus, a bright object of wonder and admiration. The Babylonian Venus was the goddess of beauty. Tradition says that the Syrian women worshiped the planet Venus from the roofs of their houses, as a means of preserving and enhancing their beauty. In Esther's case, the change of name indicates the style of beauty for which she was famous.

Rabbi Yehudah derives *Esther* from "sathes," meaning *to hide,* because she was hidden in her guardian's house, and her nationality also was concealed until she felt it opportune to reveal it.

Early in life, Esther was left an orphan and was brought up by her cousin, Mordecai, who held a minor position among the palace officials. Nothing more is known of Esther than what we have in her book. Evidently she was a young woman of commanding and commendable beauty. Esther was "fair of form and good of countenance" as the margin expresses. What was said of Mary Queen of Scots was equally true of Esther:

"All contemporary authors agree in ascribing to her the utmost beauty of countenance and elegance of shape of which the human form is capable. No one ever beheld her without admiration."

In court and empire, Esther "obtained favor in the sight of all them that looked upon her." The most beautiful of all the candidates for the King's favor, Esther possessed that dark, exotic beauty contrasting sharply with the blondness of the Persian maidens. Her peculiar gracefulness and beauty soon attracted notice, and gained for her selection as the queen of Ahasuerus. Other qualities of this one-time orphan girl are clearly evident. Esther comes before us a woman of clear judgment, of magnificent self-control, and capable of self-sacrifice. Matthew Henry comments: "Her wisdom and her virtue were her greatest beauty," and he naively adds, "but it is an advantage to a diamond to be well set."

Conspicuous in form and features, Esther seems to have been more conspicuous in her natural grace and dignity, with a rare sweetness of spirit and happy disposition making it easy for Mordecai to bring her up as his own daughter. To her can be applied the work of Sir Edwin Arnold in *The Light of the World* —

> "Thereat she rose
> Stateliest, — and Light of living Love and Truth
> Made fairer her fair face, and kindled her eyes
> To lovelier lustre."

Esther possessed those qualities of mind and spirit characteristic of Hebrew women, forming a beauty of the soul. One who is "faultlessly formed" and "exquisitely featured" can become unattractive and even repellent unless graced by the inner attribute of faith, courage and unselfishness. Much more can be said of Esther's obedience to her adopted father, even when she became queen; of her faith in the high destiny of the Hebrew nation; of her willingness to sacrifice her life in a cause she deemed just. But Esther, like all of us, had the defect of her qualities.

First of all, her marriage was a double wrong. The king himself married in contravention of the law that he must marry a wife belonging to one of the seven great Persian families. Esther was not of the royal blood. As for Esther, as a Jewess, she must have known that to marry an oriental king was a violation of the seventh commandment. While it is true that Ahasuerus was an autocrat and could choose whomsoever he pleased, Mordecai could have objected to Esther's inclusion among the maidens, a course he possibly furthered. We cannot imagine Esther being a reluctant candidate for queenly honor.

Then Vashti had not been deposed for valid reasons, and it is not an agreeable aspect to Esther's character that she willingly assented to take the place of the deposed queen, who had so bravely refused to obey the whim of her drunken husband.

With regard to the hanging of the wicked Haman, he deserved his fate, but the wholesale massacre of the enemies of the Jewish people was another matter. Scripture does not hide from us the fact that Esther was not above the vindictiveness of her age and country in her request. Five hundred men, including Haman's ten sons, had already been killed in Shushan. When Ahasuerus asked Esther if she was satisfied she had the callous boldness to ask that the Jews be given another day to take vengeance on their enemies and so three hundred more were slaughtered. Commenting on this butchery Ellicott says:

It seems impossible here to acquit Esther of simple blood-thirstiness. Before the slaughter of the 13th of Adar was actually over, it is obvious that the Jews were no longer in danger. It was known that the sympathies of the Court were entirely with the Jews, and the officers of the king consequently took their part. After one day's slaughter in which in the capital alone 500 men were killed, we may be quite certain that the Jews were master of the situation, and therefore we do not hesitate to call Esther's fresh action needless butchery.

Were anything needed to bring out the matter in its true light, it might be seen in the request that the sons of Haman might be hanged. They had already been killed (verse 10), doubtless among the first, and Esther, therefore, asks for the dead bodies to be crucified, gratuitous outrage on the dead. Because Esther was a person whom God made use of as an agent for a great purpose, we are not called upon to tone down and explain away the black spots in her history.

We realize that we must not judge Esther by our enlightened standard of Christian morality and perhaps view her action in the light of her sacrificial resolve: *If I perish, I perish.* Still, with her knowledge of divine justice she should have rested her cause with Him who said: "Vengeance is mine."

While it is not within the province of this character study to deal with the literary excellence and supreme dramatic power of the book of Esther, one is tempted to linger over the part Mordecai played in the story. As for Haman, the Jews' enemy, and the banquets of Esther, these alone form a fascinating study. Some critical scholars reject Esther as a person and also any historical value of the book of Esther. Martin Luther was so hostile to the book that he said: "I would it did not exist, for it Judaizes too much and has in it a great deal of heathenish naughtiness. It is more worthy than all of being excluded from the Canon."

To orthodox Jews Esther stands unequalled among Bible women, and they believe every word of the book. They have no doubt as to its historical accuracy, as the annual Feast of Purim proves. This Fesitval, lasting for two days, during which time the Book of Esther is solemnly read, is a time of great rejoicing, for did not Queen Esther save their race from annihilation? It is called *Purim*, meaning "The Feast of Lots," so-called for the lots cast by Haman to fix the exact time of the destruction of the Jews which he had planned.

The Book of Esther is peculiar in that God's name is not mentioned in it. Yet His over-ruling providence is evident all through it; we might call it a non-religious book in that it carries no religious term whatever. A similar feature characterizes the Song of Solomon. A remarkable tribute, however, of Esther's devout attachment to God is perpetuated upon the sarcophagus which tradition assigns to her. It takes the form of a prayer, and is attributed to Esther herself, and reads:

I praise Thee, O God, that Thou hast created me.

I know that my sins merit punishment, yet I hope for mercy at Thy hands; for whenever I call upon Thee Thou art with me: Thy Holy presence secures me from all evil.

O God! shut not my soul out from Thy divine presence! Those whom Thou lovest never feel the torments of hell.

Lead me, O merciful Father, to the life of life; that I may be filled with the heavenly fruits of Paradise.

ESTHER

Bullinger affirms that the result of the marriage of Ahasuerus and Esther was the fulfillment of Isaiah 44:28-45:4, and the birth of Cyrus, their son, the anointed of Jehovah, who surnamed him nearly 200 years before he was born, and raised him up to perform His will. Scripture, however, is silent as to any issue of this union.

There are many more female consorts we would have liked to have known about. There is the queen Nehemiah refers to as sitting by King Ahasuerus (2:6), probably Damaspia, the one legitimate queen. Some writers identify her as Esther. The feast in question was not a public one, otherwise the queen would not have been present (Esther 1:9-12).

Then there is Hephzi-bah, the wife of King Hezekiah, and mother of King Manasseh (II Kings 21:1). We also have the foreign consort of Belshazzar, whose position was one of influence, seeing her proffered advice was accepted. She has been identified as Nitocris, daughter-in-law of Nebuchadnezzar (Daniel 5:10, 12). There is also Naamah, one of Solomon's "strange women" (I Kings 11:1), the Ammonitess. But in the queens we have sought to portray we have seen the ideal and the actual. The Divine Artist has sketched for us the immeasurable majesty of womanhood and the awful possibilities of womanly degradation and moral turpitude. We have the angelic and fiendish, woman in all her alluring glory, and woman in her blackest attire and soulless nakedness.

We cannot do better than close this section on Queens with the impressive paragraph of Vallance C. Cook:

The queens have their own place in the picture, and speak to us of things every man and woman should be cognizant of. The surprising beauty of virtue and honour, the grace and glory of chivalry and sweetness, the subtle forces of courtship and marriage, the glory of parentage, the majesty of love and motherhood, the great law of heredity operating for good and evil, and the royal search for divine light and leading — all these, and many another entrancing subject, are special features impressed upon us by the story of the queens.

III

Symbolic Queens in Bible History

That the Bible uses the royal term, *queen*, in many interesting, symbolic ways is evident from a glance at a Concordance.

The queen is gold of Ophir (Psalm 45:9). Here the title is used figuratively of the Church, espoused to Christ, King of His people. She stands in the presence of her divine-human Lord, arrayed in the royal apparel of His providing. The word used for "queen" by the psalmist is *Shegal*, the same as in Nehemiah 2:6, a word implying "a foreign queen."

Their queens thy nursing mothers (Isaiah 49:23). The margin gives us "princesses" instead of "queens." As a rule kings gave their children to be brought up by their nobles (II Kings 10:5). The future aspect of Zion is in the mind of the prophet as he declares that the nation should have kings as nursing fathers and queens as nursing mothers. Other nations are to bow down to Israel the true *Ecclesia*, as the dwelling place of Jehovah, and serve her. Licking the dust denotes subjection and submission (Genesis 3:14).

A crown of glory . . . a royal diadem . . . Hephzi-bah (Isaiah 62: 1-5).

The wife of King Hezekiah was called *Hephzi-bah*, a name meaning "my delight is in her." The king's marriage synchronized with the prophecy of Isaiah (II Kings 21:1; Isaiah 54:5-8). *Beulah* meaning "married," language prophetic of the bright future of Israel as a people.

The Queen of Heaven (Jeremiah 7:18; 11:17, 19, 25).

In these passages, Jeremiah sternly declares the wrath of God upon the inhabitants of Judah and Jerusalem devoted to the worship of the host of heaven. Moses warned against the worship of the sun, moon, stars, and all the host of heaven (Deuteronomy 4:19; 17:3). Existence of such a form of worship is to be found in an earlier period (Job 31:26-28). Solomon created a shrine for the Sidonian goddess (I Kings 4:33; II Kings 23:13). Astral worship was common among Jews during the later period of their sojourn in Canaan. The ten

247

tribes in the Northern Kingdom were guilty of this idolatry (II Kings 17:16).

Many Gentile nations worshiped several astral deities, with each deity corresponding either to an astral phenomenon, or an occurrence in nature connected with the course of the stars. In Arabia, crescent-shaped cakes to represent the moon were offered to the goddess of the evening-star and to the sun-god. Could this have been a perversion of the offering of bread and cakes to God in the "meat-offering"?

Assyrian inscriptions speak of "The Lady of Heaven," a term used by Roman Catholics of Mary, the mother of our Lord. By the *queen of heaven* we understand the moon or "Ashtoreth," an aspect of worship generally associated with Baal, meaning "the sun." This *queen*, then, was the Assyrian Ishhar and the Canaanites' Asharte, the worship of which was of a grossly immoral, licentious, abominable and debasing nature. The going over of the people of Judah to some of the worst and vilest forms of heathen worship incurred the grievous displeasure of Jehovah, who had distinctly declared that His people were to have no other gods before Him. Such pagan worship was adverse to the worship of the King of heaven (Daniel 4:37).

The male and female pair, Astarte and Baal, symbolized nature's generative power, when prostitution was practiced in her worship. "The queen of heaven" was also known as "the mistress of heaven and earth." Mariolatry and astrology are modern forms of the astral worship of the Babylonians.

I sit as queen, and am no widow (Revelation 18:7). A queen who is not a widow implies a king's consort. Here the term is used metaphorically of the city of Babylon, Rome, and as used, expresses sovereign contempt and imaginary dignity and power. *Queen*, as employed by John, represents the false church or antichristian apostasy. The true Church is to be married to her Omnipotent Lord (Revelation 19:7). Walter Scott's comment on the above verse shows that pride goes before destruction:

> Religious Babylon, having been degraded from her public place by the kings of the Roman world, yet maintains her pride. Her spirit is unbroken. Her haughtiness is asserted in spite of the fact that she sits in the dust of her former grandeur, and that her final end is at hand. The kings of the earth may *lament* over her, but *help* her they cannot. Her boasting is *within*; and she says in her heart, "I sit a queen." Her public downfall had already taken place, hence the assertion of her queenly state would be out of keeping if openly expressed. "I am not a widow." Does she expect that her fortunes are to be retrieved? Utter destruction is signified in the words, "she shall be burned with Fire."

On this solemn note we close our study of "the kings and queens of the Bible," a wondrously provocative and intriguing adventure.

BOOKS OF REFERENCE

Bullinger, E. *The Companion Bible.*
The Lamp Press, London.
Cook, Vallance C. *Queens of the Bible.*
Charles H. Kelly, London.
Cooper, Professor James. *The Soldiers of the Bible.*
A. and C. Clark, London and Edinburgh.
Cottrell, Leonard. *The Lost Pharaohs, Life Under the Pharaohs.*
Pan Books, Ltd., London.
Davidson, Donald. *Mothers in the Bible.*
Marshall, Morgan, Scott, London.
Dean, Edith. *All the Women of the Bible.*
Harper and Brothers, New York.
Ellicott, C. J. *Commentary on the Whole Bible.*
Zondervan, Grand Rapids, Michigan.
Fausset, A. R. *Bible Encyclopaedia and Dictionary.*
Zondervan, Grand Rapids, Michigan.
Hallet, Mary. *Their Names Remain.*
The Abingdon Press, New York and Chicago.
Halley, Henry H. *Halley's Bible Handbook.*
Zondervan, Grand Rapids, Michigan.
Harrison, R. K. *A History of Old Testament Times.*
Marshall, Morgan, Scott, London.
Hastings, James. *Dictionary of the Bible.*
T. and T. Clark, Edinburgh.
Kuyper, Abraham. *Women of the Old Testament.*
Zondervan, Grand Rapids, Michigan.
Lockyer, Herbert. *All the Men of the Bible.*
Zondervan, Grand Rapids, Michigan.
Mackay, W. Mackintosh. *Bible Types of Modern Women.*
George H. Doran, New York.
Manning, Samuel. *The Land of the Pharaohs.*
Religious Tract Society, London.
Nicholls, Benjamin E. *Helps to Bible Reading.*
Society for Promoting Christian Knowledge, London.
Nicolson, William. *The Bible Student's Companion.*
Pickering and Inglis, London.
Odhams Press Ltd. *One Hundred Great Lives.*
Odhams Press, London.

Orr, James. *The International Standard Bible Encyclopaedia.*
  Wm. B. Eerdmans, Grand Rapids, Michigan.
Robinson, Thomas. *Scripture Characters.*
  Published 1824. Out of Print.
Scott, Walter. *Bible Handbook.*
  G. Morrish, London.
Scroggie, W. Graham. *Know Your Bible* (2 vols.).
  Pickering and Inglis, London and Glasgow.
————. *The Unfolding Drama of Redemption,* Vols. 1, 2.
  Pickering and Inglis, London and Glasgow.
Sell, Henry T. *Famous Bible Women.*
  Fleming H. Revell Co., London and Edinburgh.
White, Wilbert Webster. *Old Testament Characters.*
  Y.M.C.A. Headquarters, New York.
Wilkinson, W. F. *Personal Names of the Bible.*
  Alexander Strahan, London and New York.

INDEX

251